Nutshell Series
Hornbook Series

and

Black Letter Series

of

WEST PUBLISHING COMPANY

P.O. Box 64526
St. Paul, Minnesota 55164–0526

Accounting

FARIS' ACCOUNTING AND LAW IN A NUTSHELL, 377 pages, 1984. Softcover. (Text)

Administrative Law

AMAN AND MAYTON'S HORNBOOK ON ADMINISTRATIVE LAW, Approximately 750 pages, 1993. (Text)

GELLHORN AND LEVIN'S ADMINISTRATIVE LAW AND PROCESS IN A NUTSHELL, Third Edition, 479 pages, 1990. Softcover. (Text)

Admiralty

MARAIST'S ADMIRALTY IN A NUTSHELL, Second Edition, 379 pages, 1988. Softcover. (Text)

SCHOENBAUM'S HORNBOOK ON ADMIRALTY AND MARITIME LAW,

Student Edition, 692 pages, 1987 with 1992 pocket part. (Text)

Agency—Partnership

REUSCHLEIN AND GREGORY'S HORNBOOK ON THE LAW OF AGENCY AND PARTNERSHIP, Second Edition, 683 pages, 1990. (Text)

STEFFEN'S AGENCY-PARTNERSHIP IN A NUTSHELL, 364 pages, 1977. Softcover. (Text)

NOLAN–HALEY'S ALTERNATIVE DISPUTE RESOLUTION IN A NUTSHELL, 298 pages, 1992. Softcover. (Text)

RISKIN'S DISPUTE RESOLUTION FOR LAWYERS VIDEO TAPES, 1992. (Available for purchase by schools and libraries.)

American Indian Law

CANBY'S AMERICAN INDIAN LAW IN A NUTSHELL, Second Edition, 336 pages, 1988. Softcover. (Text)

Antitrust—see also Regulated Industries, Trade Regulation

GELLHORN'S ANTITRUST LAW AND ECONOMICS IN A NUTSHELL, Third Edition, 472 pages, 1986. Softcover. (Text)

HOVENKAMP'S BLACK LETTER ON ANTITRUST, Second Edition approximately 325 pages, April 1993 Pub. Softcover. (Review)

HOVENKAMP'S HORNBOOK ON ECONOMICS AND FEDERAL ANTITRUST LAW, Student Edition, 414 pages, 1985. (Text)

SULLIVAN'S HORNBOOK OF THE LAW OF ANTITRUST, 886 pages, 1977. (Text)

Appellate Advocacy—see Trial and Appellate Advocacy

Art Law

DUBOFF'S ART LAW IN A NUTSHELL, Second Edition, approximately 325 pages, 1993. Softcover. (Text)

Banking Law

LOVETT'S BANKING AND FINANCIAL INSTITUTIONS LAW IN A NUTSHELL, Third Edition, 470 pages, 1992. Softcover. (Text)

Civil Procedure—see also Federal Jurisdiction and Procedure

CLERMONT'S BLACK LETTER ON CIVIL PROCEDURE, Third Edition, approximately 350 pages, May, 1993 Pub. Softcover. (Review)

FRIEDENTHAL, KANE AND MILLER'S HORNBOOK ON CIVIL PROCEDURE, Second Edition, approximately 1000 pages, May 1993 Pub. (Text)

KANE'S CIVIL PROCEDURE IN A NUTSHELL, Third Edition, 303 pages, 1991. Softcover. (Text)

KOFFLER AND REPPY'S HORNBOOK ON COMMON LAW PLEADING, 663 pages, 1969. (Text)

SIEGEL'S HORNBOOK ON NEW YORK PRACTICE, Second Edition, Student Edition, 1068 pages, 1991. Softcover. (Text) 1992 Supplemental Pamphlet.

SLOMANSON AND WINGATE'S CALIFORNIA CIVIL PROCEDURE IN A NUTSHELL, 230 pages, 1992. Softcover. (Text)

Commercial Law

BAILEY AND HAGEDORN'S SECURED TRANSACTIONS IN A NUTSHELL, Third Edition, 390 pages, 1988. Softcover. (Text)

HENSON'S HORNBOOK ON SECURED TRANSACTIONS UNDER THE U.C.C., Second Edition, 504

Commercial Law—Continued

pages, 1979, with 1979 pocket part. (Text)

MEYER AND SPEIDEL'S BLACK LETTER ON SALES AND LEASES OF GOODS, Approximately 300 pages, 1993. Softcover. (Review)

NICKLES' BLACK LETTER ON COMMERCIAL PAPER, 450 pages, 1988. Softcover. (Review)

STOCKTON AND MILLER'S SALES AND LEASES OF GOODS IN A NUTSHELL, Third Edition, 441 pages, 1992. Softcover. (Text)

STONE'S UNIFORM COMMERCIAL CODE IN A NUTSHELL, Third Edition, 580 pages, 1989. Softcover. (Text)

WEBER AND SPEIDEL'S COMMERCIAL PAPER IN A NUTSHELL, Third Edition, 404 pages, 1982. Softcover. (Text)

WHITE AND SUMMERS' HORNBOOK ON THE UNIFORM COMMERCIAL CODE, Third Edition, Student Edition, 1386 pages, 1988. (Text)

Community Property

MENNELL AND BOYKOFF'S COMMUNITY PROPERTY IN A NUTSHELL, Second Edition, 432 pages, 1988. Softcover. (Text)

Comparative Law

FOLSOM, MINAN AND OTTO'S LAW AND POLITICS IN THE PEOPLE'S REPUBLIC OF CHINA IN A NUTSHELL, 451 pages, 1992. Softcover. (Text)

GLENDON, GORDON AND OSAKWE'S COMPARATIVE LEGAL TRADITIONS IN A NUTSHELL. 402 pages, 1982. Softcover. (Text)

Conflict of Laws

HAY'S BLACK LETTER ON CONFLICT OF LAWS, 330 pages, 1989. Softcover. (Review)

SCOLES AND HAY'S HORNBOOK ON CONFLICT OF LAWS, Student Edition, 1160 pages, 1992. (Text)

SIEGEL'S CONFLICTS IN A NUTSHELL, 470 pages, 1982. Softcover. (Text)

Constitutional Law—Civil Rights

BARRON AND DIENES' BLACK LETTER ON CONSTITUTIONAL LAW, Third Edition, 440 pages, 1991. Softcover. (Review)

BARRON AND DIENES' CONSTITUTIONAL LAW IN A NUTSHELL, Second Edition, 483 pages, 1991. Softcover. (Text)

ENGDAHL'S CONSTITUTIONAL FEDERALISM IN A NUTSHELL, Second Edition, 411 pages, 1987. Softcover. (Text)

MARKS AND COOPER'S STATE CON-

Constitutional Law—Civil Rights—Continued

STITUTIONAL LAW IN A NUTSHELL, 329 pages, 1988. Softcover. (Text)

NOWAK AND ROTUNDA'S HORN-BOOK ON CONSTITUTIONAL LAW, Fourth Edition, 1357 pages, 1991. (Text)

VIEIRA'S CONSTITUTIONAL CIVIL RIGHTS IN A NUTSHELL, Second Edition, 322 pages, 1990. Softcover. (Text)

WILLIAMS' CONSTITUTIONAL ANALYSIS IN A NUTSHELL, 388 pages, 1979. Softcover. (Text)

Consumer Law—see also Commercial Law

EPSTEIN AND NICKLES' CONSUMER LAW IN A NUTSHELL, Second Edition, 418 pages, 1981. Softcover. (Text)

Contracts

CALAMARI AND PERILLO'S BLACK LETTER ON CONTRACTS, Second Edition, 462 pages, 1990. Softcover. (Review)

CALAMARI AND PERILLO'S HORN-BOOK ON CONTRACTS, Third Edition, 1049 pages, 1987. (Text)

CORBIN'S TEXT ON CONTRACTS, One Volume Student Edition, 1224 pages, 1952. (Text)

FRIEDMAN'S CONTRACT REMEDIES IN A NUTSHELL, 323 pages, 1981. Softcover. (Text)

KEYES' GOVERNMENT CONTRACTS IN A NUTSHELL, Second Edition, 557 pages, 1990. Softcover. (Text)

SCHABER AND ROHWER'S CON-TRACTS IN A NUTSHELL, Third Edition, 457 pages, 1990. Softcover. (Text)

Copyright—see Patent and Copyright Law

Corporations

HAMILTON'S BLACK LETTER ON CORPORATIONS, Third Edition, 732 pages, 1992. Softcover. (Review)

HAMILTON'S THE LAW OF CORPO-RATIONS IN A NUTSHELL, Third Edition, 518 pages, 1991. Softcover. (Text)

HENN AND ALEXANDER'S HORN-BOOK ON LAWS OF CORPORATIONS, Third Edition, Student Edition, 1371 pages, 1983, with 1986 pocket part. (Text)

Corrections

KRANTZ' THE LAW OF CORREC-TIONS AND PRISONERS' RIGHTS IN A NUTSHELL, Third Edition, 407 pages, 1988. Softcover. (Text)

Creditors' Rights

EPSTEIN'S DEBTOR-CREDITOR LAW IN A NUTSHELL, Fourth Edition,

Creditors' Rights—Continued
401 pages, 1991. Softcover. (Text)

EPSTEIN, NICKLES AND WHITE'S HORNBOOK ON BANKRUPTCY, Approximately 1000 pages, January, 1992 Pub. (Text)

NICKLES AND EPSTEIN'S BLACK LETTER ON CREDITORS' RIGHTS AND BANKRUPTCY, 576 pages, 1989. (Review)

Criminal Law and Criminal Procedure—see also Corrections, Juvenile Justice

ISRAEL AND LAFAVE'S CRIMINAL PROCEDURE—CONSTITUTIONAL LIMITATIONS IN A NUTSHELL, Fourth Edition, 461 pages, 1988. Softcover. (Text)

LAFAVE AND ISRAEL'S HORNBOOK ON CRIMINAL PROCEDURE, Second Edition, 1309 pages, 1992 with 1992 pocket part. (Text)

LAFAVE AND SCOTT'S HORNBOOK ON CRIMINAL LAW, Second Edition, 918 pages, 1986. (Text)

LOEWY'S CRIMINAL LAW IN A NUTSHELL, Second Edition, 321 pages, 1987. Softcover. (Text)

LOW'S BLACK LETTER ON CRIMINAL LAW, Revised First Edition, 443 pages, 1990. Softcover. (Review)

SUBIN, MIRSKY AND WEINSTEIN'S

THE CRIMINAL PROCESS: PROSECUTION AND DEFENSE FUNCTIONS, Approximately 450 pages, February, 1993 Pub. Softcover. Teacher's Manual available. (Text)

Domestic Relations

CLARK'S HORNBOOK ON DOMESTIC RELATIONS, Second Edition, Student Edition, 1050 pages, 1988. (Text)

KRAUSE'S BLACK LETTER ON FAMILY LAW, 314 pages, 1988. Softcover. (Review)

KRAUSE'S FAMILY LAW IN A NUTSHELL, Second Edition, 444 pages, 1986. Softcover. (Text)

MALLOY'S LAW AND ECONOMICS: A COMPARATIVE APPROACH TO THEORY AND PRACTICE, 166 pages, 1990. Softcover. (Text)

Education Law

ALEXANDER AND ALEXANDER'S THE LAW OF SCHOOLS, STUDENTS AND TEACHERS IN A NUTSHELL, 409 pages, 1984. Softcover. (Text)

Employment Discrimination—see also Gender Discrimination

PLAYER'S FEDERAL LAW OF EMPLOYMENT DISCRIMINATION IN A NUTSHELL, Third Edition, 338 pages, 1992. Softcover. (Text)

Employment Discrimination— Continued

PLAYER'S HORNBOOK ON EMPLOYMENT DISCRIMINATION LAW, Student Edition, 708 pages, 1988. (Text)

Energy and Natural Resources Law—see also Oil and Gas

LAITOS AND TOMAIN'S ENERGY AND NATURAL RESOURCES LAW IN A NUTSHELL, 554 pages, 1992. Softcover. (Text)

Environmental Law—see also Energy and Natural Resources Law; Sea, Law of

FINDLEY AND FARBER'S ENVIRONMENTAL LAW IN A NUTSHELL, Third Edition, 355 pages, 1992. Softcover. (Text)

RODGERS' HORNBOOK ON ENVIRONMENTAL LAW, 956 pages, 1977, with 1984 pocket part. (Text)

Equity—see Remedies

Estate Planning—see also Trusts and Estates; Taxation—Estate and Gift

LYNN'S INTRODUCTION TO ESTATE PLANNING IN A NUTSHELL, Fourth Edition, 352 pages, 1992. Softcover. (Text)

Evidence

BROUN AND BLAKEY'S BLACK LETTER ON EVIDENCE, 269 pages, 1984. Softcover. (Review)

GRAHAM'S FEDERAL RULES OF EVIDENCE IN A NUTSHELL, Third Edition, 486 pages, 1992. Softcover. (Text)

LILLY'S AN INTRODUCTION TO THE LAW OF EVIDENCE, Second Edition, 585 pages, 1987. (Text)

McCORMICK'S HORNBOOK ON EVIDENCE, Fourth Edition, Student Edition, 672 pages, 1992. (Text)

ROTHSTEIN'S EVIDENCE IN A NUTSHELL: STATE AND FEDERAL RULES, Second Edition, 514 pages, 1981. Softcover. (Text)

Federal Jurisdiction and Procedure

CURRIE'S FEDERAL JURISDICTION IN A NUTSHELL, Third Edition, 242 pages, 1990. Softcover. (Text)

REDISH'S BLACK LETTER ON FEDERAL JURISDICTION, Second Edition, 234 pages, 1991. Softcover. (Review)

WRIGHT'S HORNBOOK ON FEDERAL COURTS, Fourth Edition, Student Edition, 870 pages, 1983. (Text)

First Amendment

GARVEY AND SCHAUER'S THE FIRST AMENDMENT: A READER, 527 pages, 1992. Softcover.

[VII]

Local Government

MCCARTHY'S LOCAL GOVERN-MENT LAW IN A NUTSHELL, Third Edition, 435 pages, 1990. Softcover. (Text)

REYNOLDS' HORNBOOK ON LOCAL GOVERNMENT LAW, 860 pages, 1982 with 1990 pocket part. (Text)

Mass Communication Law

ZUCKMAN, GAYNES, CARTER AND DEE'S MASS COMMUNICATIONS LAW IN A NUTSHELL, Third Edition, 538 pages, 1988. Softcover. (Text)

Medicine, Law and

HALL AND ELLMAN'S HEALTH CARE LAW AND ETHICS IN A NUTSHELL, 401 pages, 1990. Softcover (Text)

JARVIS, CLOSEN, HERMANN AND LEONARD'S AIDS LAW IN A NUTSHELL, 349 pages, 1991. Softcover. (Text)

KING'S THE LAW OF MEDICAL MALPRACTICE IN A NUTSHELL, Second Edition, 342 pages, 1986. Softcover. (Text)

Military Law

SHANOR AND TERRELL'S MILITARY LAW IN A NUTSHELL, 378 pages, 1980. Softcover. (Text)

Mining Law—see Energy and Natural Resources Law

Mortgages—see Real Estate Transactions

Natural Resources Law—see Energy and Natural Resources Law, Environmental Law

TEPLY'S LEGAL NEGOTIATION IN A NUTSHELL, 282 pages, 1992. Softcover. (Text)

Office Practice—see also Computers and Law, Interviewing and Counseling, Negotiation

HEGLAND'S TRIAL AND PRACTICE SKILLS IN A NUTSHELL, 346 pages, 1978. Softcover (Text)

Oil and Gas—see also Energy and Natural Resources Law

HEMINGWAY'S HORNBOOK ON THE LAW OF OIL AND GAS, Third Edition, Student Edition, 711 pages, 1992. (Text)

LOWE'S OIL AND GAS LAW IN A NUTSHELL, Second Edition, 465 pages, 1988. Softcover. (Text)

Partnership—see Agency—Partnership

Patent and Copyright Law

MILLER AND DAVIS' INTELLECTUAL PROPERTY—PATENTS, TRADEMARKS AND COPYRIGHT IN A NUTSHELL, Second Edition, 437 pages, 1990. Softcover. (Text)

Products Liability

PHILLIPS' PRODUCTS LIABILITY IN

Products Liability—Continued

A NUTSHELL, Third Edition, 307 pages, 1988. Softcover. (Text)

Professional Responsibility

ARONSON AND WECKSTEIN'S PROFESSIONAL RESPONSIBILITY IN A NUTSHELL, Second Edition, 514 pages, 1991. Softcover. (Text)

LESNICK'S BEING A LAWYER: INDIVIDUAL CHOICE AND RESPONSIBILITY IN THE PRACTICE OF LAW, 422 pages, 1992. Softcover. Teacher's Manual available. (Coursebook)

ROTUNDA'S BLACK LETTER ON PROFESSIONAL RESPONSIBILITY, Third Edition, 492 pages, 1992. Softcover. (Review)

WOLFRAM'S HORNBOOK ON MODERN LEGAL ETHICS, Student Edition, 1120 pages, 1986. (Text)

WYDICK AND PERSCHBACHER'S CALIFORNIA LEGAL ETHICS, 439 pages, 1992. Softcover. (Coursebook)

Property—see also Real Estate Transactions, Land Use, Trusts and Estates

BERNHARDT'S BLACK LETTER ON PROPERTY, Second Edition, 388 pages, 1991. Softcover. (Review)

BERNHARDT'S REAL PROPERTY IN A NUTSHELL, Second Edition, 448 pages, 1981. Softcover. (Text)

BOYER, HOVENKAMP AND KURTZ' THE LAW OF PROPERTY, AN INTRODUCTORY SURVEY, Fourth Edition, 696 pages, 1991. (Text)

BURKE'S PERSONAL PROPERTY IN A NUTSHELL, Second Edition, approximately 400 pages, May, 1993 Pub. Softcover. (Text)

CUNNINGHAM, STOEBUCK AND WHITMAN'S HORNBOOK ON THE LAW OF PROPERTY, Second Edition, approximately 900 pages, May, 1993 Pub. (Text)

HILL'S LANDLORD AND TENANT LAW IN A NUTSHELL, Second Edition, 311 pages, 1986. Softcover. (Text)

Real Estate Transactions

BRUCE'S REAL ESTATE FINANCE IN A NUTSHELL, Third Edition, 287 pages, 1991. Softcover. (Text)

NELSON AND WHITMAN'S BLACK LETTER ON LAND TRANSACTIONS AND FINANCE, Second Edition, 466 pages, 1988. Softcover. (Review)

NELSON AND WHITMAN'S HORNBOOK ON REAL ESTATE FINANCE LAW, Second Edition, 941 pages, 1985 with 1989 pocket part. (Text)

Regulated Industries—see also Mass Communication Law, Banking Law

GELLHORN AND PIERCE'S REGULATED INDUSTRIES IN A NUTSHELL, Second Edition, 389 pages, 1987. Softcover. (Text)

Remedies

DOBBS' HORNBOOK ON REMEDIES, Second Edition, approximately 1000 pages, April, 1993 Pub. (Text)

DOBBYN'S INJUNCTIONS IN A NUTSHELL, 264 pages, 1974. Softcover. (Text)

FRIEDMAN'S CONTRACT REMEDIES IN A NUTSHELL, 323 pages, 1981. Softcover. (Text)

O'CONNELL'S REMEDIES IN A NUTSHELL, Second Edition, 320 pages, 1985. Softcover. (Text)

Sea, Law of

SOHN AND GUSTAFSON'S THE LAW OF THE SEA IN A NUTSHELL, 264 pages, 1984. Softcover. (Text)

Securities Regulation

HAZEN'S HORNBOOK ON THE LAW OF SECURITIES REGULATION, Second Edition, Student Edition, 1082 pages, 1990. (Text)

RATNER'S SECURITIES REGULATION IN A NUTSHELL, Fourth Edition, 320 pages, 1992. Softcover. (Text)

Sports Law

CHAMPION'S SPORTS LAW IN A NUTSHELL,. Approximately 300 pages, January, 1993 Pub. Softcover. (Text)

SCHUBERT, SMITH AND TRENTADUE'S SPORTS LAW, 395 pages, 1986. (Text)

Tax Practice and Procedure

MORGAN'S TAX PROCEDURE AND TAX FRAUD IN A NUTSHELL, 400 pages, 1990. Softcover. (Text)

Taxation—Corporate

SCHWARZ AND LATHROPE'S BLACK LETTER ON CORPORATE AND PARTNERSHIP TAXATION, 537 pages, 1991. Softcover. (Review)

WEIDENBRUCH AND BURKE'S FEDERAL INCOME TAXATION OF CORPORATIONS AND STOCKHOLDERS IN A NUTSHELL, Third Edition, 309 pages, 1989. Softcover. (Text)

Taxation—Estate & Gift—see also Estate Planning, Trusts and Estates

MCNULTY'S FEDERAL ESTATE AND GIFT TAXATION IN A NUTSHELL, Fourth Edition, 496 pages, 1989. Softcover. (Text)

PEAT AND WILLBANKS' FEDERAL ESTATE AND GIFT TAXATION: AN ANALYSIS AND CRITIQUE, 265 pages, 1991. Softcover. (Text)

Taxation—Individual

DODGE'S THE LOGIC OF TAX, 343 pages, 1989. Softcover. (Text)

HUDSON AND LIND'S BLACK LETTER ON FEDERAL INCOME TAXATION, Fourth Edition, 410 pages, 1992. Softcover. (Review)

McNULTY'S FEDERAL INCOME TAXATION OF INDIVIDUALS IN A NUTSHELL, Fourth Edition, 503 pages, 1988. Softcover. (Text)

POSIN'S FEDERAL INCOME TAXATION, Second Edition, approximately 650 pages, May, 1993 Pub. Softcover. (Text)

ROSE AND CHOMMIE'S HORNBOOK ON FEDERAL INCOME TAXATION, Third Edition, 923 pages, 1988, with 1991 pocket part. (Text)

Taxation—International

DOERNBERG'S INTERNATIONAL TAXATION IN A NUTSHELL, 325 pages, 1989. Softcover. (Text)

BISHOP AND BROOKS' FEDERAL PARTNERSHIP TAXATION: A GUIDE TO THE LEADING CASES, STATUTES, AND REGULATIONS, 545 pages, 1990. Softcover. (Text)

BURKE'S FEDERAL INCOME TAXATION OF PARTNERSHIPS IN A NUTSHELL, 356 pages, 1992. Softcover. (Text)

SCHWARZ AND LATHROPE'S BLACK LETTER ON CORPORATE AND PARTNERSHIP TAXATION, 537 pages, 1991. Softcover. (Review)

Taxation—State & Local

GELFAND AND SALSICH'S STATE AND LOCAL TAXATION AND FINANCE IN A NUTSHELL, 309 pages, 1986. Softcover. (Text)

Torts—see also Products Liability

KIONKA'S BLACK LETTER ON TORTS, 339 pages, 1988. Softcover. (Review)

KIONKA'S TORTS IN A NUTSHELL, Second Edition, 449 pages, 1992. Softcover. (Text)

PROSSER AND KEETON'S HORNBOOK ON TORTS, Fifth Edition, Student Edition, 1286 pages, 1984 with 1988 pocket part. (Text)

Trade Regulation—see also Antitrust, Regulated Industries

McMANIS' UNFAIR TRADE PRACTICES IN A NUTSHELL, Third Edition, approximately 450 pages, 1993. Softcover. (Text)

SCHECHTER'S BLACK LETTER ON UNFAIR TRADE PRACTICES, 272 pages, 1986. Softcover. (Review)

Trial and Appellate Advocacy—see also Civil Procedure

BERGMAN'S TRIAL ADVOCACY IN A

Trial and Appellate Advocacy— Continued

NUTSHELL, Second Edition, 354 pages, 1989. Softcover. (Text)

CLARY'S PRIMER ON THE ANALYSIS AND PRESENTATION OF LEGAL ARGUMENT, 106 pages, 1992. Softcover. (Text)

DESSEM'S PRETRIAL LITIGATION IN A NUTSHELL, 382 pages, 1992. Softcover. (Text)

GOLDBERG'S THE FIRST TRIAL (WHERE DO I SIT? WHAT DO I SAY?) IN A NUTSHELL, 396 pages, 1982. Softcover. (Text)

HEGLAND'S TRIAL AND PRACTICE SKILLS IN A NUTSHELL, 346 pages, 1978. Softcover. (Text)

HORNSTEIN'S APPELLATE ADVOCACY IN A NUTSHELL, 325 pages, 1984. Softcover. (Text)

JEANS' HANDBOOK ON TRIAL ADVOCACY, Student Edition, 473 pages, 1975. Softcover. (Text)

Trusts and Estates

ATKINSON'S HORNBOOK ON WILLS, Second Edition, 975 pages, 1953. (Text)

AVERILL'S UNIFORM PROBATE CODE IN A NUTSHELL, Second Edition, 454 pages, 1987. Softcover. (Text)

BOGERT'S HORNBOOK ON TRUSTS, Sixth Edition, Student Edition, 794 pages, 1987. (Text)

MCGOVERN, KURTZ AND REIN'S HORNBOOK ON WILLS, TRUSTS AND ESTATES–INCLUDING TAXATION AND FUTURE INTERESTS, 996 pages, 1988. (Text)

MENNELL'S WILLS AND TRUSTS IN A NUTSHELL, 392 pages, 1979. Softcover. (Text)

SIMES' HORNBOOK ON FUTURE INTERESTS, Second Edition, 355 pages, 1966. (Text)

TURANO AND RADIGAN'S HORNBOOK ON NEW YORK ESTATE ADMINISTRATION, 676 pages, 1986 with 1991 pocket part. (Text)

WAGGONER'S FUTURE INTERESTS IN A NUTSHELL, 361 pages, 1981. Softcover. (Text)

Water Law—see also Environmental Law

GETCHES' WATER LAW IN A NUTSHELL, Second Edition, 459 pages, 1990. Softcover. (Text)

Wills—see Trusts and Estates

Workers' Compensation

HOOD, HARDY AND LEWIS' WORKERS' COMPENSATION AND EMPLOYEE PROTECTION LAWS IN A NUTSHELL, Second Edition, 361 pages, 1990. Softcover. (Text)

Advisory Board

[XIV]

LAND USE
IN A NUTSHELL
SECOND EDITION

By

ROBERT R. WRIGHT
Donaghey Distinguished Professor of Law
University of Arkansas
Little Rock

and

SUSAN WEBBER WRIGHT

Professor of Law
University of Arkansas
Little Rock

ST. PAUL, MINN.
WEST PUBLISHING CO.
1985

COPYRIGHT © 1978 By WEST PUBLISHING CO.
COPYRIGHT © 1985 By WEST PUBLISHING CO.

610 Opperman Drive
P.O. Box 64526
St. Paul, MN 55164–0526

Library of Congress Cataloging in Publication Data

Wright, Robert R.
    Land use in a nutshell.

    (Nutshell series)
    Includes index.
    1.   Regional planning—Law and legislation—United
States.   2.   City planning and redevelopment law—United
States.   3.   Land use—Law and legislation—United
States.   I.   Wright, Susan Webber, 1948–
II.   Title.   III.   Series.
KF5698.Z9W74   1985   346.7304'5   85–10580
                             347.30645

ISBN 0–314–92499–X

Wright & Wright Land Use 2nd Ed. NS
4th Reprint—1993

**To
our students**

PREFACE

This series of "nutshell" books was instituted by West primarily to serve the needs of law students, and this book on Land Use is written with that in mind. It is intended to be a succinct expression of the salient points to be found in this subject matter. The difficulty with being succinct, or for that matter in writing a book of this type, is that there is a tendency toward oversimplification and the avoidance of some of the more intricate and interesting aspects of the material under consideration. We feel compelled to make the same qualifying observation that Professor W. Barton Leach made in his article, Perpetuities in a Nutshell, 51 *Harv.L.Rev.* 638 (1938): "If this paper fails of its purpose it has, at least, eminent company. Lord Thurlow undertook to put the Rule in Shelley's Case in a nutshell. 'But,' said Lord Macnaghten, 'it is one thing to put a case like Shelley's in a nutshell and another thing to keep it there.' Van Grutten v. Foxwell [1897] A.C. 658, 671." Nonetheless, as an overview and as something of a summary of the material, this book should prove helpful not only to law students but also to lawyers and judges.

A caveat is essential in that regard. The subject of land use controls and urban planning is approached in different ways by editors of different casebooks. The emphasis of some varies considerably from others depending upon the subject. While this book probably bears greater relationship to the Wright and Gitelman casebook and approach than to those of others, an effort has been made to discuss practically all of the subject matter contained in the leading casebooks. Therefore, even though the casebook used and the emphasis placed upon the material may vary, students utilizing this book should find coverage of most of the material discussed in class.

Student use of this or any other text should be on a periodic basis as different topics are considered. In this manner class discussion and the understanding of the material can be supplemented by the observations contained in this book. It will also prove helpful to re-read portions of the book for review purposes at the end of the course.

The field of land use is so rapidly developing, so diverse and so much affected by various fields of law and by new trends that viewpoints or approaches to the subject will vary depending upon the professor. In developing areas of the law, it is also not unusual to find differing interpretations. This should be kept in mind in considering this material in conjunction with a particular professor's approach to the subject.

Another comment is worthwhile in regard to the somewhat summary treatment accorded the subject in this book. It would have been more time-consuming, but easier in a sense, to write an extended treatise. Law professors are accustomed to writing law review articles in which a fairly limited subject can be thoroughly explored. It is much more difficult for us to reduce the material to a limited, relatively simple version. It goes against our grain, so to speak, since almost all of our legal writing has proceeded in the opposite direction. In place of writing a great deal about relatively little, in this book we are writing relatively little about a considerable variety of material. We trust that faculty, students and lawyers who read this book will take that into account.

ROBERT R. WRIGHT
SUSAN WEBBER WRIGHT

Little Rock, Arkansas
May, 1985

*

OUTLINE

Chapter IV. Planning and the Planners

Chapter V. Regulation of Land Development

Chapter VI. Zoning

Chapter VII. Zoning and Discrimination

Chapter VIII. Aesthetics and Preservation of Historical and Cultural Resources

Chapter IX. Natural Resources

Chapter X. Environmental Controls

Chapter XI. Housing and Urban Renewal

Chapter XII. Eminent Domain and the Police Power

OUTLINE

TABLE OF CASES

References are to Pages

TABLE OF CASES

TABLE OF CASES

TABLE OF CASES

TABLE OF CASES

TABLE OF CASES

TABLE OF CASES

TABLE OF CASES

LAND USE
IN A NUTSHELL

*

CHAPTER I

THE CONTROL OF LAND USE: AN OVERVIEW

§ 1. The Past

Controls on land use are not an innovation of the 20th century. They existed in various forms in England long before we were a nation and in actuality extend back into the ancient English past. The earliest Code of Roman law, the Twelve Tables, provided for setback lines from boundaries and for distances between trees and boundaries. This was promulgated in 451–450 B.C.

Modern fiction has it that property rights have a certain absolutism about them. This stems largely from Blackstone's statement that property rights could not be violated "even for the general good of the whole community." 1 W. Blackstone, Commentaries 139 (1782). But he was speaking of the inherent right of Englishmen to own property—a fundamental, human right in Anglo-American society—and Blackstone himself stated in that regard that property could be used and enjoyed without control or diminution "save only by the laws of the land." *Id.* at 138.

What the "laws of the land" will permit in terms of controls on land use has broadened over the years, although interpretations have gone through times of extension and retrenchment as the development of the police power and the law of eminent domain illustrate. Societal and economic conditions have traditionally set the standards for a particular day. Industrialization in England led to limitations upon the use of wood for fuel. Population growth and urbanization without adequate requirements as to the quality of structures led to the Great Fire of London in the 17th century and beyond that to controls.

Controls on the use of land in America related also to particular conditions and circumstances. The cheaper and more plentiful the land, the less need there was either to compensate for controlling it or for any controls at all. In the earlier days when population was diffused and there was always more land over the horizon, it was also easy to indulge the populistic notion that property rights were sacrosanct and were somehow beyond the reach of society except in the most fundamental of situations in which landowners themselves came into conflict. Judge-made controls, such as the law of nuisance, were generally adequate. But as our situation became more complex, as cities formed and grew and reproduced like amoebas to become separate accumulations of people, property and governmental units, there arose the realization that more extensive public controls were required.

The early controls on land use in America extend back into the colonial period, but they were limited in nature and dealt with specific problems. For example, one act of the Massachusetts Bay Colony sought to prevent farm animals from feeding or running at large on a certain island because the shrubs and grass were being destroyed and the owners and the public were being damaged. Another act in Massachusetts Bay provided for assignment of slaughterhouses, tallow chandlers, and certain other nuisance-like activities to particular areas of Boston, Salem and Charlestown. These were early examples of the exercise of the police power—the power to regulate on behalf of the health, safety, morals and general welfare of the community. These regulations were not difficult for the people to swallow because they dealt with clearly defined problems on which there would be general agreement because of the nature of the activity.

Throughout the 19th century in America, the police power developed with relatively little hindrance. The alternatives for a court considering a police power control were to uphold the act or declare that it went so far as to constitute a taking of private property for public use without just compensation. (This problem is discussed at length in the chapter on eminent domain and the police power.) The early cases, which were largely state court decisions, provided great latitude in the exercise of the police power. In Brick Presbyterian Church v. City of New York, 5 Cow. 538 (N.Y.1826), the city denied the church the continued use of a cemetery when the city had many years before leased the property to the church for a church and cemetery and had covenanted with the church for such use. In Commonwealth v. Tewksbury, 11 Metc. 55 (Mass.1846), the Massachusetts Court upheld a statute which prevented landowners from removing sand or gravel from beach property. And in Commonwealth v. Alger, 7 Cush. 53 (Mass.1853), the same court upheld a statute which prohibited erecting wharves beyond certain lines in the harbor even though the landowner who challenged the statute had received his land under an ancient grant dating back to colonial times which was given for that purpose.

Although other cases were similar, these early decisions took the attitude that only a physical taking of property was compensable, and they compared the exercise of the police power by state and local governments to the nuisance maxim that no one may use his land in such a way as to interfere with his neighbor's use. (See generally on all of this, F. Bosselman, D. Callies & J. Banta, *The Taking Issue* 106–114 (1973).)

This broad interpretation of the police power was carried forward in the latter part of the 19th century by the United States Supreme Court. Although it recognized that permanent physical invasions were compensable, it denied compensation in at least one situation in which damage clearly resulted to a landowner from a public project. The most important case of that period, however, was Mugler v. Kansas, 123 U.S. 623 (1887), which involved a brewery rendered largely worthless by a Kansas prohibition statute. Using the nuisance analogy, the court reasoned that police power regulations which greatly depreciate the value of property do not amount to a taking. (See generally, Bosselman, Callies & Banta, *supra* 114–123.)

The importance of the police power, of course, is that it forms the basis for the enactment of direct regulatory statutes and ordinances—and, in particular, is the basis for the legality of zoning.

§ 2. The Contrast of the 19th and 20th Centuries

For all practical purposes, this 19th century law is largely inapplicable today. In Pennsylvania Coal Co. v. Mahon, 260 U.S. 393 (1922), Justice Holmes wrote that while property could be regulated, if regulation went too far it would constitute a taking. How far it could go was a matter of degree which had to be determined on a case-by-case basis. That the police power remained a viable tool was clearly indicated four years later when the Supreme Court upheld comprehensive zoning in Euclid v. Ambler Realty Co., 272 U.S. 365 (1926). But it was clear that the police power was not unlimit-

ed: it could not be exercised arbitrarily or capri-
ciously; it could not be unreasonable; it could not
be confiscatory.   Although *Euclid* drew upon the
earlier nuisance analogy, that analogy was no longer particularly applicable.   The *Euclid* zoning ordinance went beyond the regulation of nuisance-like
activities.   How far zoning could go, however, was
subject to the test in *Pennsylvania Coal.*

Nonetheless, the situation by the 1920's presented a rather interesting contrast with the situation
in the 19th century.   Except for a few cases such
as Rideout v. Knox, 148 Mass. 368, 19 N.E. 390
(1889), a Holmes opinion which presaged his later
expression in *Pennsylvania Coal,* the 19th century
expounded the virtue and sanctity of the private
ownership of property while permitting almost any
exercise of the police power that fell short of an
outright taking.   The first half of the 20th century
presented a similar striking contrast by expanding
the uses of the police power in its approval of
comprehensive zoning while at the same time the
courts became more inclined to find that a particular police power action encroached upon private
property rights to the point that it constituted a
taking.   As between the two, despite the dedicated
pronouncements of the 19th century relative to
property rights and despite the expansion of the
police power in the 20th century, the protection of
private property against governmental actions has
been greater in this century than in the last.

§ 3. The Inheritance

Land use controls today, however, retain a substantial inheritance from the past. The common law doctrines of nuisance and waste, as well as some others, remain available for use and are employed in the limited situations in which they apply. These controls are the subject of the next chapter. The police power, though not accorded the wide judicial berth of the 19th century, has expanded in a variety of ways. It forms the basis today not only for such purposes as zoning ordinances but also for recent environmental laws and regulations. City planning and the predecessors of the "new town" movement can be traced in rudimentary form back to the 19th century, although both flowered during the 20th century. Planning remains in a state of transition and growth, but even high school students are aware of the fact that the City of Washington originated as a planned city with particular attention being given to boulevards and traffic circles.

The feeling, popular in some circles, that planning and controls on land are somehow a break with the past and are in derogation of property rights does not therefore manifest a familiarity with the past.

§ 4. The Present

This book deals almost entirely with the present state of the law and with current trends and prob-

lems. In addition to common law devices and the
law of zoning, attention is given to planning and
the planners, subdivision development, restrictive
covenants, housing and urban development, aesthetics, natural resources, environmental problems, taxation, eminent domain and the police
power, and energy and related problems. New
forms of planning manifested in the zoning process,
such as cluster zones and planned unit developments, are considered. To what extent can zoning
be exclusionary? To what extent can aesthetics
enter into zoning or planning considerations?
What can be required of subdividers? How does
taxation affect land use? What is the interrelationship between laws pertaining to the environment or to the regulation of natural resources and
older forms of land use control? When is there a
"taking" under today's cases? If there is a "taking," can damages be recovered? What will be the
interaction between environmental laws and the
energy crisis? To what extent does regional and
state planning exist and to what extent should it
exist?

Although many of these questions and others are
answered in large measure by the current state of
the law, others are not yet answered and will not
be answered for some years to come. Land use law
is the most dynamic and constantly changing aspect of property law because it is an amalgamation
of property law and public law. Public policy

considerations affect land use law to a far greater degree than any other aspect of property law. Constitutional questions obviously play a part in that situation, and the scope and basis of constitutional review has been increasing in recent years.

Finally, it must be said that there is an interconnection between land use controls on the one hand and social, economic and constitutional trends on the other which is not usually found in traditional property law. Governmental and judicial bodies usually attempt to make land use policies responsive to emerging concerns and developing needs. Conflicts result from situations in which localities attempt to block or ignore those needs or from situations in which the response is challenged as an overextension of the police power. The complexity of urban problems and the growth of urban areas places constant tension on the land use process with the result that anyone undertaking a study of this field of law is like the pioneer approaching a new frontier. As he crosses one range of hills, there are still other hills beyond. The legal process, of course, is like that, but this course represents an intensification of that process to an extreme degree.

CHAPTER II
COMMON LAW CONTROLS ON THE USE OF LAND

§ 1. Generally

While most controls on land use result from the actions of governmental units or private developers, the use of land can also be affected by judicial determinations. These are normally negative rather than positive controls which result from lawsuits involving narrowly focused issues. Generally speaking, actions of this type occur most of the time in these two situations: (1) lawsuits involving neighbors suing neighbors or a public official acting against a neighboring landowner on behalf of the public in general, and (2) lawsuits involving individuals who share the ownership of a parcel of land.

The first type of lawsuit involves an alleged nuisance, and the second type involves an action for waste.

§ 2. Background of the Law of Waste

Actions predicated upon waste customarily involve persons who possess interests of one kind or another in the same piece of land. Persons who may be involved are life tenants and remaindermen, landlords and tenants, secured creditors and debtors (such as mortgagors and mortgagees), common or joint tenants in which one or more of the tenants are not in possession, beneficiaries and trustees, grantors and grantees, holders of the equitable title and holders of the legal title, and covenantors and covenantees. The majority view is that owners of contingent interests, such as possibilities of reverter and contingent remainders, may not bring an action for waste, but there is authority to the contrary.

If the party in possession commits certain acts upon the land which are usually but not necessarily alleged to be harmful to the rights of the party not in possession, the customary allegation is that waste has been committed. Suit may be brought for an injunction or damages or both.

The law of waste is quite old, and it assumed increased importance with the Statute of Marlborough in 1267 and the Statute of Gloucester in 1278. The early English law was very rigid with respect to the party in possession, but this rigidity has lessened in recent times. Because our situation was different, due to the large land mass and the need to clear and develop the land, American law after the early years was far less rigid.

Early English law permitted an agreement to be made that a lessee for years could hold the premises "without impeachment of waste," which allowed the lessee to cut down all the timber, for example. But in the Bishop of Winchester's case

in 1638 (1 Rolle, Abridgment 380 (T, 3)), it was held
that he could be enjoined because it was not in the
public interest to lay waste to the timber. Equity
could also enjoin wanton acts of destruction despite
the use of that term. Vane v. Lord Barnard, 2
Vernon 738 (Ch.1716). While the magic term, "impeachment of waste," was generally not employed
in the United States, it was accepted that equity
had jurisdiction where the remedy at law was
inadequate.

§ 3. Types of Waste

It is common for a student or layman to think of
waste as some act which harms or destroys a part
of the property. This is the usual type of action—
one involving an unreasonable act which produces
or will produce permanent and substantial damage. Affirmative or voluntary waste, as it is
known, is not the only type, however. Permissive
waste is passive in nature and may result from the
possessor's allowing the property to deteriorate
without taking appropriate steps to prevent it. As
mentioned, equity may enjoin threatened unreasonable or malicious acts of waste, and this is
generally called equitable waste. If the change to
the property results in increasing the value of the
land, this is referred to as ameliorating waste.

§ 4. Voluntary Waste

An act which results in permanent and substantial damage to the property and is unreasonable constitutes waste on the part of the person in possession. Whether the act is unreasonable and whether the injury to the property is of sufficient gravity to amount to waste will involve consideration of the comparative rights and reasonable expectations of the possessor and the party not in possession. This "balancing of the interests" consideration also enters into the law of nuisance.

Generally speaking, it is not waste in the United States to clear land of timber for purposes of cultivation unless the value of the non-possessor's interest is diminished or the amount of timber cut is inconsistent with that required for good husbandry. Timber may also be cut for fuel, for fences, or as ancillary to farming operations. If the land was being used for timber purposes at the inception of the lease, or if the lease was for that purpose, there is no waste in cutting it. This also applies to the removal of soil or minerals. These can also be extracted without committing waste if necessary to carry out the purpose of the lease. However, in the absence of one of these situations, such activities would normally result in waste.

It is not considered waste simply to change the appearance of land, such as from open land to cultivated land.

Modern cases generally allow alterations to structures, or occasionally the destruction or replacement of existing structures, if the value of the property would be enhanced. Thus, ameliorating waste is usually not waste in the sense that it would give rise to an action at law or in equity. A situation of this type may result when conditions have changed quite substantially in the neighborhood where the property is located. In the leading case of Melms v. Pabst Brewing Co., 104 Wis. 7, 79 N.W. 738 (1899), the Wisconsin Court upheld the removal of a house and the leveling of a lot by a life tenant on the basis that there had been a radical and permanent change in surrounding conditions which justified the action taken.

§ 5. Permissive Waste

A possessor can be held responsible for poor husbandry resulting from inaction on his part. The duty of care is that of a man of ordinary prudence. Aside from allowing open land or cultivated land to diminish in value, permissive waste can result to structures from failing to make repairs or otherwise protect the premises against deterioration or destruction. Permissive waste can result in almost any situation when there is a failure by the possessor to act to preserve the property when he is found to have a reasonable duty to act.

§ 6. Remedies

Although statutes may vary somewhat, an action
for waste normally involves a suit at law for damages, an equitable action for injunctive relief, or a
combination of the two. It is not uncommon to
seek damages for acts already committed and to
ask for an injunction against future acts. The
usual allegations in equity with respect to irrepara-
ble harm and the inadequacy of the remedy at law
are required to secure an injunction unless a statute provides for some other test. Some statutes
provide for temporary relief if acts of waste are
threatened or are being committed.

The measure of damages, in general, is the
amount by which the acts of the possessor have
diminished the value of the interest of the party
not in possession. This is not easy to measure in
situations in which a long period of time will
elapse before the plaintiff is entitled to possession.
Where a life tenant is in possession, actuarial
tables are sometimes employed to determine the
probable duration. The amount of recovery is also
affected by statutes, some of which allow double or
treble damages in situations involving malicious or
wanton conduct.

In one case involving the use of a building as a
smallpox hospital, it was held that this was an
injury to the reversion and that the plaintiff
should recover the resulting diminution in value

for every valuable use to which the building might reasonably be put.

§ 7. Background of the Law of Nuisance

The law of nuisance began to develop shortly after the Norman Conquest, and in the late 12th century, the royal courts began to handle such disputes. The early dual relief of damages and specific abatement was superseded by trespass on the case, allowing damages only, which forced the plaintiff to seek injunctive relief in equity. Most of today's nuisance cases seek injunctive relief coupled with a prayer for special damages.

Unlike an action for waste in which the parties each possess an interest in the same piece of property, a nuisance action involves a suit by a neighboring landowner or by a public prosecutor suing on behalf of the people seeking to control or limit the use of land owned by the defendant. The basis of the suit is the maxim, *sic utere tuo ut alienum non laedas,* which means that no one may use his property in such a way as to injure his neighbor (or neighbors in the area generally). A claim of a nuisance thus involves the assertion of something in the nature of a negative interest—the interest of an adjoining or nearby property owner in not being adversely affected by the misuse of the land in question. It is somewhat comparable to a judicially created restrictive covenant in which each landowner is burdened by the limitation.

§ 8. Public and Private Nuisances

A private nuisance is an unreasonable interference with the use or enjoyment of land without there being a trespass or physical invasion. Practically speaking, it will be asserted by A in a suit against B, in which A alleges that certain acts by B constitute a nuisance as to A and his property. These acts may or may not affect other property in the area.

A public nuisance has wider-ranging implications. It is of sufficient magnitude to affect adversely the health, morals, safety, welfare, comfort or convenience of the public in general. Water pollution, air pollution, the storage of explosives under dangerous conditions, a house of prostitution, the emission of loud noises or bad odors, and obstruction of public ways, are examples. Statutes will in some instances define what constitutes a public nuisance.

A nuisance may be both public and private at the same time. In other words, activity may be sufficient to constitute a public nuisance and still substantially interfere with the use of adjoining land to the point that a landowner may bring an action predicated upon allegations of a private nuisance.

All nuisance actions do not result from affirmative acts. A landowner may fail to maintain his property in a reasonably suitable condition, as in

the case of a failure to maintain a horse lot or a pig
pen or a dog kennel, or of a failure to prevent the
danger of fire with respect to tall grass and brush
during dry weather. An ultrahazardous use of
land, whether intentional or due to neglect, could
impose absolute liability permitting injunctive relief.

"Private nuisance" refers to the property interest or extent of interests affected rather than to
the type of conduct.

From a strictly legal standpoint, a physical invasion of property gives rise to an action of trespass.
But trespass and nuisance sometimes are difficult
to distinguish. Gases, odors, dust particles, chemi-
cal particulates, and noise waves are invasions
which produce trespasses in a technical sense, but
the cases normally deal with such problems
through nuisance doctrines.

§ 9. Nuisances Per Se and Per Accidens

A nuisance per se is simply an activity or structure which constitutes a nuisance in and of itself.
It may be defined as such by statute or it may
constitute an immoral or extrahazardous activity.
Obviously, a nuisance per se is often a public
nuisance as well, and it may constitute a private
nuisance. Most nuisances per se have resulted
from the courts declaring them to be such on
numerous occasions, such as funeral parlors in
residential districts.

A nuisance per accidens is a nuisance in fact, *i.e.,* it must be proven to be a nuisance. It would probably not constitute a nuisance under all circumstances. Most of the allegations of private nuisances involve alleged nuisances per accidens, but a nuisance per accidens may be alleged on behalf of the public as well. The burden of proof is on the plaintiff to show that the activity or structure complained of is sufficiently obnoxious or sufficiently interferes with the use of his land that it amounts to a nuisance.

§ 10. Nuisances in Rural Areas

Whether an activity or operation is considered a nuisance will vary depending upon its location. Not every activity that would constitute a nuisance if located in town or in a fairly well-settled area will be considered a nuisance in the open country or even on the fringes of a city. On the other hand, some operations are so noxious that they have difficulty finding a place to hide.

These situations often lead to application of the "balancing of hardships" or "balancing of the equities" doctrine. In an old California case, cement was being manufactured in an area close to the quarries when the surrounding area was developed for growing citrus fruits. The cement dust was ruining the citrus trees and affecting the homes of the plaintiffs. The court felt that despite the loss which would result from closing the plant, to per-

mit the cement company to continue its operations
would amount to a taking of private property and
could not be permitted. Hulbert v. California Portland Cement Co., 161 Cal. 239, 118 Pac. 928 (1911).
By contrast, in a fairly recent Arizona case, there
was a conflict between a developing urban area
known as Sun City and a large cattle operation,
and the court balanced the hardships by requiring
the cattle feedlot to be moved to more distant land
of the defendant but also requiring the developers
to indemnify the feedlot owners for damages and
expenses resulting from the injunction. Spur Industries, Inc. v. Del E. Webb Development Co., 108
Ariz. 178, 494 P.2d 700 (1972). Both of these cases
involved operations which had sought isolation
from other activities.

Another more modern case which contrasts with
Hulbert, supra, is Boomer v. Atlantic Cement Co.,
26 N.Y.2d 219, 309 N.Y.S.2d 312, 257 N.E.2d 870
(1970), which illustrates another attempt to balance the equities. The opinion in *Boomer* focused
on the economic consequences in shutting down a
plant which was polluting the air but which involved a $45,000,000 investment and the employ-
ment of over 300 people. Since there would be
heavy economic loss in closing the plant in contrast
to a relatively slight loss to the nearby landowners,
the court chose to award permanent damages.
The dissent argued that this amounted to an impermissible private taking for private use. In any

event, *Boomer* and *Spur* represent the modern trend of the cases in making every effort to balance the hardships in order to avoid severe economic loss to the wrongdoer.

Although these cases do not illustrate it, operations which put forth large amounts of dust and gases or which emit foul odors are much "safer" from potential injunctions if they are located in open or rural areas. Cases involving emissions of this type have often held in favor of the industry or have given the plant a chance to improve its conditions. Moreover, in some cases damages have been allowed without enjoining the operation as in *Boomer*.

Even in rural areas, however, it makes a difference if the alleged nuisance is interfering with residential use as opposed to agricultural or commercial activity. If the area is viewed as residential in nature, even though it is rather sparsely settled, injunctive relief is more likely to be granted. But if the area is basically open country, the mere fact that there is a house or two in the vicinity will generally not suffice for injunctive relief in the absence of substantial interference or an extreme situation. Thus the Tennessee Court in a fairly recent case refused to enjoin a proposed crematory in a largely rural area, although the decision was based partly on the concept that a mere possibility or fear of future injury is not enough. State ex rel. Cunningham v. Feezell, 218

Tenn. 17, 400 S.W.2d 716 (1966). Cases involving
racetracks and drive-ins demonstrate varied results depending largely on how substantial the
court views the impact on the complainants and
how the court chooses to balance the equities.
Cases involving pigs, cattle and other such animals
illustrate the importance of the question of whether the area is rural or is in the process of becoming
residential.

The Restatement of Torts indicates that factors
to be considered in nuisance cases include the
adequacy of the injunction and other remedies,
unclean hands or laches on the part of the plaintiff, the relative hardship to the parties, the interests of third parties and the public, and the ability
to frame and enforce the decree. If there will be a
loss of jobs, loss of purchasing power, loss of taxes,
and substantial harm to the owners of such an
industry, these factors should be taken into account in assessing the public interest. Obviously,
consideration of such factors would lead to a balancing of the equities.

§ 11. Nuisances in Residential Areas or on the Urban Fringe

Nuisance situations become more obvious when
the area is well-established as residential in nature. In fact, mixed uses and the relative lack of
control over development have been factors which
have affected the denial of injunctive relief in

areas on the urban fringe. Even in situations in which a solid residential development is affected, as in the Sun City case, the tendency is to try to balance the hardships or permit the defendant to take measures to correct the condition.

These cases involving the fringe areas of a city often present the problem of "moving to the nuisance." One of the oft-cited cases on that subject, however, Bove v. Donner-Hanna Coke Corp., 236 App.Div. 37, 258 N.Y.S. 229 (1932), involved a house which had been built in an industrial area. Although the house was built before the coke plant, the court denied relief stating that this had been an industrial area for many years and that the plaintiff knew that when she bought the property. In the Sun City case, the court noted that if the developer were the only party harmed, it would feel justified in following that doctrine, but that people who had bought homes from the developer should not have to suffer. The key to the moving to the nuisance rule seems to be that if someone intentionally and knowingly locates in an industrial area or the like, the doctrine applies; but if there is a natural growth outward by the city until it begins to be affected by an alleged nuisance, then the doctrine does not apply.

This concept also affects the cases previously discussed relative to locating in a rural or agricultural area. If that is intentionally done, a homeowner should not then be heard to complain that the adjoining farm has cows or pigs which smell bad. (Of course, the result would be different if the situation had changed or intensified after the homeowner moved in.) Some states have adopted so-called "right-to-farm" laws designed to protect agricultural operations from nuisance suits.

A related issue is whether a federal law provides the exclusive remedy when a plaintiff is seeking relief on the basis of state nuisance law. In Marshall v. Consumers Power Co., 65 Mich. 237, 237 N.W.2d 266 (Mich.App.1975), the court found that the Atomic Energy Act was for protection against radiation hazards and did not preempt state nuisance law concerning other aspects of construction of a nuclear power facility.

If an area is not clearly established as residential, and contains mixed uses, courts will not normally enjoin such activities as gasoline stations, junkyards and funeral homes (although they will enjoin particularly noxious or harmful uses). The same result will likely occur if an area is in transition from residential to commercial. Even where an area was predominantly residential, the Pennsylvania Court decided to limit the operations of a grocery store rather than keep it out. Essick v. Shillam, 347 Pa. 373, 32 A.2d 416 (1943).

Despite the dictum in the West Virginia case of Parkersburg Builders Material Co. v. Barrack, 118 W.Va. 608, 191 S.E. 368 (1937), courts will generally not issue an injunction based on aesthetic considerations alone. The funeral home cases, however, present certain aesthetic overtones since they seem largely predicated on the mental attitudes of the public. Funeral homes can be enjoined as nuisances in neighborhoods which are exclusively, predominantly, or essentially residential. By contrast, in the absence of a health hazard of some type, cemeteries are normally not subject to injunction. Other types of operations which are deemed particularly unpleasant or threaten the mental health and property values of people in the neighborhood are also sometimes enjoined. Examples include a mental sanitarium, a venereal disease clinic, and "halfway houses" for paroled convicts (although there are seemingly contrary decisions on the latter). Normally, a mere fear of future injury from an alleged nuisance per accidens is not enough for injunctive relief. But that rule does not apply to funeral homes and certain other operations which produce mental apprehension that the courts feel is genuine and common among average people.

§ 12. Nuisances in Commercial and Industrial Areas

As indicated previously, there is usually little relief for someone who intentionally locates in an industrial area. But conflicts arise between otherwise lawful businesses or types of industry when one emits offensive odors or dangerous gases which affect or endanger the health of people working or doing business in the vicinity. Sometimes a commercial operation will be located apart from other businesses but gradually come into contact with the business area as a result of normal growth. This situation can lead to an injunction if, for example, the operation gives off offensive odors.

Many of the situations in industrial districts today are covered by air and water pollution statutes and regulations. However, unless a statute expressly states that the remedies under it are exclusive, the mere passage of it is generally not enough to divest courts of their common law jurisdiction over nuisance actions.

In considering injunctive relief the balancing doctrine applies, and courts may consider the comparative economic impact which will be involved. It is not unusual for courts to take halfway steps by requiring the defendant to clean up its operation, or make adjustments in it, or conform to the most modern methods and utilize modern technology in an effort to diminish the effect of the activity.

§ 13. Public Facilities

Country clubs and public parks have been sued in nuisance actions because of errant golf balls, litter, crowds, and noise. Plaintiffs have at times been unsuccessful because of the requirement that the interference with the use and enjoyment of property must be substantial and continuous. An occasional interference is not sufficient to establish a nuisance. As in other instances involving "moving to the nuisance," courts are unlikely to extend relief to those who elect to live adjacent to a golf course, park, or playground. However, damages suffered as a result of the defendant's negligence in operating the facility or supervising others can result in liability independent of a finding of nuisance.

If construction of a highway has blocked access to a right of way or has otherwise interfered with a property owner's use of his land, a proper remedy might lie in an action for nuisance. One court even held that the remedy of summary self-help abatement (without breach of peace) is available to those who suffer from nuisances created by public entities as well as from those created on private land by private citizens.

§ 14. Nuisances in Zoned Areas

The fact that an activity of a certain type is permitted in an area under the zoning ordinance does not mean that it may not be enjoined if it develops into a nuisance. The Colorado Court stated that the fact the zoning permits such an operation means that it cannot be considered a *public* nuisance. Green v. Castle Concrete Co., 181 Colo. 309, 509 P.2d 588 (1973). Actually, it would only be proper to say that it is not a nuisance *per se*. An otherwise legitimate activity could be conducted in such a way as to threaten the health or safety of the community in general and thus constitute a public nuisance. Obviously, it might also constitute a private nuisance.

Cases stating that a permitted use under zoning may still constitute a nuisance have involved such operations as funeral parlors, a taproom restaurant that attracted delinquents, a garbage dump, and a rock quarry. Some of these cases go beyond the idea that the key to whether a zoned business is subject to injunction depends on how it is operated. In the case of the funeral home, for example, the zoning was only given some weight as bearing on the issue and otherwise had no relevance. These are peculiar cases, however, and in few instances would an activity be enjoined from an area in which it could exist under the zoning law unless it had developed clear nuisance characteristics.

Some non-conforming uses which are permitted in certain areas because they predated the zoning can be eliminated by injunction if they constitute nuisances. However, the mere fact that they are non-conforming is not sufficient to justify injunctive relief.

Zoning laws and nuisance doctrine sometimes come into conflict with First Amendment rights. This is frequently the case when a zoning ordinance does not allow adult bookstores or when a neighboring property owner alleges that such a bookstore constitutes a nuisance. Until the materials in such bookstores are determined to be obscene in violation of law, the operation of the bookstore is generally protected. Statutes declaring these stores to be public nuisances have on occasion been declared unconstitutionally vague. The same problems arise concerning activities such as adult movies and stage presentations.

First Amendment questions also arise where the activities of religious groups are alleged to be nuisances or to violate zoning ordinances. The latter problem is discussed in Chapter VI.

§ 15. Nuisance Doctrine and Environmental Regulation

When a jurisdiction has enacted a pollution control act, a question arises concerning whether the act provides the exclusive remedy as to the activities it is designed to regulate. If the legislation provides an exclusive remedy, plaintiffs may not bring common law actions for nuisance. The better rule is that such legislation be construed as providing remedies in addition to the common law action for nuisance unless the act specifically states that its remedies are to be exclusive. However, the United States Supreme Court, in City of Milwaukee v. Illinois and Michigan, 451 U.S. 304 (1981), held that the Federal Water Pollution Control Act preempted the federal common law of nuisance.

A related issue is whether a federal law provides the exclusive remedy when a plaintiff is seeking relief on the basis of state nuisance law. In Marshall v. Consumers Power Co., 65 Mich.App. 237, 237 N.W.2d 266 (1975), the court found that the Atomic Energy Act was for protection against radiation hazards and did not preempt state nuisance law concerning other aspects of construction of a nuclear power facility.

§ 16. Other Judicial Controls on Land

In addition to the law pertaining to nuisance and waste, the judge-made or statutory law of lateral support, water rights, adverse possession, implied easements, drainage of surface waters, trade and agricultural fixtures, redemption and the rights of mortgagees, improvements by tenants, and duties in regard to fencing animals, all affect the way in which land can be used.

CHAPTER III

PRIVATE LAW DEVICES

§ 1. Generally

Even though many controls on land use result
from the actions of governmental units, some very
significant planned limitations result from "private" land use restrictions. Generally speaking,
these create a right in the land of another. Unlike
most of the common law controls discussed in the
previous chapter, private law devices can be positive in nature as well as negative, since they compel a landowner to take affirmative measures as to
the use of land subject to the restrictions. They
are "private" in the sense that they are created by
land developers rather than by public agencies.

Private law devices take several forms, and
while courts sometimes confuse the terms as well
as the nature of the various devices, it is important
to understand how the devices differ from one
another and the legal consequences which arise
from the use of a particular legal device.

§ 2. Defeasible Fees

One way to impose controls on land use is by the
creation of estates in land called defeasible fees.
In the fee simple determinable, Blackacre is conveyed to the grantee for as long as a certain

situation exists or does not exist, and if such prescribed use ceases or if the prohibited event occurs,
then the land automatically reverts to the grantor
and his heirs. The grantor and his heirs retain a
possibility of reverter. In the fee simple upon
condition subsequent, the land is conveyed "upon
condition that" or "provided that" a certain condition perpetually is met or a specified event does
not or is not permitted to occur, and if the condition is no longer fulfilled or the event occurs, then
the grantee and his heirs have a power to terminate the estate (which is often called a right of
entry for condition broken).

These estates usually encumber land titles need-
lessly, often adversely affect alienation, do not take
into account unexpected future situations, and
should almost always be avoided. They are not
favored at law or in equity, and courts will construe such estates to give rise only to covenants
whenever the language of the conveyance permits.
In addition, the limited scope of such devices renders them practically useless for the creation of
effective land use controls.

Some states have passed desirable statutes which
extinguish possibilities of reverter and rights of
entry after a specified period of time if the event in
question has not occurred.

§ 3. Easements Compared to Covenants

An easement is an interest in the land of another which is created by language of transfer, *i.e.,* grant, reservation, or conveyance. Easements run with the land and can be affirmative, negative, appurtenant, in gross, implied, or prescriptive. Moreover, new types or new forms of easements or what are called easements are periodically created and recognized. Scenic easements are an example. The concept of "reciprocal negative easements" resulted from the use and recognition of covenants in deeds as binding upon all landowners in a neighborhood. These are not easements in the traditional legal sense based upon the usual terminology employed in these instruments.

More akin to this latter situation is the modern subdivision development. A land developer, having platted his subdivision into lots, blocks, and streets, imposes certain limitations on the use of all lots in the development. He will likely provide, among other things, for single-family dwellings with no detached outbuildings, for the dwellings to be constructed at least a specified distance from the street and from the side and back lot lines, for dwellings of a minimum square footage, as well as for an extensive variety of other limitations. These provisions are filed for record along with the approved plat and bill of assurance and constitute covenants which restrict the use of each lot. They are reciprocal in that each owner of a lot in the subdivision may enforce them against another lot owner. They "run with the land," in the sense that these rights continue upon the sale of a lot to a third party. Restrictive covenants are today generally considered interests in land. Although Arkansas declined to award damages for their breach in an eminent domain action, California and other states properly have held to the contrary. (Arkansas State Highway Commission v. McNeill, 238 Ark. 244, 381 S.W.2d 425 (1964); Southern California Edison Co. v. Bourgerie, 9 Cal.3d 169, 107 Cal.Rptr. 76, 507 P.2d 964 (1973).)

While a restrictive covenant or a reciprocal negative easement may preclude someone from certain activity on a parcel of land, easements traditionally at law are affirmative and constitute a grant in the sense that they grant certain rights to A with regard to the land of B. One of the most common types of easements today is the affirmative grant to a utility company to run its lines across the owner's property.

Easements may be perpetual, for a specific term, or may be terminated by operation of law. An easement which is dependent on certain circumstances or is for a particular purpose may be extinguished if the circumstances no longer exist or if the purpose cannot be carried out. An easement could also cease to exist under the doctrine of merger, as when the owner of the easement acquires the fee title.

Recently, easements have also been used for public objectives such as for the preservation of open space, conservation, and the protection of scenic views.

§ 4. Easements Appurtenant and in Gross

An appurtenant easement is connected with the ownership of nearby land, and its principal characteristic is that there is a dominant tenement, the owner of which benefits from the easement, and a servient tenement which is subject to the easement. For example, if A and B own adjacent land and A has a right of way across B's land, A has the dominant tenement and B has the servient.

An easement in gross does not have dominant and servient tenements because it is not connected with the ownership of nearby land. At common law such an easement was personal to the grantee and could not be assigned or inherited. There is a growing trend toward assignability, and commercial easements in gross are regarded as assignable by the Restatement. Easements in gross are traditionally not favored in the law, and an easement will be presumed to be appurtenant if there is any doubt.

Conservation easements are normally not appurtenant because generally there is no publicly owned land nearby which can serve as the dominant tenement. A scenic easement along a highway can be an appurtenant easement because the publicly owned highway serves as the dominant tenement.

Easements in gross are not altogether satisfactory for conservation purposes because the old common law rule that such easements are non-assignable prevails in some jurisdictions, although others have modified the rule by holding that such easements are assignable where the clear intent of the grant was to create an assignable easement.

Problems which have arisen in the area of conservation easements include those of notice of the easement to subsequent purchasers of the fee when the easement is not recorded, the possibility that it might terminate by court declaration of a change of conditions, and the control which the fee owner retains over the land. The owner retains any right not specifically granted.

§ 5. Implied and Prescriptive Easements

If a property owner sold part of his land to someone whose only access or only reasonable access to it was across the remaining land of the grantor, an easement of necessity would be implied to exist across the grantor's land. Equity will "imply" the existence of an easement in situations in which it would be inequitable not to do so. In this situation, however, if the grantee had other reasonable means of access to existing roads, the way of necessity would not be implied.

Some easements are implied because of the probable intent of the parties when, at the time of severance of the dominant and servient tenements, there was an obvious and continuous servitude burdening the servient tenement and favoring the dominant one.

Easements may also be acquired by prescription, or adverse use, for the required period. The use must be without the owner's consent and with his knowledge. A prescriptive easement can be acquired by the public as well as by private persons and can be appurtenant to other land or in gross.

Although the rule in England is different, in the United States there are no implied or prescriptive easements for light and air. Therefore, a property owner who wishes to build a building which would block his neighbor's access to sunlight or air is not restricted by any implied or prescriptive easement. However, in one case the court found that a landowner had stated a cause of action in private nuisance by alleging that a neighbor proposed to build a home which would block sunlight from the plaintiff's solar collector, even though the proposed home would conform to existing deed restrictions and ordinances. Prah v. Maretti, 108 Wis.2d 223, 321 N.W.2d 182 (1982).

§ 6. Equitable Servitudes and Restrictive Covenants: Generally

Unlike easements, equitable servitudes are created by language of promise in the form of a covenant between parties. An action at law for damages can be brought for breach of covenants that run with the land, touch and concern the land, and involve privity of estate. Yet equitable servitudes render covenants enforceable in equity even when they do not run with the land on the theory that it would be unconscionable to permit a landowner who takes with notice of a restrictive covenant to avoid the covenant when the intent was clear that the burden should pass to him. Enforcement of equitable servitudes through injunctive relief is regarded by some as having no contractual basis even though the servitude itself arises from a covenant. It is based on the concept of notice as contained initially in the old English case of Tulk v. Moxhay, 41 Eng.Rep. 1143 (1848).

§ 7. Real Covenants Running with the Land

Real covenants which are enforceable at law must run with the land, touch and concern the land, and involve privity of estate. Where there is doubt concerning whether a covenant runs with the land, a court will consider whether the original parties to the covenant intended for the covenant to be personal as to them or for it to run with the land. Clark v. Guy Drews Post of the American

Legion, 247 Wis. 48, 18 N.W.2d 322 (1945). However-
er, intent alone is not enough, and in order for a
covenant to run with the land, it is also necessary
to show that the covenant "touches and concerns"
the land and that there is privity of estate between
the party seeking to enforce the covenant and the
one to be bound.

The requirements of touching and concerning
the land and privity of estate are at times difficult
to meet if they are narrowly applied. Courts have
therefore been willing to look to the substance
rather than the form of such covenants. Thus, a
covenant to pay an annual charge on land to a
homeowner's association was held to run with the
land although under the common law rule, such a
covenant did not touch and concern the land and
there was no privity of estate between the homeowners' association and the defendant landowner.
Neponsit Property Owners' Ass'n v. Emigrant Industrial Savings Bank, 278 N.Y. 248, 15 N.E.2d 793
(1938).

§ 8. Equitable Servitudes

If a covenant does not meet the requirements at
law of running with the land, touching and concerning the land, and privity of estate, it may still
be enforceable in equity under the concept of notice originally enunciated in the English case of
Tulk v. Moxhay, as mentioned earlier. This concept is that if a party purchases land with notice of

the covenant, he should stand in equity in no different position from that of the earlier owner. In short, it would be inequitable not to require performance.

Equitable servitudes can exist in a variety of ways: by a general scheme of development involving plat and covenant recordations, by inference of a general scheme as the result of the developer placing certain restrictions in most or practically all of the deeds (perhaps joined with his expression of intent to pursue a common scheme), by covenants contained in the original deeds, or by restrictions found in separate, usually contemporaneous, agreements among the owners of the lands. Under modern recording statutes, recordation of any instrument which forms part of the chain of title provides constructive notice of the servitude and enables it to be enforced in equity. In the case of a general scheme of development, inquiry notice may also be involved as discussed in this chapter.

Anyone involved in the building scheme, or anyone whose land is affected by deed or covenant, may enforce the equitable servitude against anyone else whose land is burdened.

The difference between equitable servitudes and real covenants which run with the land is of less importance today due to the modern practice of recording subdivision plats and restrictive covenants.

Retention by a developer of a power to eliminate or modify a restrictive covenant unilaterally or by subsequent agreement with one or more of his grantees will customarily be held to vitiate the restrictive covenants and eliminate any presumption of a common scheme of development.

§ 9. "Inquiry" Notice of Restrictions

Ordinarily a landowner who purchases a lot in a restricted subdivision will have notice of restrictions in his abstract of title because the restrictions will be filed with a subdivision plat and a bill of assurance.

However, in older subdivisions landowners often had notice of restrictions only through covenants in their deeds. The problems that arise with this method of planning a subdivision stem from situations where different covenants are inserted in different deeds or where some deeds contain the restrictive covenants and others do not. Where a general scheme of development is evident from a view of the area, a landowner who has no restrictions in his chain of title would normally be placed on notice to inquire concerning covenants binding other landowners in the subdivision. If such restrictive covenants are found to exist, they create what are known as reciprocal negative easements which benefit and bind all landowners, whether or not the covenants appear in a particular chain of title. Reciprocal negative easements are imposed

only where a common grantor conveyed land subject to restrictions which were intended to benefit
and bind all land in the subdivision. Thus a landowner whose lot is benefited by the restrictions and
who is put on inquiry notice will be bound by
similar restrictions even though they do not appear
in his chain of title. See Sanborn v. McLean, 233
Mich. 227, 206 N.W. 496 (1925).

The term "reciprocal negative easements" does
not refer to easements in a strictly legal sense
because easements are created by language of
grant, transfer or conveyance. Reciprocal negative
easements are akin to restrictive covenants and
equitable servitudes.

§ 10. Restrictions as Constituting an Interest in Land

There has been some disagreement as to whether
a restrictive covenant or equitable servitude creates a property interest of such a type as to make
it compensable in a condemnation proceeding
which vitiates the restriction. The majority view
is that such an interest is compensable because it
extinguishes a valuable property interest and produces loss of value to the land benefited. See
Southern California Edison Co. v. Bourgerie, 9 Cal.
3d 169, 107 Cal.Rptr. 76, 507 P.2d 964 (1973). The
minority view, which is arguably based more upon
considerations of public policy than upon eminent

domain law, takes the position that such an interest is not compensable.

§ 11. Construction of Restrictive Covenants

Restrictive covenants are generally strictly construed by courts in the sense that a landowner may use his land for any purpose which is not specifically prohibited by the restrictive covenants or by the police power. Therefore, a land developer who wishes, for example, to restrict his subdivision to single family residences should not limit the use merely to "residential" but to "single family residential."

This rule of strict construction of covenants has caused problems where covenants must be applied to situations which were not contemplated at the time the covenants were executed. Courts have not been consistent in determining whether a covenant restricting the use of land to "residential purposes only" prohibits the erection of a condominium. A holding that a condominium (or apartment house) is prohibited goes beyond a strict construction of the wording of the covenant and is questionable. However, if in such a case there is also a restriction against subdividing lots, a condominium might be excluded on the basis that it involves a subdivision of land in the form of airspace.

Generally speaking, a residential restriction barring churches and synagogues is upheld as constitutional and not void as against public policy. This type of restriction merely prescribes certain uses and is therefore distinguishable from a racially restrictive covenant, which excludes people. Nevertheless, courts have on occasion voided restrictions against churches. As noted in the chapter on zoning, zoning ordinances excluding churches in residential districts are more vulnerable to constitutional attack.

§ 12. The Effect of Parol Representations Regarding Covenants

If parol representations are proved, usually they can be enforced, although the grounds for such enforcement are at times less than clear because of two converging views giving effect to oral covenants. One view is that such covenants are enforceable because they create contracts relating to the use of land. This view, which disregards the Statute of Frauds, is easily applicable where the person claiming the benefit of the promise can take the position of a third party beneficiary to a contract, as where the owner of a lot in a subdivision claims the benefit of a parol restriction imposed upon a subsequent purchaser in the subdivision. Problems can arise, however, in the application of this contract theory where it becomes necessary to expand the concept of third party beneficiaries to subsequent as well as prior purchasers.

Courts have also enforced parol restrictions even while ruling that an interest in land has been created. This view would perhaps apply the Statute of Frauds but accompany it with such usual exceptions as fraud or part performance. In Bristol v. Woodward, 251 N.Y. 275, 167 N.E. 441 (1929), Cardozo wrote that parol restrictions were effective since what had evolved into an interest in land retained enough of its contractual origin to overcome the bar of the Statute of Frauds. This is an interesting hybrid approach which overcomes the excess of technicalities in the interest of a just result.

§ 13. Standing to Enforce Restrictions

Since restrictive covenants, appurtenant easements, and equitable servitudes are all intended to benefit nearby or adjacent land, the rule in a majority of jurisdictions is that in order to sue to enforce one of these restrictions the plaintiff must own land which is benefited by it. See London County Council v. Allen, L.R. (1914) 3 K.B. 642, Ann.Cas. 1916C, 932. This concept has been applied to deny standing to one who had been a developer of a subdivision and had sold all the land in the subdivision except the entrance way, but who still owned land in adjacent subdivisions. Kent v. Koch, 166 Cal.App.2d 579, 333 P.2d 411 (1958). Essentially, this rule follows a negative easement concept as to equitable servitudes.

The minority rule permits a developer who has imposed restrictions, but no longer owns land in the development, to sue to enforce the restrictions on the grounds that an interest was reserved by the conveyance which was not destroyed when the covenantee conveyed all of the land to be benefited, that the breach of the restrictions alone is enough to provide standing to sue, and that no damages resulting from the breach need be proved. Van Sant v. Rose, 260 Ill. 401, 103 N.E. 194 (1913).

§ 14. Termination of Restrictive Covenants

Some developers provide that restrictive covenants in a subdivision will terminate after a specified period of time (usually 25 or 30 years) unless a majority or larger percentage of the landowners reaffirm them, or alternatively, that the covenants may be terminated at the end of such period if a majority or larger percentage of the landowners file an instrument to that effect. There are other variations on such provisions.

The reason for such provisions is that in their absence, the only way restrictive covenants can be terminated is by court decree. In such a situation, a court of equity would have to find that the character of the subdivision had changed so drastically since the covenants were imposed that it would be inequitable and without any appreciable value to the property owners to enforce them any longer. This "change of conditions" reasoning is similar to that applied in the law of waste and in zoning cases. The issue almost invariably arises in situations in which outer lots in the subdivision are affected by nearby commercial development. While courts will take such conditions into account in determining the current situation within the subdivision, they will generally not invalidate the covenants to benefit buffer or outer lots unless the residential character of the total subdivision has been impaired. Estoppel, waiver, laches and acquiescence are other doctrines which enter in where the covenants have been violated on a substantial basis without complaint.

Most courts will not invalidate restrictive covenants simply because zoning regulations permit some other use. If the covenants are more restrictive, they will normally be enforced. A rezoning, however, is some evidence that the character of the subdivision has drastically changed. In a rare situation in which the zoning was more limiting than the covenants, the stricter zoning regulations would apply if they were not arbitrary or unreasonable. As a matter of simple logic, with regard to the issue of whether a rezoning by itself could vitiate a restrictive covenant, it should be apparent that if the exercise of the police power destroyed property rights, it would amount to a taking.

Although tax forfeitures and tax deeds normally extinguish prior rights, the interests of other landowners in a subdivision, as dominant tenants, could not be extinguished by a tax sale and tax deed of one of the lots. Thus a tax deed does not terminate an equitable servitude, the benefit of which is possessed by other landowners, nor should it terminate the servitude in the lot sold for taxes since the purchaser of the tax deed should have the benefit of the restrictions as well. A condemnation action would potentially eliminate restrictive covenants on the lot, since the taking is total, but it should properly also involve compensation for loss suffered by other landowners in the subdivision due to the termination of the servitude.

CHAPTER IV

PLANNING AND THE PLANNERS

§ 1. Background

Planning is the process which ultimately results in a comprehensive or master plan or an interrelated group of plans followed by ordinances regulating the use of land in a metropolitan area. These ordinances involve the exercise of the police power through zoning, regulation of subdivision developments, street plans, plans for public facilities, building regulations and the like. Properly, planning should precede zoning, since zoning and other regulatory ordinances merely amount to the execution of the planning process. To be effective, planning should stem from comprehensive studies of the urban area with particular reference to projected growth trends and public needs over the next ten years or more, which of course will be based largely on what has happened, what is happening, and what appears likely to happen in relation to the urban area. These studies will result in what is known as the "master plan," "comprehensive plan," "general plan," or just "the plan." This plan has been appropriately referred to by Professor Charles Haar of Harvard as an "impermanent constitution"—impermanent in the sense that it must be rewritten periodically to conform to new studies and new trends in urban development. But it is a "constitution" in the sense that the validity of zoning ordinances and rezoning will depend in large measure on whether they conform to the master plan. Contemporaneous with the master plan will come the "official map" in states having statutes providing for official maps. The map will show the location of major streets, public facilities both in existence and projected, and other such landmarks. Subdivision developers will have to plan their own developments in accordance with the official map. Some statutes provide for a number of maps—showing major street locations, parks and playgrounds, police and fire stations, and the like. All of this, plus continuing study by urban planners, forms a part of the planning process from which ultimately emanates specific ordinances enacted pursuant to such planning.

§ 2. Content of the Master Plan

Traditional master plans of urban communities take into account the location and type of activities taking place on the land and the design and type of physical structures and facilities serving these activities. Long-range projections of population and employment trends are considered. This is the approach of the Standard City Planning Enabling Act (SPEA), an early model for many states, and it serves a number of objectives, such as prediction of physical facility needs, allocation of land to desired activities, and preservation of open space for aesthetic and recreational needs. This planning process is designed to enable a locality to plan for construction of schools, streets, water and sewage facilities, fire and police protection, and other public amenities, while the private use of land is controlled by zoning and subdivision ordinances enacted in compliance with the plan.

The recent Model Land Development Code, the ultimate impact of which remains to be seen, provides for a "Local Land Development Plan" which is broader in scope than the traditional master plan, since it not only takes into account the physical development of a community but also reflects consideration of economic and social data of the area and the economic and social impact of developmental proposals. Unlike the older SPEA, the Model Land Development Code assumes that planners for a local government may or will be required to deal with state or regional planning agencies which are increasingly prevalent. The Model Code requires specification of short-term objectives so that planners will be involved in achieving goals as well as formulating them. This act further requires that the local governing body keep the plan current by adopting land development reports at regular intervals. The Code offers the potential for a major step forward in planning and development.

§ 3. Legal Effect of the Master Plan

The local governing body adopting a master plan derives its authority from a state statute or statutes which either enable or require local governments to adopt and enforce plans through local legislative enactments. A few states, such as Arkansas, Indiana, Kentucky and Minnesota, have enabling acts which require a locality to adopt a plan as a prerequisite to such land use controls as zoning and subdivision regulation. However, most states, and the Model Land Development Code, do not make planning a mandatory prerequisite to land use regulation although the planning process is given great weight in the Code.

The master plan, which is often formulated by a planning commission operating under the aegis of the local governing body, has no legal effect until it is adopted by the governing body. Cochran v. Planning Board of City of Summit, 87 N.J.Super. 526, 210 A.2d 99 (1965). After it is legally adopted, it is somewhat akin to a constitution, since subsequent land use regulation must be compatible to or in conformity with the plan.

Any master plan contemplating development over a period of years requires periodic amendments which modify it based on trends and developments which have occurred and which were not contemplated at the time the plan was adopted. Where special legislative procedures for adoption of a plan are required, it has been held that the

same procedures must be followed for amendments
to the plan and that the city's general powers to
amend ordinances are not applicable.   Dalton v.
City and County of Honolulu, 51 Haw. 400, 462
P.2d 199 (1969).

§ 4. The Official Map

The official map sets out in detail existing and
planned streets, sewers, water lines, parks and
playgrounds and other public facilities.   It often
establishes set-back lines for future streets and
may also establish set-back lines for the widening
of existing streets.   There may be separate official
maps—*i.e.,* street maps, parks and playgrounds,
and the like.

Historically, the official map preceded the master plan, but in the planning process the master
plan ideally comes first.   The drafters of New
York's 1926 official map act and of a 1935 model
act, Edward M. Bassett and Frank B. Williams,
have distinguished the official map from the master plan as follows: the plan provides general
information and includes many factors not shown
on the map, while the map reflects accurate de-
tails; the plan is plastic, while the map is rigid.   In
some jurisdictions, such as New York and Wisconsin, the map is legally binding and the plan is not,
for the plan must be adopted by the planning
commission only and is thus unofficial, while the
official map must be adopted by the local gov-

erning body. This procedure or policy is not universal by any means, however. Moreover, the differences in legal effect between the plan and the map should not be overemphasized because a knowledgeable landowner will generally not build in the bed of a future street even if it is included only in an unofficial document.

As in the case of most master plans, before an official map can have any legal effect it must be adopted by the local governing body, and that body must have authority to adopt and enforce it. Such authority is derived through state enabling statutes which give localities the right to adopt official maps for the purpose of reserving land for future streets, sewers, water lines, parks, schools and other public needs, and to control development in reserved areas by requiring landowners to obtain building permits as a prerequisite to building in an area reserved on the map. Failure to obtain a permit generally results in no compensation for the unauthorized structure at the time the reserved land is actually taken. Compensation should occur in circumstances in which a landowner secured official approval which was erroneously given but which he relied upon in good faith to his detriment.

As a practical matter, cities cannot afford to pay a landowner compensation at the time the land is reserved for a future public purpose, and the vast majority of states have statutes which provide for

compensation at the time the land is actually tak-
en by the locality. In the few jurisdictions which
provide for compensation at the time the land is
"reserved" by the filing of the official map, the
right to reserve is rarely exercised.

Official map enabling statutes have been upheld
constitutionally on grounds that the enactment of
the map is within the police power of the state
since it is for the protection of the health, safety,
and welfare of the community. Where the party
attacking the statute can show no injury resulting
from the reservation of some of his land on the
map, the map will not be stricken as an unconstitutional taking of property without compensation.
Headley v. City of Rochester, 272 N.Y. 197, 5
N.E.2d 198 (1936). A probable exception would be
if all of the owner's land were reserved or if the
reservation served to create an incumbrance on the
title. Forster v. Scott, 136 N.Y. 577, 32 N.E. 976
(1893). In most instances a landowner must ex-
haust his remedies by seeking a building permit or
a variance as a prerequisite to alleging that a map
ordinance constitutes a taking without compensation. Some unfavorable decisions have also been
based on the court's conclusion that potential hardship will result.

To withstand constitutional attack it is essential
that official map laws include savings provisions to
protect individual landowners from hardship resulting from the reservation of their property on

the map. Such provisions typically permit the
local authority to issue a building permit in a
reserved area where failure to do so would result
in unnecessary hardship, such as where compliance with the map would render impossible a fair
return from the property. State ex rel. Miller v.
Manders, 2 Wis.2d 365, 86 N.W.2d 469 (1957). The
standards for what constitutes an unnecessary
hardship are somewhat similar to those applied to
the granting of zoning variances. As in zoning,
some states allow the permit to be issued if there
would be "unnecessary hardship" or "practical difficulties" involved.

§ 5. State and Regional Planning

There is an increasing tendency away from local
planning and toward regional or statewide planning. Proposed federal legislation, which has not
been enacted (but has come close), would spur this
tendency. Some states have already enacted statutes designed to promote state or regional planning. Small states, such as Vermont and Hawaii,
have adopted somewhat disparate statutes embracing the state planning concept. The Vermont statute has strong environmental overtones and contemplates the adoption by an environmental board
of a rather broad state land use plan. The Hawaii
statute involves a somewhat more traditional classification of lands by a state land use commission,
although it too has environmental overtones in its

attention to conservation of certain areas and consideration of similar factors. Hawaii reviews its
situation every five years, which is desirable due to
changing circumstances.

Regional planning is more conducive to the situation of states encompassing large land areas or to
situations involving metropolitan areas which encompass portions of two or more states. Examples
of the latter include such areas as the New York
City-Newark-Philadelphia complex, the Los Ange-
les-Long Beach metropolitan area, and the Chicago
metropolitan complex which actually extends into
Northern Indiana and upward toward Wisconsin.
A single metropolitan area which involves two or
more states requires the use of such devices as
interstate compacts and the passage by more than
one state legislature of identical statutes creating
agencies or "authorities" with powers over situations involving more than one state.

Some intrastate regional planning results from
the recognition in progressive jurisdictions that in
a metropolitan area comprehensive planning is not
possible without taking into account the situation
of all of the communities which comprise the metropolitan area. Every city of any size has suburban or satellite communities. To plan only for the
central city, without considering the situation of
the satellite communities, would make no sense.
This situation exists not only in major metropolitan areas, such as those mentioned previously, but

also in such medium-sized or smaller metropolitan areas as Central Arkansas (Little Rock-North Little Rock and environs), Central Oklahoma (Oklahoma City-Norman and environs), the Tri-Cities area of Northeastern Tennessee and Southwestern Virginia, the Raleigh-Durham area of Central North Carolina, the Madison area in Wisconsin, the Phoenix-Tempe area in Arizona, and many more.

Unfortunately, most planning and land use controls are still predicated upon essentially local powers and considerations. The lack of regional planning and zoning, as indicated in the chapter on zoning and discrimination, has caused some courts to mandate housing requirements for all outlying communities or townships in order to overcome discrimination on the basis of socio-economic status and race. If regional planning and zoning existed, each regional planning area could disperse land uses in a reasonable way within the area without providing for every type of housing component in every township or community.

An example of a state which has looked more toward regional planning is Minnesota, which some years ago provided by statute for regional development commissions, the result of which would permit coordinated development of the Minneapolis-St. Paul metropolitan area including comprehensive planning involving review of the actions of local governmental units.

Interstate compacts today often have an environmental underlay as illustrated by the California decisions involving the Lake Tahoe area. On the other hand, many interstate compacts which affect land use simply involve such public facilities as the interconnection through bridges, tunnels and the like of the New York City-Newark area.

A useful summary of the Lake Tahoe Regional Planning Compact, the Vermont statute, and the Adirondack Park Agency Act is set out in D. Hagman, *Urban and Land Development* 117–120 (1973). The powers of the different governing bodies vary in some respects, but there are many basic similarities with regard to planning for the particular area involved.

The history of these various entities seems to be that when they are created, lawsuits usually or often result which test their constitutional validity or the scope of their powers. The outcome may be determined by how liberally a court is willing to construe its state constitution, which quite often will contain relatively antiquated provisions "freezing" the prerogatives of counties and cities into a particular mold and allowing relatively little flexibility. In Mogilner v. Metropolitan Plan Commission, 236 Ind. 298, 140 N.E.2d 220 (1957), the Indiana Court took the liberal approach in considering a statute authorizing a single planning and zoning department for the entire county in every county containing a city of the first class. The metropoli-

tan planning commission was to develop a plan for
the entire county. The act was attacked on numerous "particulars" which included the "taking"
issue, equal privileges or immunities and equal
protection, procedural due process, separation of
powers, vagueness, the old rule about every act
embracing one subject, and violation of constitutional provisions as to where county administrative
powers must be vested. Despite these and other
laundry list allegations, the act was upheld.

The Lake Tahoe compact was upheld in People
ex rel. Younger v. County of El Dorado, 5 Cal.3d
480, 96 Cal.Rptr. 553, 487 P.2d 1193 (1971). This
case had strong environmental overtones, and the
California Court pointed out that the basic concept
of the compact was to provide for the planning,
conservation and resource development of the region as a whole without destroying the environment. Once again, constitutional arguments put
forth the sanctity of local governmental powers.
This argument took numerous forms, including tax
privileges, preemption of local governmental powers, and improper delegation of powers. Equal
protection was argued, as were matters pertaining
to appointment rather than election of the governing body, a "one person-one vote" argument as
to county representation, and some offshoots of the
foregoing. The court was impressed by the goals
the legislature sought to achieve, the fact that they
could best be achieved on a regional basis, and the

unique problems of the area due to its interstate nature.

The more progressive approach is to uphold such regional schemes wherever there is no direct conflict with state law. Not only is regional planning desirable in general, but in many situations planning is ineffective without it.

§ 6. Local Planning

Despite the trend in recent years toward recognition of the need for regional planning or state planning, most planning still takes place at the local level. This can create conflicts between counties and cities exercising overlapping jurisdiction as well as between neighboring municipalities which are part of a suburban or metropolitan area. This is illustrated by Borough of Cresskill v. Borough of Dumont, 15 N.J. 238, 104 A.2d 441 (1954), which involved four adjoining boroughs and in which an amendatory ordinance of one borough changing a residential zone to a business district did not take into account the contiguous residential areas of the plaintiff boroughs. The court upheld the standing of the other boroughs to bring the suit and held that Dumont had to give consideration to the situation of its neighboring boroughs. The ordinance was invalidated as amounting to "spot zoning" and thus not in accord with the comprehensive plan. In Wrigley Properties, Inc. v. City of Ladue, 369 S.W.2d 397 (Mo.1963), it was held that a proposed zoning change authorizing a shopping center was more for the benefit of other cities and towns than for Ladue. Thus, to the contrary of Dumont, the locality could not be penalized to aid its neighbors. In another case, Township of River Vale v. Town of Orangetown, 403 F.2d 684 (2d Cir.1968), rezoning in a town in New York gave rise to an action brought by a neighboring community in New Jersey, which was held to have standing to sue.

Regardless of these cases, however, zoning decisions remain largely local in nature and usually remain unaffected by situations prevailing outside of the municipal boundaries.

In terms of the operational planning framework within a community, there will usually be a planning commission with a staff (or a planning department), or some other form of planning agency under another name. The members of the commission will customarily be appointed by the municipal governing body, and there will usually be a full-time technical staff of trained city planners (whose status will be discussed at greater length in a subsequent section). Recommendations of the commission are subject to the action of the city governing body when they propose ordinances or seek to revise existing ordinances. One unfortunate feature of the planning process is that local planning commissions are often composed to a large extent of the very people who are most affected by the decisions—building contractors, developers, real estate brokers, and architects (who often work with developers on projects). This is particularly true in smaller or medium-sized urban areas.

Federal aid, and urban renewal and redevelopment in particular, in effect demand that a community engage in comprehensive planning and develop various types of local plans. This situation tends or helps to freeze local planning into a particular mold. But whatever name is employed (such as "internal development plan" or "general plan"), statutes or regulations of government agencies are usually only referring to what is commonly called the master plan.

The Model Land Development Code also provides for a "local development plan," but its description of it is general enough to allow for more flexibility in permitting differing views of the planning process. (See §§ 3–101 and 3–106, Model Land Development Code.)

§ 7. National Planning

Probably the closest semblance to anything that may be called national planning today is in the area of the environment stemming from such acts as the National Environmental Policy Act (NEPA). (Environmental controls are discussed in a later chapter and will not be dealt with here.) These controls, however, are somewhat negative in nature in the sense that they are directed toward

protecting the environment and thereby preventing a particular harm rather than promoting a
positive, comprehensive plan. Of course, there is
also planning associated with national parks, national rivers, and government lands in general.
But there is no comprehensive national land use
program at the present time which would affect
state, regional or local planning. Federal laws and
policies, other than NEPA and related acts, affect
what is done on a local basis—as in the case of
housing, urban renewal and federal taxation. But
the effects are peripheral in nature and ancillary
to the basic intent of such statutes and policies.

During the great depression of the 1930's, there
was a National Resources Board which advocated
national planning. Moreover, during the depression and World War II, our economy in particular
became one which was planned to a very large
extent and remains so today. Beginning in the
mid-1950's and developing extensively in the 1960's
and early 1970's, urban planning was heavily influenced by massive federal aid for such programs as
low-income housing and community development
involving urban renewal and rehabilitation, model
cities, acquisition of open space, and the construction of neighborhood and water and sewer facilities. Most of these programs were suspended or
terminated in 1973, except for funding for existing
projects. However, the Housing and Community
Development Act of 1974, P.L. 93–383, consolidated

urban renewal and several community development programs into a new approach designed to
give localities more control. Federal aid in other
areas affects local land use activities through funding for such projects as airports, water and sewer
facilities, highways and mass transportation, public facilities of various kinds, and various conservation or environmental activities. But all of this is
an ad hoc kind of approach, and there has never
been an overall, cogent national land use policy.
(See generally on this subject, Vestal, Planning for
Urban Areas: The Fight for Coherency, 56 *Iowa
L.Rev.* 19 (1970).)

Congress has in recent years developed an increased awareness of this problem, however. This
was manifested in 1970 by the Urban Growth and
New Community Development Act, 42 U.S.C.A.
§ 4501 et seq., and by the introduction of a bill
intended to establish a national land use policy.
The urban growth act noted the rapid and uneven
growth of urban centers and related problems,
observed that federal programs affect urban development and require coordination, and concluded
that the federal government should develop a national urban growth policy. It set forth certain
worthwhile objectives relative to wise use of physical and human resources, maintaining economic
strength in all areas, reversing trends of population migration, dealing with problems of poverty
and employment, encouraging good housing, im-

proving the role of the federal government in community and urban planning, strengthening governmental institutions to contribute to balanced urban growth, and improving coordination among federal programs. It required an urban growth report from the President in every even-numbered year. This act seems to have had relatively little impact on federal activities or legislation in Congress. Federal programs which affect urban areas remain fragmented.

Despite the introduction of bills in Congress establishing a national land use policy and the backing of them on occasion by the administration, they have failed to pass both houses of Congress, although by increasingly narrow margins. Essentially, such bills would require the states to develop planning procedures, assess resources, develop certain types of data, inventory the land needed and useful for certain purposes, identify critical areas and problems, hold public hearings, and create a land use planning agency. The states would be required to develop planning and regulatory programs taking into account the various factors which planners normally consider. The federal government would establish an office and an advisory board to oversee the state programs and would make grants. Local planning obviously would be affected and, to some extent, directed in certain ways. Obviously, such a program would lead to much more land use planning on a larger scale and would take into account state, regional, and occasionally national considerations.

The Model Land Development Code "looks" in much the same direction although without the federal component. It is apparent that the trend is toward a more coordinated, public control of land use on a much wider scale.

§ 8. Publicly Owned Land

An enormous amount of land, particularly in the western states, is owned by the United States. It approximates one-third of all of our acreage. Most of this is under the jurisdiction of the Interior Department (particularly the Bureau of Land Management) or the Forest Service. Aside from the control and planning emanating from those agencies, bills have been introduced from time to time that would require the development of land use plans principally to protect and preserve public lands.

There have been some proposals which would lead to disposition of federal land to private owners, and this could eventually come to pass. Environmentalists, however, have opposed bills potentially disposing of public lands. The pressure of the energy crisis promoted the idea of selling or leasing mineral producing properties for private development. This led and will most certainly lead in the future to a clash of values.

[67]

§ 9. New Towns

Casebooks generally deal with new towns separately and apart from planning and in greater detail than they will be considered here. *E.g.:* J. Beuscher, R. Wright & M. Gitelman, *Land Use* 1081–1101 (2d ed.1976); and D. Hagman, *Urban and Land Development* 1048–1126 (1973). However, a "new town" or "new community" is the most planned of all communities since it is planned from its inception and develops according to the plan.

Under the English concept, a new town was an independent planned community which existed without interdependence on a nearby city and was large enough to permit various types of housing, economic and social opportunities, and public facilities. During the planning process, the allocation of space to various uses was determined. Such towns were started in open country and were surrounded by "green belts."

In the United States, however, new towns are customarily satellite communities lying within the orbit of or near to a substantially larger metropolitan area. They are developments on a large scale usually undertaken by a development corporation. They follow a plan providing for various kinds of housing, businesses, schools, churches and social and cultural facilities. They are carefully designed to promote the amenities of nature and eliminate or greatly minimize the undesirable attributes of urban life. They may or may not provide land for industry.

The new town concept is generally credited to Ebenezer Howard, an English stenographer and inventor, who developed a concept for "Garden City" which would alleviate overcrowding and reestablish the balance between the country and the city. He presented this idea in a book written shortly before the turn of the century. Before he died in 1928, he had seen two new towns come into being in England. The concept which he developed later became national policy there, and new towns are being built or planned in most modern nations today.

In America, even before the concept of Howard's Garden City, there were towns which were developed as "company towns" by industries wishing to locate outside of urban areas. Examples are Gary, Indiana, built by U.S. Steel, and Kohler, Wisconsin, which was the work of the Kohler Company. But these early company towns were not fully planned and did not control growth. Pullman, Illinois, however, was a company town which provided various cultural and social facilities, with housing varying according to income. Kingsport, Tennessee, was an advance beyond Pullman in that it provided for democratic local government and an early planning body, although the plan and the early zoning restrictions used were not adequate. Crossett, Arkansas, a smaller company

town planned by Harland Bartholomew and Associates of St. Louis, was more of a model of planning
than probably any of the others.

Somewhat different from the company towns
and in some respects the forerunner of the modern
suburb were the real estate communities which
sought to create residential developments on the
edge of cities. These communities eliminated industry and attempted to isolate themselves from
urban growth through planning and through various restrictions. Although these were business
ventures, these communities became self-governing, developed a sense of community, and maintained property values.

The first of the garden city new towns in
America was Radburn, New Jersey, created in the
late 1920's by Clarence Stein and Henry Wright.
(This followed an experience by Stein of several
years earlier when he developed a planned neighborhood in New York City called Sunnyside Garden Apartments.) The Radburn plan attempted to
segregate roads and services from pedestrian, park
and open space areas.

The federal government followed the Radburn
concept during the Franklin Roosevelt administration by building three planned communities—
Greenbelt, Maryland; Greenhills, Ohio; and
Greendale, Wisconsin. But the two leading examples of new towns in the United States today were
privately financed—Reston, Virginia, and Colum-

bia, Maryland. Both seek to follow the garden
concept enunciated by Howard, although the planning techniques which have been applied are far
more advanced and sophisticated.

New communities involve a physical development which provides a full scale of urban activities
but utilizes greenbelts, a variety of carefully
planned uses, open space and a limited population
or area, a complete range of social and public
services, a development which is economically stable and will provide an adequate return on the
investment, and a politically self-governing unit.
They are intended to provide for a multiplicity of
uses and income groups. They obviously entail a
carefully conceived plan which is long-range and
continuing.

The Urban Growth and New Community Development Act of 1970, *supra,* created a Federal Community Development Corporation which was empowered to make grants and loans to new town
developers. The New Communities Act of 1968, 12
U.S.C.A. §§ 371, 1464; 42 U.S.C.A. §§ 1492, 3901
et seq., provided for guarantee of financial obligations incurred by developers of new towns. New
towns have also benefited from federal housing
legislation particularly when they provide for low-
cost housing as a component part of the development.

As might be expected, new towns have spawned
little litigation. However, in Sierra Club v. Lynn,

502 F.2d 43 (5th Cir.1974), cert. denied 421 U.S. 994 (1974), the San Antonio Ranch new town, which involved a bond issue guaranteed by HUD, was attacked by environmentalists who argued that the development would pollute an underground water formation which was the sole water supply for San Antonio. Substantial efforts had been made by HUD and the developer to assure that the underground aquifer would be unaffected, and the court sustained the district court decision to permit the project. The case is perhaps most significant because the court of appeals went into the purposes behind the Urban Growth and New Community Development Act and found them commendable. In Clem v. Cooper Communities, Inc., 344 F.Supp. 579 (E.D.Ark.1972), the court was concerned with the governance of an improvement district in Cherokee Village, Arkansas, which was created for the purpose of maintaining roads, streets, and recreational facilities and providing fire protection. An Arkansas law providing for appointment of the commissioners by the circuit court was sustained against an argument that the equal protection clause required that the commissioners be elected by popular vote. It was also contended that the development company would control the district. The court upheld the statute. Generally to the contrary, however, is Burrey v. Embarcadero Municipal Improvement District, 5 Cal.3d 671, 97 Cal.Rptr. 203, 488 P.2d 395 (1971).

The governance problem is a serious one in many planned communities. The developer wishes to control matters as long as possible in order to carry out his plan. The people are used to democratic procedures and are not used to a fashionable, well-planned equivalent of a company town. Developers err when they do not adequately provide for a transitional sharing of control.

§ 10. The Planners

The planning function ultimately gave rise to a planning profession. In the beginning, planning was chiefly the province of architects and engineers. While they were not cast aside by any means, there gradually began to develop a specialized group, which might or might not have such backgrounds, who had devoted their education and experience solely or largely to urban planning. Moreover, universities developed schools of urban planning.

The City Beautiful Movement in the early 20th century has been referred to as the rebirth of planning. Basically, this form of planning dealt with civic centers, thoroughfares and parks. Plans for public buildings and open spaces were connected with parkways and boulevards. This emphasized the necessity of relating buildings to their sites. It made manifest the need for comprehensive city planning. It also recognized the connection between planning and socioeconomic considerations. It was limited, however, by the high costs incidental to it and the absence of public controls over private actions (such as subdivision ordinances). The movement gave rise to two permanent additions to the American scheme of planning: planning commissions and professional advisors. Architects and engineers served the latter function in the early years. Planning commissions were given an added boost by the Standard City Planning Enabling Act promulgated by the Department of Commerce in 1928. Lawyers, along with engineers and architects, became increasingly involved in the process in the 1920's, state enabling legislation became common along with city planning, and comprehensive zoning blossomed.

Universities began to offer courses in city planning early in the century, beginning at Harvard. These early courses were generally related to offerings in landscape architecture, and modern schools of city planning did not develop until later. By the beginning of the depression of the 1930's, however, comprehensive planning had become fairly well accepted, spurred on not only by the Commerce Department's model acts, but also by the work of such lawyer pioneers as Edward M. Bassett and Alfred Bettman.

The American Society of Planning Officials (ASPO) came into being in 1934 and was the institutional vehicle of the new profession. Moreover, thinking coalesced during the depression years to connect physical planning with social and economic factors as well as to recognize the need for continuity in planning. The post-World War II era gave rise to growth of planning activities by providing more staff support and more funding. The concept of a full-time resident staff of professionals, which had come into fruition before the war, was implemented in much greater measure after it. Schools of city planning grew in number and in curricular sophistication. Planning studies increased in number and in depth, particularly with regard to transportation. Moreover, as the federal government entered the picture on a major basis, impetus to the formation of planning staffs increased. The Housing Act of 1954 was particularly significant in this respect. (See, more specifically on the foregoing discussion, the material in Wright & Gitelman, *Land Use* 312–317 (3d ed.1982).

Modern approaches to planning are often characterized by the attitudes or thought processes of the planners involved. A planner may be of the traditional school and wish to deal largely with the physical environment. At the other extreme is the social planner who wishes to utilize the planning process to further social welfare goals. In between is a physical planner who is sensitized to social needs and will take such criteria into account. On the fringes is the social policy planner who is concerned only with the social effects of physical planning and with great questions of social policy and programming. (See the material in D. Hagman, *supra* 31–34 (1973).) These views must be tempered somewhat by the Code of Professional Responsibility of the American Institute of Planners (AIP), which recognizes the obligation to take into consideration the needs of disadvantaged groups but also speaks of accommodating the client's or employer's interest with the public interest. The tone of the Code would seem to exclude purely social concerns if those considerations could not be accommodated without emasculating reasonable planning procedures.

§ 11. The Legal Status of Planners

The planning profession is so new that it is still struggling to establish its acceptability and to carve out its appropriate niche. Governmental bodies and courts are at times inclined to look upon the planners with some scepticism and to view them as somewhat less recognizable as an independent profession when compared to law, architecture and engineering. (Courts perhaps forget, or are unaware, that the greatest of all English architects, Sir Christopher Wren, was actually a geometry professor at Oxford.)

This peculiar attitude is manifested in New Jersey Chapter, American Institute of Planners v. New Jersey State Board of Professional Planners, 48 N.J. 581, 227 A.2d 313, appeal dismissed, cert. denied 389 U.S. 8 (1967). The case involved a statute exempting architects, engineers and land surveyors from having to pass an examination for a planner's license. The work of the licensed planner was defined statutorily to relate largely to the development of master plans and the offering of professional planning services related to the plan and to land development in general. The AIP objected on the basis of equal protection, pointing out the requirements for planners as to substantial education and experience. (Of course, the architects, engineers and surveyors already had to take licensing examinations related directly to their fields. But the planners argued that planning was a distinct and separate profession.) Noting that modern planning had its roots in architecture and engineering, the court upheld the exemption.

Aside from recognition, a more specific problem relates to the work of planners. Practically speaking, they participate quite heavily in drafting land use ordinances of various kinds—sometimes doing the job exclusively, perhaps with some advice and assistance from the city attorney's office or from outside counsel. An ordinance involving zoning or subdivision regulations is, of course, an amalgam of the application of planning principles, requirements relating to topography and land formations, mathematical formulas and ratios, and legal requirements and considerations. It is complicated and technical, but it is also a legal document. Most attorneys and most planners do not possess the expertise to draft a comprehensive zoning or subdivision ordinance by themselves. These facts are recognized by the AIP. Therefore, when a planner participates in drafting or drafts such an ordinance or appears as an advocate before governmental bodies, is he practicing law?

The case law is sparse on this point. Generally speaking, laymen cannot appear before state agencies in a representative capacity in adversary proceedings. Moreover, in one lower court case in Illinois, a consent decree prohibited a Chicago planning firm from drafting zoning ordinances. In a lower court Pennsylvania case, a planner was held not to have the authority to practice before the board of adjustment. Consequently, it would appear that planners who are not lawyers are constricted in what they may do outside of their capacity as employees or consultants to planning boards or similar agencies.

What the planner does in his capacity as an advisor, however, unavoidably laps over into the legal arena. The planning staff must advise the planning commission on particular applications for rezoning, for example. This often involves the issue of whether this would constitute "spot zoning," which is purely a legal concept, or "strip zoning," which may have legal consequences. The staff must concern itself with whether applications for special use permits (or permits with equivalent nomenclature) fall within the provisions of the ordinance allowing such permits, or whether an application for a variance meets the legal criteria applied to it. Planners thus inevitably deal with a narrow field of law, and if they are not attorneys they should operate in cooperation with the city attorney's office or with independent counsel.

CHAPTER V

REGULATION OF LAND DEVELOPMENT

§ 1. Property Rights and the Police Power

Contrary to popular adage, property rights have never been absolute in Anglo-American law. But in England after the Magna Carta private property could not be taken for public use without due process of law and later not without compensation to the owner (according to Blackstone). Similarly, the 5th Amendment to the United States Constitution, which also applies to the states through the 14th Amendment, prohibits the taking of property without just compensation as do almost all of the state constitutions. Yet the mere regulation of the use of property does not traditionally entitle the owner to compensation and is justified by the proper exercise of the police power, a concept applied as early as the case of the Charles River Bridge v. Warren Bridge, 11 U.S. (Pet.) 420 (1837). The police power is generally defined as the power to legislate for the health, morals, safety, and welfare of the community, and this power can be exercised even though it imposes burdens on the use and enjoyment of private property.

Land use was regulated rather severely throughout the nineteenth century. Justice Holmes, then on the Massachusetts Supreme Court, pointed out in 1889, however, that the power of eminent domain and the police power differed only in degree and no clear line could be drawn between the two. Rideout v. Knox, 148 Mass. 368, 19 N.E. 390 (1889). In 1922, Holmes wrote that "while property may be regulated to a certain extent, if regulation goes too far it will be recognized as a taking." Pennsylvania Coal Co. v. Mahon, 260 U.S. 393, 415 (1922).

Since the holding in *Pennsylvania Coal,* the Supreme Court has not enunciated a clear test for determining when a land use regulation amounts to a taking. The fact that the regulation causes a substantial diminution in the value of the land is not controlling, as long as the property can still be used to the economic benefit of the owner. See, *e.g.,* Penn Central Transportation Co. v. New York City, 438 U.S. 104 (1978); Hadacheck v. Sebastian, 239 U.S. 394 (1915). However, in *Penn Central,* Justice Brennan listed factors which should be considered in determining whether the regulation is a taking: (1) the economic impact, with particular regard to the extent to which the regulation "has interfered with distinct investment backed expectation"; (2) the character of public activity, in the sense that a physical invasion may more readily be identified as a taking "than when interference arises from some public program adjusting the benefits and burdens of economic life to promote the common good"; and (3) the history of sustaining reasonable police power regulations "that destroyed or adversely affected recognized real property interests" and "which have been viewed as permissible governmental action even when prohibiting the most beneficial use of the property," as in the zoning cases.

Some lower courts have found that regulations placing land in public "reservation" for possible future condemnation are takings if landowners are deprived of the use of their property for an unreasonably long time. Generally a one-year reservation period is considered reasonable, while a three-year period has been held to be a taking.

Ordinances controlling land development have also been attacked on grounds that they violate the due process and equal protection clauses of the 14th Amendment by depriving the owner of the most beneficial or profitable use of his land. But as long as the regulation operates to protect the health, safety or welfare of the community, as long as it is not arbitrary, capricious, or unreasonable, and as long as it operates uniformly upon all landowners similarly situated, it will be upheld. Thus where a city ordinance prohibited the operation of a livery stable within a designated area, the ordinance was upheld on grounds that it was not clearly unreasonable or arbitrary, that it operated uniformly on all landowners in the area, that the area was not arbitrarily selected, and that it is within the police power to regulate such activities within a thickly populated area. The court pointed out that even though the operation of such a business is not a nuisance per se, it can be a nuisance in fact and in law under certain circumstances. Reinman v. City of Little Rock, 237 U.S. 171 (1915). The burden of proving that an ordinance is unconstitutional is on the party seeking to invalidate it, and an ordinance has been upheld as a valid police regulation where the landowner failed to show how enforcement of the ordinance would diminish the value of the property, even though the city had failed to show why the ordinance was necessary or reasonable. Goldblatt v. Town of Hempstead, 369 U.S. 590 (1962).

A leading New York decision, Fred F. French Inv. Co. v. City of New York, 39 N.Y.2d 587, 385 N.Y.S.2d 5, 350 N.E.2d 381 (1976), held that a regulation which rendered the property unsuitable for any reasonable productive use was violative of due process and thus void. The court refused to find that the regulation was a "taking" on grounds that a regulation without actual appropriation or occupation can never be a taking in eminent domain. The decision indicates that Justice Holmes was merely using a metaphor when he held in *Pennsylvania Coal* that a regulation can become a taking. This is in keeping with what scholars had generally believed up until recent federal and U.S. Supreme Court decisions.

§ 2. Compensation or Damages for Unconstitutional Land Use Regulation

A question which has not been answered by the United States Supreme Court is whether a landowner whose property has been subject to an unconstitutional land use regulation is entitled to compensation in an inverse condemnation action. In San Diego Gas and Electric v. City of San Diego, 450 U.S. 621 (1981), the Court left the issue unresolved, but two of the justices who currently serve on the Court joined in a dissenting opinion by Justice Brennan which requires compensation under the just compensation clause of the Fifth Amendment for a regulatory taking. This approach might be consistent with the literal words of Justice Holmes in *Pennsylvania Coal,* but has been rejected in state court decisions such as *Fred F. French Inv. Co., supra,* and Agins v. City of Tiburon, 24 Cal.3d 266, 157 Cal.Rptr. 372, 598 P.2d 25 (1979). Thus, there are two opposing lines of thought. One is that a regulation may be a taking in eminent domain for which just compensation is due under the Fifth Amendment. The other is that a regulation is never a taking in eminent domain because it is enacted pursuant to the police power, and the proper remedy for an unconstitutional regulation is injunctive or declaratory relief, not compensation. The latter view may be said to be the near unanimous view of state courts. The former view reflects probably the dominant view in the federal courts.

A closely related question is whether damages may be awarded under 42 U.S.C.A. § 1983 to a landowner aggrieved by an unconstitutional land use regulation. A few courts have awarded such damages under this statute, which reads as follows:

Every person who, under color of any statute, ordinance, regulation, custom or usage, of any State or Territory, subjects, or causes to be subjected, any citizen of the United States or other person within the jurisdiction thereof to the deprivation of any rights, privileges, or immunities secured by the Constitution and laws, shall be liable to the party injured in an action at law, suit in equity, or other proper proceeding for redress.

Awarding damages against cities for violations of Section 1983 is a fairly recent development. In Monell v. New York City Department of Social Services, 436 U.S. 658 (1978), the Court held that cities are "persons" subject to suits under Section 1983. In Owen v. City of Independence, 445 U.S. 622 (1980), the Court held that in Section 1983 suits cities do not enjoy qualified immunity for good faith acts. There is no exhaustion of remedies requirement to bring this type of action.

The Fifth Circuit Court of Appeals, citing Brennan's dissent in *San Diego*, held that a landowner should be entitled to damages under Section 1983 for denial of a rezoning if the denial constituted a taking. Hernandez v. City of Lafayette, 643 F.2d

1188 (5th Cir.1981), cert. denied 455 U.S. 907
(1982). That Circuit reached a similar conclusion
in Wheeler v. City of Pleasant Grove, 664 F.2d 99
(5th Cir.1981) cert. denied 456 U.S. 973 (1982).
However, the First Circuit has held to the contrary, holding that "voiding the offending restriction
will make the owner whole" and refusing to follow
the Brennan dissent in *San Diego.* Citadel Corporation v. Puerto Rico Highway Authority, 695 F.2d
31 (1st Cir.1982), cert. denied 104 S.Ct. 72 (1983).
Thus, there is a clear split of authority between the
Fifth and First Circuits, and the United States
Supreme Court has not yet decided the issue of
Section 1983 damages for regulatory takings in a
definitive case. However, in Lake Country Estates, Inc. v. Tahoe Regional Planning Agency, 440
U.S. 391 (1979), the Court did find that a cause of
action under Section 1983 was stated against a
planning agency for unconstitutional land regulations, although it did not discuss the appropriate
remedy.

A number of issues have not yet been resolved
with regard to Section 1983 actions involving land
use regulations. For example, the Supreme Court
might rule that a direct cause of action is available
under the Fifth and Fourteenth Amendments for a
regulatory taking, or the Court might rule that
Section 1983 damage actions are the sole remedy
for plaintiffs seeking monetary relief. Further-
more, it is possible that the Court will adhere to

the line of authority which holds that monetary relief is unavailable for regulatory takings because such "takings" are actually violations of due process, not of the just compensation clause.

Another important issue in this area is the extent to which the Court will apply federal abstention in land use disputes, including Section 1983 actions. A strong argument favoring abstention is that land use controversies involve important public policy issues on a local level and that local tribunals are more knowledgeable and better suited for resolving land use disputes. On the other hand, those who advocate that courts not abstain in these cases point out that federal courts are the primary protectors of constitutional rights. Until the Court decides the issue in a definitive case, abstention in land use cases probably will remain an unresolved question.

It is generally agreed that an inverse condemnation suit may not be brought against an entity that does not have the power of eminent domain. It is possible that suits for damages under Section 1983 for land use regulations that are "takings" will be similarly barred.

In the event that Section 1983 damages are recognized for regulatory takings, the appropriate measure of damages will be an issue. Compensation in eminent domain is based upon the market value of the property taken, while damages under Section 1983 are compensatory. The difference

between these two might be substantial in a temporary regulatory taking, because frequently the
plaintiff can show no actual damages.

Although clearly there is no exhaustion of remedies requirement for a Section 1983 suit, it is
possible that a cause of action will not lie in the
event that there is an adequate state procedure
and thus no infringement on constitutional rights.
In Parratt v. Taylor, 451 U.S. 527 (1981), the Supreme Court found that there was no violation of
due process when a prison inmate's hobby materials were lost by the negligence of prison employees
because the state had provided a post-deprivation
state remedy. Although some authorities contend
that the *Parratt* holding applies only to alleged
procedural due process violations, a similar rule
has been applied in inverse condemnation actions
where there is an adequate state procedure for
obtaining just compensation for physical takings.
E.g., Collier v. City of Springdale, 733 F.2d 1311
(8th Cir.1984). Therefore, perhaps local governments can avoid Section 1983 suits for regulatory
takings by establishing procedural and remedial
safeguards that insure against infringements of
constitutional rights.

Despite the ultimate resolution of the issue of
compensation or damages for regulatory takings, it
is possible that damages for regulations violative of
other constitutional rights, such as due process and
equal protection, will be available under Section

1983. Thus, even a regulation that is not a "taking" might result in liability for a local government.

The development of law in this area might have a dramatic impact on land use. Those who oppose compensation or damages for regulatory takings believe that such would inhibit local governments from attempting innovative and effective land use controls. Those who favor compensation or damages believe that such is constitutionally mandated and is an appropriate remedy for a landowner who has suffered actual damages. They argue that the aggrieved landowner should at least receive damages for the period of deprivation of his rights—*i.e.*, from the time the regulation was challenged until the time when he received relief.

§ 3. Regulation of Flood Plains, Wetlands and Open Lands

The regulation of flood plains and open lands is closely related to the protection of natural resources and to environmental controls which are the subjects of later chapters. Such regulation is considered here as it relates to the regulation of urban development on the edge of cities or rivers. But the considerations involved cannot be entirely severed from considerations relating to the preservation of natural resources and environmental concerns. Both in fact help justify flood plain regulations.

Ordinances establishing flood plains and open lands are often attacked, as are other types of zoning ordinances, as constituting an unconstitutional taking of property without compensation. However, these ordinances differ from others in that the restrictions imposed are often more severe and the economic effects more drastic to landowners than is true of ordinances restricting land to other types of uses. Flood plain ordinances are usually passed with the view of protecting surrounding areas from flooding or protecting wetlands flora and fauna, which is also an environmental goal.

In Morris County Land Improvement Co. v. Township of Parsippany-Troy Hills, 40 N.J. 539, 193 A.2d 232 (1963), the court struck down an ordinance which prohibited landowners in Troy Meadows, a low, swampy area, from filling land except with materials taken from the zone itself and provided that special exceptions would be allowed only in aid of a permitted use. Permitted uses were few in number. They included the raising of plants and fish, outdoor recreational uses, and conservation uses. The court found that many of the permitted uses were public or quasi-public in nature and that the private landowner was effectively prevented from obtaining a reasonable return on his property. The purpose of the ordinance was to use the area as a water detention basin for flood control and to preserve the land as open space for such public benefits as a nature refuge established within the zone by a conservation organization. In light of the purpose of the ordinance and of its effect upon the plaintiff-landowner's use of its land within the zone, the court found the ordinance to be confiscatory.

An ordinance establishing a flood plain district was struck down in Dooley v. Town Plan and Zoning Commission of Fairfield, 151 Conn. 304, 197 A.2d 770 (1964), on grounds that the effect of the ordinance upon plaintiff landowners was confiscatory. Uses for property affected by the ordinance were limited to parks, playgrounds, marinas, boat houses, landings and docks, and club-houses. The court found that as applied to plaintiffs these restrictions resulted in a severe depreciation of the value of the property since potential buyers were restricted to what amounted to public or semi-public uses. Except when allowed by special exception, the regulations prohibited excavation, filling, and removal of soil, earth and gravel. Although evidence showed that much of the property was subject to periodic flooding, much of it was on high ground which was not even flooded in a hurricane that had struck the area in 1938, and this land could be used for houses. It was also noteworthy that before the defendant had changed the zoning classification, it had levied a sewer assessment of over $11,000 against some of the property and that as long as the property remained privately owned the regulations prevented the sewer system from being utilized.

Both of these cases quoted from the opinion of Justice Holmes in Pennsylvania Coal Co. v. Mahon, 260 U.S. 393 (1922), to the effect that where a valid police power limitation ends and a taking begins is a matter of degree, to be determined on a case by case basis. In *Dooley,* the fact that a substantial amount of the land was suitable for houses and not subject to flooding was damaging to the ordinance. In the *Parsippany-Troy Hills* case, the court suggests that the zoning is really directed toward accomplishment of public aims or goals which should be satisfied by condemnation rather than flood plain limitations. It would seem that the land described in the *Parsippany-Troy Hills* opinion should be subject to flood plain zoning if any ever could. It was a marsh. But the severity of the limitation on the landowner, joined with the apparent public purpose, led the court to conclude that the township should pay for the land if it wanted to so limit its use. By Holmes' yardstick, *Parsippany-Troy Hills* would make one wonder if one could ever create such a district.

In the short span of time between these two cases and the present, however, concern mounted over the state of the environment. While there had been legislation aimed at protecting the environment prior to the late 1960's, public concern mounted to lead to more sweeping federal and state legislation. This concern and the resulting legislation in turn began to affect court decisions.

In Harbor Farms, Inc. v. Nassau County Planning Commission, 40 A.D.2d 517, 334 N.Y.S.2d 412 (1972), petitioner's subdivision plat was disapproved upon ecological grounds. The petitioner's land was on a peninsula that flooded at high tide. It was perhaps the only part of the peninsula that was not developed, and the petitioner had complied in all respects with the zoning ordinance. The plat was disapproved because the planning commission found that a proposed land fill operation would lessen the flow of water in an adjacent channel, that the septic tanks and tile fields would pollute the water in the channel, and that the use of storm water drainage outfalls to conduct drainage into the channel would result in added pollution problems. The court found that the evidence upon which the commission based its findings were not substantial. Noting that the planning commission apparently intended to prohibit development of petitioner's property in order to maintain it in its marshland state, it held that the commission could not completely deny the petitioner the use of his property but could only specify reasonable conditions upon petitioner's right to develop it. The case was remanded for reconsideration of what reasonable restrictions might be imposed. Certainly, the tenor of the opinion is far different from that of the *Dooley* and *Parsippany-Troy Hills* cases.

While the court recognizes the taking problem, it also recognizes justifiable concern over environmental problems.

The movement toward protecting the environment resulted in legislation which, while enacted to fulfill environmental goals, provided the vehicle for regulation of wetlands and coastal areas. An example of this is seen in Just v. Marinette County, 56 Wis.2d 7, 201 N.W.2d 761 (1972). Wisconsin had passed a Navigable Waters Protection Act, and a shoreland zoning ordinance promulgated under it was upheld in the *Just* case. The purpose of the ordinance was to protect navigable waters and the public's interest in them from degradation and deterioration resulting from the uncontrolled use and development of shorelands. One provision of the ordinance required a conditional use permit for the filling of more than 500 square feet of wetlands contiguous to water and the filling or grading of more than 2,000 square feet on slopes of twelve percent or less. In upholding the ordinance the court distinguished, as did the courts in *Parsippany-Troy Hills, Dooley* and *Harbor Farms,* between a valid exercise of the police power and an unconstitutional taking without compensation. But unlike these cases, the Wisconsin Court quoted Professor Ernst Freund's analysis that property taken by eminent domain entitles the owner to compensation because the property is taken for public benefit, while property restricted by the police power entitles the owner to no compensation because the restriction is for the prevention of a public harm. Characterizing the ordinance as one preventing harm which might result from the change in the natural character of the area, the court reasoned that the regulation did not prohibit indigenous uses consistent with the nature of the land. The court recognized holdings in which ordinances establishing flood plains and open spaces were stricken as unconstitutional, but it indicated that too much stress is placed upon the right of a landowner to change commercially valueless land where the change damages the rights of the public.

Cases which hold similarly to the *Just* case include Candlestick Properties, Inc. v. San Francisco Bay Conservation and Development Commission, 11 Cal.App.3d 557, 89 Cal.Rptr. 897 (1970), in which the court upheld the denial of a permit to place fill in the bay, and Potomac Sand & Gravel Co. v. Governor of Maryland, 266 Md. 358, 293 A.2d 241, cert. denied 409 U.S. 1041 (1972), which upheld wetlands legislation prohibiting dredging on plaintiff's property.

Another case in which a court attempted to formulate a test to be used is Spears v. Berle, 48 N.Y.2d 254, 422 N.Y.S.2d 636, 397 N.E.2d 1304 (1979), in which "Spears' Bog" had been classified as wetlands and a permit was denied to extract humus, sand and stone from it. The purpose of the wetlands statute was to balance ecological and economic considerations. The New York Court of Appeals applied the test that it had used in the *Fred F. French* case, *supra,* to the effect that regulation is too burdensome when the property is rendered unsuitable for any reasonable income, productive or other similar use and thereby destroys its economic value. The case was remanded for a hearing on the taking issue. It would be difficult to say in *Just* that the economic value of the property was not destroyed, except insofar as it could be used largely in its natural state. In other words, its economic value for development was almost entirely gone. Only through the argument that a public harm was being prevented and no public benefit was being gained could the court avoid the taking issue. The Wisconsin decision would thus seem to run more along the lines of 19th Century thinking that in the absence of a physical taking, reasonable police power regulations should be upheld, while the New York decision seems more in line with Holmes' thinking in *Pennsylvania Coal.*

It is noteworthy, however, that most of these cases illustrate an increased sensitivity on the part of courts when the aim is to preserve wetlands and protect the ecology as opposed to cases which seek to prevent development because the land tends to flood. The impact of the environmental movement seems apparent, and legislation of this type seems to affect judicial attitudes and the ground rules for

adjudicating such cases. These statutes have led
to an expansion of the police power in that when
courts uphold them, they are saying that no taking
is involved and that the state has legitimately
exercised its police power. Thus, where the older
flood plain ordinances often failed, with the courts
emphasizing the severity of the limitation and
speaking in terms of confiscation of property, legislation preserving wetlands has succeeded, with the
courts emphasizing the public interest and the fact
that the general welfare is legitimately being
served. As for the older group of cases, the problem of an overly restrictive approach remains.
However, some cases have upheld some rather
strict flood plain regulations. An absolute prohibition of structures in a flood plain along a river was
upheld in Turner v. County of Del Norte, 24 Cal.
App.3d 311, 101 Cal.Rptr. 93 (1972). In Turnpike
Realty v. Town of Dedham, 362 Mass. 221, 284
N.E.2d 891 (1972), flood plain restrictions were
upheld in a swampy area reminiscent of that involved in the *Parsippany-Troy Hills* case. While
there is still that fine line to be drawn between the
police power and a taking, the recent cases have
shown a tendency toward a broadening of the police power in flood plain cases. Although this may
simply have been a pour-over effect of the environmental cases and statutes, it is a significant trend.
This does not mean that just any flood plain ordinance will be approved. It does mean, however,

that reasonable controls in swampy areas or in areas of demonstrated propensity toward flooding stand a much better chance of being approved today than they did twenty or twenty-five years ago.

§ 4. Regulation of Urban Growth

With the rapid expansion of population from major urban centers into satellite cities and what were once slumbering nearby towns, some of the municipalities on the metropolitan periphery have passed subdivision ordinances providing controls leading to "phased" or "timed and sequential" growth. When a city attempts to regulate its composition and rate of growth in this manner, the validity of its ordinances are determined by a multiplicity of considerations. Where city services and facilities are in short supply in the face of a rapidly expanding population, courts have recognized a legitimate need for planned, orderly urban growth. Yet at the same time any regulation with the purpose of simply excluding additional population without providing for planned growth would likely be held unconstitutional on the ground that it impinges upon the right to travel and move freely from town to town and from state to state. See Edwards v. California, 314 U.S. 160 (1941). In addition these ordinances must be reasonably related to promoting the health, safety, or general welfare of the community and must not be arbitrary or capricious.

In the landmark case of Golden v. Planning Board of Town of Ramapo, 30 N.Y.2d 359, 334 N.Y.S.2d 138, 285 N.E.2d 291, appeal dismissed 409 U.S. 1003 (1972), the court upheld a zoning ordinance which had been amended to provide for timed and sequential growth on grounds that it was within the state's enabling legislation, although specific provisions for such an ordinance were not included in any statute. The court looked to the overall public purpose of subdivision regulation, which is to guide development in such a way that the community needs for housing, public services and public facilities will be met adequately and in an orderly, convenient fashion. The court found that the amendments in question were consistent with this purpose and were therefore permissible under the enabling legislation.

The town of Ramapo controlled growth by requiring the availability of certain facilities and services as a condition precedent to subdivision development. A subdivider was required to obtain a special permit which would not be issued until the proposed development had accumulated fifteen "development points." The number of points accumulated was determined by a sliding scale measuring the availability of essential facilities and services. While the city had the burden to provide these services and facilities, the developer could

provide them at his own expense if he wished to
hasten development. Under no circumstances
would any of the affected land be restricted for a
period longer than eighteen years, and the scheme
contemplated that special permits would be issued
as essential facilities and services became available. The provisions of the ordinance were in compliance with the town's comprehensive plan.

Noting that the ordinance under review involved
a substantial restriction on the use of land for a
substantial period of time, the court nonetheless
found that the restrictions did not amount to an
unconstitutional taking. The land was not restricted as to all uses, and any landowner could
erect a single-family dwelling. Any diminution in
value to land subject to restrictions might be offset
by an appreciation in value when the restrictions
were lifted. Even if this were not the case, the
court pointed out that where land has diminished
in value because of imposition of restrictions, the
owner will be compelled to bear the burden where
the restrictions are for the public good.

The *Ramapo* decision recognized the unconstitu-
tionality of any ordinance aimed at exclusion, but
the court found that the amendments sought "to
maximize growth by the efficient use of land"
through timed and sequential growth. The court
found that the town was not attempting to keep
population out but was realizing the need to have a

well-ordered growth to prevent deterioration and blight.

A second important decision involving timed and sequential growth was Construction Industry Ass'n of Sonoma County v. City of Petaluma, 522 F.2d 897 (9th Cir.1975), cert. denied 424 U.S. 934 (1976). There the City of Petaluma was faced with an accelerating rate of population expansion, most of which was in single-family dwellings. The "Petaluma Plan" constituted a group of resolutions by the city council requiring that each year only 500 "development units" could be approved for construction and establishing a "greenbelt" around the city to serve as a boundary for urban expansion for at least five years. The purpose of the plan, according to the City, was to promote orderly development of the city, to prevent sprawl, and to provide for variety in building types and densities and for a wide range in prices and rents. For purposes of the plan a "development unit" was defined as part of a project involving five or more units, so that single-family dwellings not part of a project involving five or more units were not included in the limitation and apartments of four units not a part of a larger project were likewise not included. The plan required that the 500 units be allocated equally between the eastern and western parts of the city and between single-family and multi-family units. From eight to twelve percent of the approved units were to be constructed for low and moderate income persons. A complicated point system, measuring factors such as architectural design, recreational facilities, environmental design, and availability of low and moderate income units, was developed to determine which proposed projects would be approved.

The plan was attacked on grounds that it was unconstitutional because it was exclusionary and because it violated due process by being arbitrary and capricious. Relying upon the holdings in Village of Belle Terre v. Boraas, 416 U.S. 1 (1974), and Ybarra v. Town of Los Altos Hills, 503 F.2d 250 (9th Cir.1974), the court upheld the plan. In *Boraas* the Supreme Court had upheld a village ordinance requiring that all residences be single-family (as narrowly defined by the ordinance) on grounds that preservation of quiet family neighborhoods serves a legitimate interest within the police power. In *Los Altos Hills* an ordinance requiring a minimum lot size of one acre was upheld on grounds that it served a legitimate governmental interest in the preservation of a rural environment. The *Petaluma* court reasoned that the plan was less exclusionary than the ordinances upheld in *Boraas* and *Los Altos Hills,* which it thought effectively prohibited future growth, and that the plan served a legitimate government interest within the concept of the public welfare because it sought to preserve the small town character, open spaces, and low density population, and to promote growth at an orderly rate. The court declined to find that the plan violated due process and viewed it as within the police power.

The Petaluma Plan was also attacked on grounds that it violated the commerce clause of the Constitution. Since the plan was a legitimate exercise of the police power, the court found it not to be violative of the commerce clause where it did not discriminate against interstate commerce nor operate to disrupt its uniformity. (The district court had viewed it as violative of Edwards v. California, *supra.*)

The decisions in *Ramapo* and *Petaluma* show that timed and sequential growth ordinances will be upheld as long as they are within the authority of enabling legislation, serve to promote the public welfare, possess legitimate features designed to permit orderly growth, and do not give rise to unconstitutional exclusion. Within the ambit of the public welfare are restrictions aimed at promoting orderly growth, a rural environment, a small town atmosphere, and quiet family neighborhoods. Decisions such as these give rise to the question of whether regional or state planning should be utilized to control and direct urban growth. The dissenting opinion in *Ramapo* argues that such decisions should not be left to individual localities. The *Petaluma* opinion points out that if every municipality in the region surrounding Petaluma were to adopt a plan such as the Petalu-

ma Plan, the impact on the housing market would
be substantial. This is a serious consideration and
illustrates the desirability of planning on an area-
wide scale. Moreover, such considerations may
affect the validity of such plans under appropriate
circumstances. Too much area-wide timed and
sequential growth might prove unconstitutionally
exclusionary in its total regional effect.

In Associated Home Builders of the Greater
Eastbay, Inc. v. City of Livermore, 18 Cal.3d 582,
135 Cal.Rptr. 41, 557 P.2d 473 (1976), the court
upheld an initiative ordinance prohibiting the issuance of further building permits until school, sewage and water facilities complied with certain standards. Unlike the ordinances in *Ramapo* and
Petaluma, this one imposed no time limitations for
meeting the required standards. The plaintiff
failed to carry the burden of proving that the
ordinance did not reasonably relate to the public
welfare, and the court allowed the ordinance to
stand on its presumed constitutionality. However,
the dissent pointed out the lack of a timetable and
the exclusionary effects, which could constitute
violations of the state and U.S. constitutions. This
case contrasts sharply with decisions such as National Land and Investment Co. v. Kohn, 419 Pa.
504, 215 A.2d 597 (1965) and Southern Burlington
County NAACP v. Township of Mount Laurel, 67
N.J. 151, 336 A.2d 713, appeal dismissed 423 U.S.
808 (1975), which are discussed under the topic on

exclusionary zoning. Possibly the court in *Livermore* was giving special consideration to the fact that this was an initiative ordinance passed by the voters, a procedure commonly employed in California.

In *Ramapo, Petaluma,* and *Livermore* the issues involved restrictions imposed by cities in the path of urban growth. The cities were faced with population growth resulting from the socio-economic conditions of the area. But where a municipality is not in the path of urban growth and passes ordinances to restrict the use of its land to preserve its character, the considerations determining the validity of the ordinances are somewhat different from the considerations in *Ramapo* and *Petaluma.* In one case rural property owners formed a municipal water district for a negative purpose—to retard population growth by preventing their land from being included in adjacent water districts which had sufficient water to supply the rural area. The landowners who formed the district did not want supplemental water to be available because they believed that additional water would result in urbanization. The petitioners in the case owned land within the district, and they sought to have their land excluded from the newly created district so that it could be annexed to one of the adjacent districts. They received no water from the new district. The district's board of directors denied the petition, but the trial court held for the

petitioners. On appeal the denial was upheld and
the district court was reversed on grounds that the
board of directors was serving in a quasi-legislative
rather than a quasi-judicial capacity. It was reasoned that the board was elected by landowners in
the district and was compelled to protect their
interests and could not look only to the interest of
petitioners. Even though the new water district
supplied no water, the court found that it could
exist for negative purposes, *i.e.,* to prevent land
within it from becoming part of the two adjacent
districts. The court held that the board's action
was not arbitrary, capricious, or entirely lacking in
evidentiary support and that the board had followed the procedure required by law. Wilson v.
Hidden Valley Municipal Water District, 256 Cal.
App.2d 271, 63 Cal.Rptr. 889 (1967). As questionable as this may appear in a rural locale, it would
seem diametrically opposed to the result to be
expected in an urban setting. See, *e.g.,* Robinson v.
City of Boulder, 190 Colo. 357, 547 P.2d 228 (1976),
in which Boulder was held obligated as the sole
public utility for the area to supply water to an
adjoining rural development.

Another instance in which a court might apply
standards different from those applied in *Ramapo*
and *Petaluma* is where a town imposes restrictions
which are intended to keep developers from building homes intended to be "second homes" or vacation homes for the urban affluent. When a six-

acre minimum lot restriction was passed to keep
such developers from a rural New England town,
the court upheld the limitation even though it
could find no reason why a six-acre limitation was
imposed instead of some other. Noting that it was
guided by no precedent and that the problem presented was not the same as that where restrictions
are imposed in the path of a natural population
expansion, the court found the six-acre limitation
legitimate under the local circumstances and until
further study and planning could be implemented.
The avowed purpose of the limitation included
preservation of the ecological balance of the area,
promotion of orderly, logical growth and avoidance
of population density, all of which the court found
to be within the concept of the general welfare.
Steel Hill Development, Inc. v. Town of
Sanbornton, 469 F.2d 956 (1st Cir.1972). This case
does not square very well with the criteria usually
employed in minimum lot size cases (discussed
elsewhere in this book). The usual requirement is
that the minimum must have a reasonable relationship to the police power and must not be arbitrary or capricious. The limitation in *Sanbornton,*
like the water district in *Hidden Valley,* when one
cuts through the verbiage about preserving the
ecological balance and promoting orderly growth,
was intended to keep people out. The six-acre
minimum related to that objective rather than to
police power considerations. As is demonstrated

in the discussion on minimum lot sizes, however, there is no clear-cut uniform standard, particularly when you move into a rural or semi-rural setting and courts begin taking into account such factors as ecological, historical, cultural and aesthetic considerations. The tendency to approve large minimum lot sizes is much greater in that situation than when the setting is urban, suburban, or one which lies in the path of urban growth.

Although dealing with regulation of subdivision developments and with overall town growth, these cases interrelate with those discussed in this book under the topic of exclusionary zoning. These regulations are basically exclusionary, and that fact gives rise to constitutional problems. There is a fine line that must be drawn between plans or devices which are deemed legitimate in terms of promoting orderly growth within reasonable confines and situations in which the action of the community is viewed as unconstitutionally exclusionary. Therefore, such cases as *Ramapo* and *Petaluma* have to be considered in conjunction with the cases in which the exclusionary action of the community was invalidated. Compare, for example, *Southern Burlington County NAACP v. Mount Laurel, supra,* and U.S. v. Black Jack, Missouri, 508 F.2d 1179, cert. denied 422 U.S. 1042 (1974), discussed in the material under exclusionary zoning. Both invalidated ordinances which had the result of greatly limiting permissible land uses and of keeping out most members of minority racial groups as well as the lower income public in general. The comparison of such cases with the "timed and sequential growth" cases leads to the conclusion that while suburban communities in the path of growth may validly limit growth while concomitantly developing municipal services, they may not pass ordinances intended to discriminate on the basis of race. See Village of Arlington Heights v. Metropolitan Housing Development Corp., 429 U.S. 252 (1977). New Jersey went even further in *Mount Laurel* and held that ordinances which effectively exclude lower economic groups are invalid under the state constitution. In *Arlington Heights,* the United States Supreme Court did not go that far, and it limited constitutional violations to those involving racially discriminatory intent as opposed to those having a racially discriminatory effect, although it indicated that under federal housing legislation, the statutory imperative might be such that a civil rights violation would result from the effect of excluding low-income housing from a community. In this latter situation, upon remand, the Seventh Circuit established criteria under which a community might be held to have improperly discriminated in regard to provision for low-income housing without violating the equal protection or due process provisions of the Constitution. Any future timed and sequential growth plan must take this factor into account

although the decision in *Arlington Heights* generally serves to sustain plans of the type approved in
Ramapo and *Petaluma.* See Wright, Constitutional Rights and Land Use Planning: The New and
the Old Reality, 1977 *Duke L.J.* 841, 864 (1978).

Another comparison might appropriately be
made in the *Sanbornton* situation with respect to
such cases as Appeal of Girsh, 437 Pa. 237, 263
A.2d 395 (1970). The latter case invalidated restrictions which were less severe than those in
Sanbornton. *Girsh,* like *Sanbornton,* sought to
maintain the character of the community. But
unlike *Sanbornton,* the community in *Girsh* stood
in the path of urban development.

The clear message to be derived is that whether
a community is thinking in terms of limiting urban
growth while its public facilities are developed or
of maintaining the character of the community
itself, there is a direct interrelationship with exclusionary practices which in some cases have been
invalidated. Whether it is a zoning regulation or a
subdivision regulation or a regulation of overall
town development, the question of unconstitutional
exclusion is relevant and should not be ignored.

§ 5. Environmental Controls and the Land Development Process

Land developers must seek approval from local
governmental bodies for their subdivisions and other developments, but increasingly they must also

seek approval of various other agencies of government whose purpose is environmental protection.
The extent to which environmental laws and regulations apply to land development has been the
focus of litigation in several respects. For example, development of land bordering a pond was held
to be a "commercial" development within the
meaning of the Maine Site Location Development
Law, even though the development was for home-
sites, because the development of the property was
commercially motivated in that the developer
hoped to make a profit. The act required that
commercial or industrial developments in excess of
twenty acres be approved by an environmental
improvement commission on the basis of several
factors, all of which the court found to be within
the police power. The court also found that the
act's application only to developments in excess of
twenty acres was a reasonable classification and
not violative of due process. In re Spring Valley
Development, 300 A.2d 736 (Me.1973).

A similar decision extending the requirements of
an environmental act to land development was
Friends of Mammoth v. Board of Supervisors of
Mono County, 8 Cal.3d 1, 104 Cal.Rptr. 16, 500 P.2d
1360 (1972), involving a condominium project with
over 180 units, a restaurant and specialty shops
housed in six buildings of six to eight stories.
Local approval had been obtained, but the court
concluded that the state environmental quality act

also applied and compliance was required. In another case, the alleged adverse impact upon the environment by a thirteen story condominium project was alleged to be the obstruction of the view, shadow effect, excessive bulk and excessive relative scale. Polygon Corp. v. City of Seattle, 90 Wash.2d 59, 578 P.2d 1309 (1978). It was held that the state environmental act applied even though the project complied with zoning requirements.

These and similar cases illustrate the problem posed for a land developer in meeting these added requirements and also the different interests involved. Land use planning might dictate that a facility be located in a certain place or configuration so as not to impact adversely on other land uses, while an environmental agency concerned with air quality standards might opt for some other location. See, in general, City of Highland Park v. Train, 519 F.2d 681 (7th Cir.1975). It may legitimately be urged that a developer should only have to secure approval of a single agency charged with considering all aspects of the development including environmental concerns.

It may also be urged with some validity that environmental legislation should not be employed solely as a tool to defeat a proposed project. Thus, the argument that before beginning construction of a large housing project the Navy had to comply with NEPA by filing an environmental impact statement, was rejected because, to make such requirement, the potential effect on the environment must be "significant." Town of Groton v. Laird, 353 F.Supp. 344 (D.Conn.1972). The town was attempting to use NEPA as a device to prevent non-compliance with local setback and dwelling area requirements. "NEPA is not a sort of meta-zoning law," said the court, and was "not designed to enshrine existing zoning regulations on the theory that their violation presents a threat to environmental values."

The conflicts posed by these cases suggest that environmental requirements which are very desirable and generally work fairly well in connection with pollution of streams and waterways and air pollution caused by substantial emissions into the atmosphere are more controversial and subject to question in involving proposed land uses which do not pollute the water or air. The *Friends of Mammoth* and *Polygon* cases may be questioned on the basis that aesthetic considerations largely were at stake as opposed to pollution questions. The principal impact on the environment in *Friends of Mammoth* seems to have been on the natural beauty of the area, although other considerations were raised, such as water and sewage requirements. In *Polygon,* the impact seems to have been on the aesthetics and surroundings in the general area. While it is understandable that residents of single-family dwellings or low density condominiums would not want a high rise condominium project in the neighborhood, it would seem arguable that this is a planning and zoning question and that environmental questions of this particular nature should be addressed in that context or in the context of rezoning the property to a less intensive use.

It is apparent that how broadly particular courts tend to view environmental requirements, based on their own set of values, is an important factor. A related issue is whether aesthetic considerations alone are sufficient to justify the exercise of the police power, which is a subject taken up in a later chapter.

§ 6. Subdivision Regulations

Subdivisions are cities at their growing points. Annexations and the development of suburban communities very much affect the appearance and configuration of a city; but within the city itself, as within peripheral, developing suburbs, the subdivision is the major point of growth. Its appearance and character, its provision or lack of it for essential facilities and services, will directly impact from a social and economic standpoint upon the life of the total community. The very permanence of subdivisions and potential problems that are avoided or created by such development are legitimate public concerns.

Governmental authority to regulate subdivision developments is not normally questioned today.

Legal questions today customarily relate to the reasonableness of the requirements and whether such requirements are appropriate in a particular factual context. To the extent that the question of the power to regulate enters in, it would normally relate to whether the city had exceeded its authority under state law, under its own ordinances, or under the police power generally. The fact that this is so illustrates how far we have come since the 1920's. The older cases raised such questions as to whether a developer could be required to dedicate additional right-of-way alongside property being developed or whether this requirement amounted to a taking. The answer the courts gave was that the streets needed to be widened for public safety reasons to accommodate the development and that the city was not trying to compel a dedication but was simply imposing reasonable conditions on the developer before permitting his plat to be filed of record. Ridgefield Land Co. v. Detroit, 241 Mich. 468, 217 N.W. 58 (1928). Thus, dedication was deemed to be voluntary and for the purpose of gaining the privilege of having the plat recorded.

The principle that the plat recordation is a privilege to which reasonable conditions may be attached extends not only to street dedications, but also to such requirements as the paving, curbing and guttering of streets, the width and surfacing quality of the proposed streets, sewer and water facilities in the subdivision, easements for public utilities, and similar regulations. These are subdivision exactions, which are justified on the basis that the subdivision will increase the public cost of providing services and that a developer who profits from the subdivision should bear at least a reasonable part of the burden of these increased costs and should also develop according to requirements which are aimed at reducing the cost impact on the city and at maintaining a suitable quality of life.

There are powers of cities other than the power to condition recording of plats and the general police power considerations which are involved in this process. The city has the power to condition acceptance of street dedications. In other words, if the developer wants to dedicate street easements in his subdivision to the city in return for the city agreeing to maintain them in the future, then he is required to construct the streets to meet certain specifications. The streets must also be located in accordance with the master street plan. Moreover, the community has the power to protect its right to tax real estate, and thus the accuracy of the plat and the ability of the taxing authorities to list the land correctly on the tax rolls are matters of importance. Trawalter v. Schaefer, 142 Tex. 521, 179 S.W.2d 765 (1944).

The subdivision process, involving the division of tracts into blocks, lots, streets, open land, recreational areas, and the like, necessarily involves standards which are prerequisites for filing the plat and developing the land. This process differs from zoning in that the latter regulates the uses that are permitted and the type of building development that can take place. On the other hand, both are concerned with the orderly use of land and with the prevention of deterioration of property values and demand on community services. Some subdivision controls are directed at assisting the subdivision in comporting with the surrounding locality. This is why the street design must be such as to connect to and interact with major streets on the master street plan. The impact of the subdivision on the need for added or expanded fire and police protection, water and sewer requirements, schools, parks and recreation are also concerns which must be addressed.

Subdivision regulations are of value to the developer in providing an attractive and profitable new venture in which, in the future, the streets, water and sewer facilities, police and fire protection, will be the city's responsibility and not his. Moreover, he may sell his lots or houses by reference to a recorded plat, which is also beneficial to the city since it simplifies its record-keeping for tax purposes. As for homeowners, such regulations assure them of the orderly development of the area according to certain basic requirements for their safety and comfort. Conscientious developers are protected from fly-by-night operators as are the prospective homeowners.

Through this process, subdivisions receive many of the same planning considerations as do zoning decisions. Unlike zoning and rezoning, which theoretically at least is a purely public process, subdivision development is in some respects a joint enterprise of private developers and those who regulate on behalf of the public. The restrictive covenants unilaterally imposed by the developers on the subdivisions bear many comparisons to zoning requirements although such covenants generally go beyond zoning limitations. The point is, however, that the total process obviously has substantial public involvement through the regulatory process.

In connection with this process, one of the problems of cities relates to annexation of land in which some rural subdivisions have already been developed following either less rigid county requirements or no requirements at all. Cities sometimes refuse to accept sub-par streets or water and sewer facilities in such subdivisions as a part of the city system unless brought up to city requirements. As long as such developments can occur outside of the city's jurisdiction, the problem will remain. With respect to such rural land, a subdivider must do more than just file a plat to gain any vested rights that will not be affected by annexation. In other words, he has to institute the development process or, upon annexation, the subdivision regulations will apply to his plat. Dawe v. City of

Scottsdale, 119 Ariz. 486, 581 P.2d 1136 (1979).
Generally speaking, where the developer has made
substantial expenditures and has proceeded with
the project based on issuance of such permits as
are necessary, he cannot be prevented from proceeding by subsequent governmental action. This
is based on varying theories—vested rights, equitable estoppel, detrimental reliance—but how much
development must take place before a developer is
free to proceed will necessarily vary with the facts.
If the developer has spent substantial sums on a
fairly well-developed project and acted in accord
with existing regulations, subsequent ordinances
cannot impose new requirements. But he must
generally do more than simply file his plat or even
start clearing the land.

Another problem is the fact that the subdivision
process, by definition, quite commonly relates only
to dividing land into two or more lots as opposed to
land development in general. If an ordinance or
statute is so limited, it may be held that a non-
subdividing developer does not have to comply with
the regulations. City of Corpus Christi v. Unitari-
an Church, 436 S.W.2d 923 (Tex.Civ.App.1969).
Statutes and ordinances should be written to apply
to development in general as well as to subdivisions.

§ 7. Subdivision Exactions

As mentioned in the previous section, exactions result from subdivision requirements which cause the developer to have to make certain expenditures to comply with the regulations imposed upon him in return for being able to file his plat, dedicate and receive acceptance of his streets, connect his water and sewer lines to the public system, and generally gain approval of his subdivision. They are "exactions" in the sense that they exact from the developer costs which are required by the city.

Exactions raise issues which are based on the taking question. When does an exaction "go too far" and exceed what a city may reasonably require a subdivider to do in return for approval of his project? Today, such requirements as surfacing, curbing and guttering streets to prescribed standards, or constructing water and sewer facilities are commonly accepted. These are what might be called traditional exactions. Problems more commonly arise with land dedications or payment of fees in lieu of such dedications or with off-site improvements.

Jurisdictions may vary on how they construe municipal powers. Some jurisdictions regard statutes authorizing use of the police power by cities and counties as being in derogation of the common law and to be strictly construed. Some statutes, however, state that such regulations are to be construed liberally to effectuate their objectives.

This question of whether the requirements of an ordinance are within the limits of the enabling statute or are ultra vires is frequently a basis for litigation. In jurisdictions with strong traditions of municipal "home rule" the courts do not strictly require the ordinances to be within the enabling acts. See, *e.g.*, Ayres v. City Council of City of Los Angeles, 34 Cal.2d 31, 207 P.2d 1, 11 A.L.R.2d 503 (1949), in which an ordinance was upheld on grounds that its requirements were consistent with the subdivision map act and were reasonable even though they were not specifically authorized by statute.

Traditional Exactions

Cases illustrate how much the attitude toward exactions has changed over the past thirty years or so. In Petterson v. City of Naperville, 9 Ill.2d 233, 137 N.E.2d 371 (1956), the dispute concerned city requirements of curbs and gutters and storm water drainage facilities over which both the county and city exercised jurisdiction. It was held that cities may be given extraterritorial jurisdiction and that the requirements were reasonable within the intent of a statute allowing "reasonable requirements with reference to streets, alleys, and public grounds." The court rejected arguments that this was an illegal tax or a taking. As mentioned, the case also stands for the proposition that a city may be given extraterritorial authority to regulate developments and may enforce its exercise, even though the county has concurrent jurisdiction and has approved a plan with lesser requirements. Requirements of the type involved in this case are seldom contested today, but this case and the older *Ridgefield Land* case, *supra*, illustrate that the tradition of such exactions is not a very old one.

Exactions of this type illustrate the fact that as long as the requirements are not ultra vires with respect to the enabling act and as long as they are reasonable, their imposition will be upheld as a condition to subdivision approval. The developer may be offered the choice of installing the improvements before final plat approval, of furnishing escrow money to cover the cost of improvements as a condition to plat approval, or of furnishing a surety bond guaranteeing installment of improvements.

Other traditional improvements involve such requirements as surfacing streets of a certain width and to certain specifications, installing water and sewer lines of certain sizes and specifications, providing for public utilities to supply electricity and gas, requiring sidewalks, and in general making requirements which are directly related to the health, safety and general welfare of the people who will occupy the subdivision as well as the general public.

But even with these more traditional forms of exaction, questions as to the reasonableness of the requirement (as opposed to the nature of it) may arise. For example, what if a developer seeks approval of a water line of a certain size to connect to the city system, but the city council or planning commission requires a larger line because of the potential demand that will be created by future development outside of the subdivision? This situation combines imposition of a traditional requirement with a requirement that the developer provide for future demand generated by nearby subdivisions yet to be developed. Because the city has a responsibility for growth management, the city's action will normally stand unless its requirement is unreasonable and arbitrary or unless there is some defense such as estoppel which may be asserted. See Wright Development, Inc. v. City of Wellsville, 608 P.2d 232 (Utah 1980). Similarly, the city can dictate the width of minor residential streets within the subdivision based on reasonable street classifications set forth in the master street plan. It can also make reasonable requirements as to the quality, composition and thickness of the street surface. Cases have held that developers can be required to pay the cost of on-site water main extensions into new areas. The question is whether this is reasonable or whether it is an arbitrary or discriminatory requirement. Moreover, cases have held that if the developer employs poor building practices in his construction of improvements, he may be held liable by the municipality. Town of Brookfield v. Greenridge, Inc., 177 Conn. 527, 418 A.2d 907 (1979).

As mentioned in the previous section, although requirements may be imposed retroactively where the plat has been approved in certain limited circumstances, courts may find the city estopped, or that the developer has a vested right to proceed if he has changed his position in reliance on earlier requirements or on the fact that there were no requirements. Compare Brous v. Smith, 304 N.Y. 164, 106 N.E.2d 503 (1952) with Spindler Realty Corp. v. Monning, 243 Cal.App.2d 255, 53 Cal.Rptr. 7, cert. denied 385 U.S. 975 (1966).

Off-Site Improvements

The question of what is a reasonable requirement is more likely to be litigated where off-site improvements are involved. Requirements for off-site improvements are not presumptively invalid— the reason being that the development of a subdivision has ripple effects on the community, and sometimes a direct impact, beyond the physical boundaries of the subdivision. The construction of water and sewer lines, for example, if adequate only to serve a single development, may retard future growth which must depend in part on connecting to those same facilities. By then, these in-place facilities are part of the city water and sewer system and may have to be replaced to accommodate future growth. It is not unreasonable to require the original developer to install adequate lines in order to prevent such future difficulties. Similarly, reasonable requirements may vary de-

pending on such factors as topography, soil conditions, population density, and whether the subdivision is in the projected mainstream of outward
growth.

The problem of allocating costs to a developer for
off-site improvements necessitated in part by his
subdivision is illustrated by some New Jersey
cases. In Divan Builders, Inc. v. Planning Board of
Wayne Township, 66 N.J. 582, 334 A.2d 30 (1975),
the ordinance provided that the cost of required
off-site improvements would be allocated between
the subdivider, other property owners, or any one
or more of them. The court upheld assessment to
developers of off-site improvements as being permitted under the enabling act where such improvements were necessitated by the effect of the development. If the improvement was a municipally
financed general improvement, the subdivider
would pay the difference between the cost of the
improvement and the total amount by which all
properties serviced by it, including the subdivision,
would be specially benefited. If constructed as a
local improvement, he would in addition pay the
amount by which the subdivision property was
specially benefited. A third way would be for the
developer to do it at his expense with a formula
providing for partial reimbursement if the improvement specially benefited other property. The
court in *Divan* decided that there was possible
discrimination in cost apportionment because no

part of the cost of this general improvement was allocated to other properties which were specially benefited. In another case, 181 Inc. v. Salem County Planning Board, 133 N.J.Super. 350, 336 A.2d 501, modified on appeal 140 N.J.Super. 247, 356 A.2d 34 (1976), the plaintiff was required to dedicate land bordering a road as a condition precedent to approving its site plan for construction of a law office. The county required dedication of frontage along every county road without regard to present need or proposed use. The court found this invalid under the "rational nexus" test, holding that the developer can only be required to bear that part of the cost which bears a rational nexus to the needs created by and benefits conferred upon the subdivision. Since his limited activity did not appear at present or in the immediate future to place such burden on the road as to require its improvement, then the requirement was invalid.

The New Jersey holding in *Divan,* essentially to the effect that a developer may be required under one formula or another to pay a reasonable pro rata share of an improvement made necessary in whole or in part by his activity, seems to be equitable and justified. The theory is that since the developer is placing an additional burden on public facilities and, perhaps in concert with other developers, creating the need for new facilities, then he should bear his fair share of the cost. To do otherwise would be to place a burden on the city and on landowners in existing subdivisions to subsidize the developer by picking up the tab for the spillover costs created by his activity. (To the contrary, developers might argue that they should not be penalized for risking capital expenditures to provide homes for newcomers by having to pay for public facilities needed as a result of population growth. Further, they might argue, how can you attribute to a single development, with any degree of precision, the increased public burden?) Be that as it may, the tendency seems to be toward obtaining contribution from developers for the off-site burdens of such activity.

The rational nexus test provides a limitation on this in that the chargeable costs must reasonably relate to the activity of the developer. While this also seems fair, the problem with it is illustrated by the *181* case. It is obviously true that an office for a lawyer or even several lawyers will not alone generate such activity as to require improvement of a road. But if each small business operation along the road, as it developed, could successfully contend the same thing, then the total burden might ultimately compel its improvement or enlargement without any contribution from those along its borders. Moreover, if some businesses were required to contribute land along the road while others were not, then the result of the dedication process would be to leave periodic gaps.

Many courts have employed the rational nexus test in these situations. The connection to the developer's activity must not only be reasonable, but also the requirement must be for presently contemplated improvements and not be for the purpose of banking the land for future use. See, *e.g.,* Simpson v. City of North Platte, 206 Neb. 240, 292 N.W.2d 297 (1980). A separate test is the "specifically and uniquely attributable" test, which upholds assessment for required improvements only where the need is specifically and uniquely attributable to the development. Obviously, while bearing some similarity, this is a much less flexible test than the rational nexus test, would seem to provide a greater burden for the city to meet, and would seem to eliminate in most cases the combining of the burden imposed by more than one developer and the allocation of costs accordingly. A third test is the "reasonable relation" requirement, which places the burden on the developer to establish that the required dedication bears no reasonable relation to the police power. See Wald Corp. v. Metropolitan Dade County, 338 So.2d 863 (Fla.App. 1976), where the latter two tests are rejected in favor of the rational nexus test.

If the rational nexus test could be broadened to alleviate the problem illustrated by the result in the *181* case, which is to say that it could take into account reasonably foreseeable future needs resulting from the combination of a variety of individual developments, then it would seem to be the fairer test. The "specifically and uniquely attributable" test places too great a burden on the city, and the "reasonable relation" test does the same with respect to the developer.

Non-Traditional Exactions

Some cities have passed ordinances requiring dedication of land by the developer for parks, playgrounds, recreational areas, schools or other public facilities, or requiring the payment of fees in lieu of such dedications to cover the cost or part of the cost of such facilities. The amount of land to be dedicated is usually determined by the size of the subdivision or the number of lots in it or both. As in the case of ordinances requiring improvements, these ordinances have been attacked on the basis that they constitute an unconstitutional taking without just compensation. Exactions of this nature have produced mixed results in the courts, and in that and some other respects they bear a close relationship to exactions for off-site improvements.

Illinois was one of the earlier jurisdictions to grapple with these exactions. In Pioneer Trust and Savings Bank v. Village of Mount Prospect, 22 Ill.2d 375, 176 N.E.2d 799 (1961), the court applied the "specifically and uniquely attributable" test to a requirement that land be dedicated for a school and playground and held that the need was not shown to be specifically and uniquely attributable to this subdivision. The court relied in part on an earlier Illinois case invalidating an attempt to allow subdividers to pay a certain sum per lot in return for not dedicating land for schools.

Having given due consideration to this decision and a similar Kansas holding, however, and having accepted application of the "specifically and uniquely attributable" test, Wisconsin reached a contrary result in Jordan v. Village of Menomonee Falls, 28 Wis.2d 608, 137 N.W.2d 442, appeal dismissed 385 U.S. 4 (1966). The ordinance here required dedication of land for schools, parks and recreational facilities, or in lieu of dedication, a certain fee per lot. Both the dedication and in lieu fee requirements were upheld. The fees were upheld as not constituting a taking or an unconstitutional property tax. While the results are dissimilar, both Illinois and Wisconsin adopted the same test, and Illinois presumably would reach the same result if it found the requirements of the test to be met. The Wisconsin Court reasoned that the enabling act permitted the ordinance and that the requirements were a reasonable exercise of the police power where it is shown that the development of the subdivision would increase the need for schools and parks. This rule would uphold payment of fees for public facilities which *may or may not* be located near the subdivision for which the fees were exacted, and it is essentially the rule incorporated in the Model Land Development Code for situations where dedication is not feasible. However, location away from the subdivision area, or the failure to specify in the ordinance that such facilities will be located within reasonable proximity of the subdivision, could result in a successful challenge to the ordinance predicated upon the taking argument, an allegation of an abuse of the police power, or both. It is logical to assume that if the subdivision and perhaps neighboring subdivisions create the burden, then the burden should be alleviated in the same vicinity. Otherwise, it is arguable that subdivision-produced income is being diverted to sustain existing city obligations in older areas, and the legitimacy of the exactions in such circumstances becomes suspect. Moreover, the fees in *Jordan* were to go into two special funds for school and park purposes. If instead the funds were to go directly into the general fund, that would also seem to provide a basis for challenging the ordinance.

Not all courts have passed on such exactions, but there is a clear split of authority. The more recent cases seem to show a slight trend in favor of allowing such exactions. Some cases which invalidate such dedications or in lieu fees do so on the basis that the action is ultra vires with respect to the state enabling act. A good many cases, both pro and con, are cited in R. Wright & M. Gitelman, *Cases and Materials on Land Use* 616–618 (3d ed. 1982).

An economic factor to be considered in connection with this problem is the fact that subdivision exactions increase the cost of housing at a time when housing has become increasingly less affordable for large segments of our population. If the developer has to bear the costs, he will attempt to pass along to the purchasers of his lots and houses a pro rata allocation of such costs. This squeezes developers by narrowing the potential market, which may in turn depress development or diminish the quality of construction or both. On the other side of the economic coin, some potential purchasers find themselves increasingly unable to enter the market particularly in an economy of high interest rates. The contrary argument in favor of exactions, as stated previously, is that the public should not have to subsidize developers in their entrepreneurial activities by assuming exterior public burdens produced by such developments. Moreover, the public should not permit shabby developments. These are problems of substantial economic and social concern which have a way of influencing courts as well as legislative bodies.

CHAPTER VI

ZONING

§ 1. Background

Zoning is the principal tool employed in urban planning. Although zoning was utilized in such European countries as Germany and France in the 19th century, the first comprehensive zoning ordinance was that adopted in 1916 by New York City and upheld in a case decided in 1920. Lincoln Trust Co. v. The Williams Bldg. Corp., 229 N.Y. 313, 128 N.E. 209 (1920). Other states followed suit and broadened the process. Wisconsin permitted zoning outside of corporate limits in 1923 and authorized rural zoning in 1929.

The validity of zoning is predicated on the police power—the power to regulate for the advancement and protection of the health, morals, safety or general welfare of the community. Whether a particular zoning regulation will be upheld depends generally on whether it represents a valid exercise of the police power. If the application of the regulation to the property in question is unreasonable, arbitrary and capricious, it will be held invalid. If it deprives the property of all or practically all reasonable use, then it will be invalidated on the basis both that it is unreasonable and that it constitutes a taking of the property without just

[*133*]

compensation. Under the test framed by Justice Holmes in Pennsylvania Coal Co. v. Mahon, 260 U.S. 393, 415 (1922), and followed in varying degrees since then, the extent of the police power and its valid use will depend on the particular facts of the case at hand. The same is true with respect to whether a particular type of regulation is a valid exercise of the police power.

Prior to comprehensive zoning, the police power was used for relatively simple regulatory measures relating to fire zones, building controls and limitations on certain nuisance-like uses in locations where they were not compatible. For example, Reinman v. Little Rock, 237 U.S. 171 (1915), upheld an ordinance prohibiting a livery stable within a certain area, and Hadacheck v. Sebastian, 239 U.S. 394 (1915), upheld an ordinance which prohibited operation of a brickyard or brick kiln within certain limits in Los Angeles. Comprehensive zoning of the last 60 to 70 years, however, has involved the creation of a variety of use, height and area restrictions in districts throughout a municipality.

After comprehensive zoning came into use, it received varied treatment at the hands of state courts. It was upheld in New York, as we have seen, and in Wisconsin shortly thereafter in State ex rel. Carter v. Harper, 182 Wis. 148, 196 N.W. 451 (1923), which opinion is a rather classic statement of the rationale supporting comprehensive zoning. Maryland, however, struck down the Baltimore zoning ordinance, viewing zoning as an encroachment upon constitutionally protected property rights.

Comprehensive zoning was upheld by the Supreme Court in the landmark case of Euclid v. Ambler Realty Co., 272 U.S. 365 (1926), which drew upon the nuisance analogy of pre-zoning cases to uphold the basic validity of such ordinances under the police power and which decision, in particular, emphasized the need to protect single-family dwellings from commercial, industrial or multi-family encroachment. Ever since *Euclid,* such zoning has commonly been referred to as "Euclidian" or "Euclidean" zoning. A year and a half after *Euclid,* the Supreme Court invalidated a zoning provision as being unreasonable and unconstitutional as it applied to a particular tract of land. Nectow v. Cambridge, 277 U.S. 183 (1928). This case provided what then became the customary manner of attacking such an ordinance—i.e., the ordinance is confiscatory or is unreasonable and arbitrary in the way in which it has been applied to a specific parcel of land. (This is the logical application of *Pennsylvania Coal, supra.*) The customary remedy to the invalidity was to require rezoning in such a way as to permit the landowner to make reasonable use of his property.

§ 2. Enabling Acts and Zoning Ordinances

The general rule is that to be valid a zoning ordinance must be authorized by enabling authority, and the validity of the provisions of the ordinance may be tested on the basis of whether they are "ultra vires" or are within the confines of the enabling authority. While such enabling authority may be found in a state constitution or a municipal charter, it is customarily the result of a state statute authorizing local zoning ordinances, providing the basis for the creation of planning or zoning commissions and boards of adjustments and their authority, and prescribing certain criteria for such ordinances and their adoption. The original basis for much of the zoning legislation in most states was the Standard Zoning Enabling Act which was prepared as a model act in the 1920's by the U.S. Department of Commerce. This act is often referred to simply as the "Standard Act."

State enabling legislation differs somewhat on whether the enactment of the zoning ordinance be preceded by a study of conditions in the community followed by a report or reports on such conditions and the development of the comprehensive plan on which the zoning ordinance will be based. States which require such a procedure, which is considered to be the better practice, are placing an emphasis on planning with zoning to serve as the instrument of planning. After a study of population trends, existing land use patterns, traffic conditions and problems, the location of major business districts and commercial areas, drainage or sewage problems, the location of public buildings, single-family areas, and so forth, a master plan is developed and after public hearings on the proposed plan following notice to the public, the plan is ultimately adopted. The zoning ordinance is then written based on the needs and requirements of the master plan or comprehensive plan, and after notice and public hearings, it is adopted. A number of cases have held that unless such a process is followed, any zoning ordinance which is adopted is invalid. This is based on the view that zoning is not an end in itself but is a tool of planning. But, as stated, this rule is not universal. Some states do not require that a planning process precede adoption of the zoning ordinance. Also, because of the problem of controlling the development of discordant land uses until the planning process is completed, interim zoning of a temporary nature is sometimes permitted. Unless interim zoning is specifically authorized by the enabling act, however, it may be held invalid.

In all of this, the provisions of the enabling act will control the outcome. If it does not require comprehensive planning as a condition precedent to adoption of a zoning ordinance, then no such process need be followed. If it does, then the zoning ordinance must await the completion of the planning process. While planning properly should precede the zoning ordinance, it would seem desirable to permit interim zoning for a period not to exceed one year.

§ 3. Spot Zoning

Once a zoning ordinance has been adopted and the land has been zoned, problems arise with regard to proposed amendments changing its application to specific parcels or with respect to granting relief from its provisions for certain lots. Such amendments or relief often give rise to allegations of "spot zoning."

Spot zoning, by definition, is invalid because it amounts to an arbitrary, capricious and unreasonable treatment of a limited area within a particular district. As such, it departs from the comprehensive plan. It singles out a parcel of land for special treatment or privileges not in harmony with the other use classifications in the area and without any apparent circumstances which call for different treatment. Spot zoning almost invariably involves a single parcel or at least a limited area. However, the "floating zone" device which is discussed later in this chapter was successfully attacked as constituting spot zoning even though that device normally involves substantial acreage. Eves v. Zoning Board of Adjustment, 401 Pa. 211, 164 A.2d 7 (1960).

An allegation of spot zoning may arise from situations involving amendments to the ordinance, variances, special use permits or special exceptions or similar devices discussed in later sections. Any change may be subjected to such a contention except possibly for one involving comprehensive revision of a substantial area or of the master plan based on new studies and new information. Even then, some small part of the revision may come under attack.

Allegations of spot zoning are defended against with such contentions as that the change is in accord with the master plan, that conditions in the area have changed drastically since the original zoning thereby justifying the change as to the parcel or parcels involved, that the action taken by the city zoning authority was fairly debatable and entitled to be upheld unless clearly erroneous and arbitrary, that the parcel or parcels are afflicted by some condition peculiar and unique to them which justifies the change, that the change meets the criteria of the ordinance allowing a conditional use or special use permit or special exception, that the zoning would be confiscatory or an unreasonable hardship to the landowner unless the change were granted, and that (in the case of larger parcels) the change is in the public interest and promotes the general welfare.

There is some indication that where the boundaries of several communities run together, one community may rezone in such a way that it constitutes spot zoning in terms of the adverse and unreasonable effect upon adjoining communities. Borough of Cresskill v. Borough of Dumont, 15 N.J. 238, 104 A.2d 441 (1954).

§ 4. Zoning Amendments

The most obvious way to effect a zoning change is to amend the ordinance. There may be a single, major amendment as the result of new studies. The usual situation, however, involves periodic amendments resulting from applications from interested landowners. This process involves a legislative act on the part of the council or board according to the majority view.

Amendments are tested by essentially the same standards as the zoning ordinance, *i.e.*, whether the restriction is arbitrary or whether it bears a reasonable relationship to the police power. No vested rights accrue in neighboring landowners to have land zoned the same way it has been. While a change in the character of an area is often a predicate for rezoning, it is not an essential element to rezoning if the amendment is reasonable. Moreover, a landowner seeking a rezoning amendment does not normally have to establish that denial of his request would be confiscatory as to use of his land (although he would clearly be entitled to the amendment if that could be shown). If the relative gain to the public is small when compared to the hardship to the property owner, the amendment will likely be granted. See, *e.g.*,

Duggan v. Cook County, 60 Ill.2d 107, 324 N.E.2d 406 (1975).

Periodic amendments may result in allegations of spot zoning, in which the change from single-family residential to multi-family residential, for example, is essentially preferential in nature and cannot be reasonably justified. On the other hand, if the amendment in question involves rezoning in accord with a plan which has taken into account the changing circumstances inherent in or imping-ing upon a single-family zone, then it is more likely to survive an allegation of spot zoning. Of course, an amendment following negotiations with the owner may give rise to an allegation of contract rezoning if that course is pursued, although a re-zoning with unilateral conditions attached might permit a different result, as will subsequently be discussed.

The Model Land Development Code seeks to dis-courage amendments involving small parcels. Sec-tion 2–205 contains rather broad provisions autho-rizing the revision of district boundary lines upon the making of certain findings by the land develop-ment agency.

The question of standing to attack a zoning amendment is rarely raised. It is usually the nearby neighbors who object or bring suit. Their allegations usually relate to diminution in value of their property if the proposed change is permitted and other adverse effects upon their property which would result from a different, proposed use. If the objectors include a neighborhood property owners association, again the question of standing is seldom reached; but in questioning the standing of such an association, the courts would look to its capacity to assume an adversary role, its size and composition, the potential effect on the group it represents, and whether membership is open to all property owners in its neighborhood.

§ 5. Contract or Conditional Rezoning

These terms are sometimes used interchangeably, particularly by courts which are in the process of invalidating a rezoning on this basis. Some courts have sought to distinguish between the two, holding "contract zoning" (or rezoning, actually) to be invalid while sustaining conditional rezoning. Thus, the Maryland Court has referred to "impermissible conditional zoning," while other states have approved unilaterally imposed conditions or rezoning which is subject to revocation if certain conditions are not met. *Cf.:* Montgomery County v. National Capital Realty Corp., 267 Md. 364, 297 A.2d 675 (1972), with State ex rel. Zupancic v. Schimenz, 46 Wis.2d 22, 174 N.W.2d 533 (1970) and Arkenberg v. Topeka, 197 Kan. 731, 421 P.2d 213 (1966).

The basis of the invalidity of contract rezoning is that a city cannot bargain away its police power. A process of negotiation between the municipal

government and a private person leading to zoning
reclassification of land in order to accommodate
private interests has been viewed as amounting to
spot zoning and thus invalid. Based on this thinking, some jurisdictions have held that rezoning on
the express condition that the owner impose certain restrictions on the use of his premises is also
illegal. The idea is that the conditions must be
imposed, if at all, by the zoning ordinance.

Courts which have sustained conditional rezoning have segregated situations in which the city
has unilaterally imposed conditions which must be
met for the rezoning to take place or has rezoned
the land conditionally subject to revocation of the
action if the conditions are not met. Sylvania
Electric Products v. Newton, 344 Mass. 428, 183
N.E.2d 118 (1962); Church v. Islip, 8 N.Y.2d 254,
203 N.Y.S.2d 866, 168 N.E.2d 680 (1960). These
special restrictions are justified on the theory that
they require the owner to perform some act or
make some improvements which will justify a different classification and which will avoid harm to
neighboring property or to the planned use of the
surrounding area. Cases upholding such reclassification view the conditions as reasonable and not
arbitrary and as a valid exercise of the city's police
power. Perhaps implicit in those cases is the
thought that to deny rezoning which would be
reasonable if certain conditions existed or could be
created would, in itself, be arbitrary. Contract

rezoning, on the other hand theoretically involves a situation similar to a bilateral contract in which both the city and the landowner enter into an express agreement involving mutual obligations.

The distinction is obviously tenuous. Any owner or developer seeking rezoning will undergo a period of discussion and negotiation of sorts with the planning staff and possibly the planning commission or even the city board. What appear to be unilateral conditions have often been hammered out over a period of time involving numerous discussion sessions. On the other hand, the advantage of conditional rezoning lies in the flexibility afforded planning officials in seeking to accommodate landowners in such a way as not to interfere with the master plan or harm adjoining landowners. It affords a middle ground rather than a strict "yes" or "no."

There is a split of authority on conditional rezoning with its validity having been accepted largely in Midwestern and Northeastern jurisdictions. Contract rezoning is another form of spot zoning and is invalid. The basic question is whether a given jurisdiction will "spin off" conditional rezoning into a separate category or classify both forms as essentially the same and as illegal.

It should be noted that conditions are commonly attached to the granting of variances and special use or conditional use permits or special exceptions. Therefore, why should any distinction be made between rezoning subject to conditions and administrative relief granted subject to conditions? Presumably, it goes back to the old idea that rezoning is a legislative act and (in a jurisdiction making no distinction between contract and conditional rezoning), the legislative body cannot bargain away the police power. Granting a special use permit, special exception or conditional use permit is viewed as an administrative or quasi-judicial act. Just as the distinction that many states make between illicit contract rezoning and permissible conditional rezoning is somewhat narrow, so also is the legislative-administrative distinction that is made between rezoning and the granting of a special or conditional use. In a minority of jurisdictions which regard the rezoning of small parcels as being administrative in nature, which it largely is, then there is no reason not to permit conditional rezoning. But even some of the states which make the distinction between rezoning and the administrative process view conditional rezoning as permissible.

The Indiana legislature adopted a statute which has the effect of allowing or requiring an owner to make written commitments relative to rezoning and which also has the effect of legalizing conditional rezoning by statute.

§ 6. Variances

The variance is the most controversial, most abused, and usually the most used administrative relief that can be granted in requests for zoning changes. A variance is granted when "unnecessary hardship" would result to the landowner if it were denied. Some statutes allow variances based upon either "unnecessary hardship" or "practical difficulties," but this seeming liberalization of the rule is likely illusory since cases which find "practical difficulties" to exist will be translated in other jurisdictions to mean "unnecessary hardship." "Mere" hardship is not enough to amount to unnecessary hardship, however. Devereaux Foundation Inc. Zoning Case, 351 Pa. 478, 41 A.2d 744, appeal dismissed 326 U.S. 686 (1945).

These hardship conditions which lead to the granting of variances should be peculiar and unique to the land in question. If such conditions existed over a wide area, the proper remedy would be rezoning. An appropriate variance situation, however, involves a single lot or a relatively small area which suffers from peculiar, unique circumstances.

There are area variances and use variances. The former is the least controversial and least abused because it is generally granted due to some odd configuration of the lot or some peculiar natural condition which prevents normal construction in compliance with zoning restrictions. The relief is usually a simple relaxation of the requirements as to set-back or minimum floor area or the like. A use variance on the other hand involves a change in the permitted use—as from single-family residential use to multi-family use or to one of the higher classifications of commercial use. A use variance can only be sustained where unnecessary hardship (or, in some states, practical difficulties) would result, and since this must be hardship which is unique and peculiar to the lot, use variances are often attacked as constituting spot zoning. Some jurisdictions have applied the unnecessary hardship test to use variances and the practical difficulties test to area variances, which is both reasonable and descriptive of the different nature of the problem.

Abuses involving the use variance led one city to abolish the device, but the state supreme court ruled that the use variance could not be abolished under the state enabling act (even though the enabling act made no specific requirement along that line). Nuckolls v. City of Tulsa, 560 P.2d 556 (Okl.1976). Since hardship cases could have been handled under other administrative devices designed to relieve hardship, and through the amendment process, the decision was unnecessary and unfortunate. Moreover, some state statutes do not permit use variances at all. Perhaps it was the desire to prevent abuse which led one court to define unnecessary hardship as a deprivation of all beneficial use amounting to confiscation. R-N-R Associates v. Zoning Board, 100 R.I. 7, 210 A.2d 653 (1965). This definition perhaps requires too much, but the burden on the applicant would seem to deter the wholesale granting of variances.

The hardship which justifies granting a variance must stem from the application of the ordinance to the property in question and not from actions of the applicant which amount to self-induced hardship. Moreover, if the "unique and peculiar" circumstances of the situation actually apply to the entire area or neighborhood, the appropriate corrective device is rezoning rather than a variance.

The Pennsylvania Supreme Court quoted these requirements for a variance: "The sole justification for the grant of a variance is that a strict application of the terms of the zoning statute will result in an 'unnecessary hardship', and even then, the variance can be granted only if 'the spirit of the ordinance may be observed, the public health, the public safety and the general welfare secured and substantial justice done'. He who seeks a variance has the burden of proving justification for its grant. The 'hardship' which must be proven must be an 'unnecessary', not a 'mere' hardship, as well as 'unique or peculiar to [the property involved] as distinguished from the impact of the zoning regulations on the entire district'. The fact that an increase or decrease in value will result from the grant or refusal of a variance will not,

standing alone, constitute a sufficient hardship."
In re Cresko, 400 Pa. 467, 162 A.2d 219 (1960). If
every board of adjustment and every court were
more aware of these factors and applied them more
rigorously in place of bending them to meet the
economic aims of developers and landowners, use
variances would no longer constitute a synonym
for evasion of zoning restrictions. As matters
stand today, zoning is as much characterized by
the variances from it as by the adherence to it.

§ 7. Special Exceptions and Special Use or Conditional Use Permits

Some writers have attempted to distinguish between special exceptions and special use permits by
defining the former to involve authority by the
planning board or board of adjustment to permit
certain deviant uses where it can make certain
findings provided for in the ordinance, and by
defining special use permits as involving situations
requiring particular attention and special treatment due to the neighborhood or city-wide ramifications of the special use. As a practical matter,
the cases illustrate that about the only difference
in special exceptions, special use permits, and conditional use permits is the term employed in a
particular enabling act or ordinance. See Tullo v.
Township of Millburn, 54 N.J.Super. 483, 149 A.2d
620 (1959). The ordinance will specify the conditions and findings which are required to grant such

relief, and the relief will be granted only when those conditions are found to exist. Presumably, an implicit condition always would be that the relief granted must neither ravish the master plan for the neighborhood nor amount to such preferential treatment as to constitute spot zoning. One major line of attack on such actions would be that it was unreasonable and capricious for the board to find that the criteria of the ordinance was met or not met in granting or denying the special permit or special exception.

The Model Land Development Code allows special development permits based upon a finding of compatibility with surrounding areas and with developments already permitted under the general provisions of the ordinance.

It is common for boards to attach conditions to the granting of special exceptions or special use permits in order to preserve the integrity of the neighborhood. The same is true of variances. See Montgomery County v. Mossburg, 228 Md. 555, 180 A.2d 851, 99 A.L.R.2d 222 (1962).

The difference between variances and special exceptions or special use permits is that variances allow a prohibited use based on unnecessary hardship, while these special permit procedures are allowed in situations specified or described by the zoning ordinance in the event certain facts are found to exist.

The term "*special* exception" should not be confused with a plain *exception* in a zoning ordinance. The latter usually involves a non-discretionary determination in that the ordinance simply provides that certain types of structures or uses are excluded from the application of all or part of the ordinance.

Some cases have involved questions as to whether the special permit procedure embodied in a local ordinance is authorized by state enabling legislation. While the cases have varied, the better view is that unless the local provisions for such procedure are so loose as to involve a delegation of what is traditionally viewed as legislative authority, the issuance of special use permits should be permitted if the prescribed standards are met (including the very basic requirement that the master plan not be violated). Otherwise, municipalities are deprived of a method of alleviating the rigidity of traditional zoning regulations.

§ 8. Floating Zones

The floating zone is described in the ordinance in such a way that its characteristics and the requirements for its establishment are defined, but its location remains undesignated. It can come into being when the board finds that a situation exists which allows the location of that type of zone in a particular area. Then, the criteria of the ordinance presumably having been met, the floating zone ceases to "float" and is located by a zoning amendment.

This device was upheld in New York and Maryland, but it was invalidated in Pennsylvania as constituting spot zoning and as not being in accord with the comprehensive plan. Rodgers v. Village of Tarrytown, 302 N.Y. 115, 96 N.E.2d 731 (1951); Huff v. Board of Zoning Appeals, 214 Md. 48, 133 A.2d 83; Eves v. Zoning Board, 401 Pa. 211, 164 A.2d 7 (1960). In the *Rodgers* case, garden apartments (provided for in the "floating zone" ordinance) were permitted in a single-family residential area where the criteria of the ordinance had been met and where the court thought the action taken formed a part of a comprehensive zoning plan as opposed to spot zoning.

The floating zone is somewhat of an historical antecedent of the modern cluster zone and planned unit development. Its purpose is to provide greater flexibility to the municipality in dealing in a specified, limited way with needs which are expected to occur but cannot presently be accomodated effectively or with as much intelligence now as later.

Floating zones should normally be upheld if permitted by or not in conflict with the master plan, if the criteria and standards provided for them are adequate, and if the action taken is not arbitrary or unreasonable. The type of development should make some difference, since it would appear to be easier to "float" a multi-family residential development into a single-family residential area than to "float" an industrial area or a high density commercial area into disparate zones. But this did not form the basis for the ruling in Pennsylvania. Nor, for that matter, did it form the basis for the favorable ruling in Maryland. The keys to the question of whether a floating zone provision will be upheld probably relate to the interpretation courts are willing to accord to the enabling statute, the criteria employed in the ordinance, and the general attitude of the court toward the issue of the appropriate amount of flexibility to be accorded local authorities.

By way of example, in one case a proposed rezoning involved a floating zone which was upheld against allegations that it amounted to an improper delegation of legislative authority, was lacking in uniform regulations, failed to define standards for project approval, and constituted spot zoning. The court stated that there were uniform restrictions within the type of zone involved, general standards to be considered, and that the fact that spot zoning might occur in a particular circumstance would not invalidate the zoning. Treme v. St. Louis County, 609 S.W.2d 706 (Mo.App.1980).

§ 9. Planned Unit Developments and Cluster Zones

These are relatively recent devices intended to ameliorate the rigidity of Euclidian zoning. Their applicability and importance is best understood by reference to subsequent sections in this chapter relating to setback lines, side-lot lines, minimum lot sizes, and the like. Traditional zoning located structures on similarly sized lots in similar locations much as Washington's head might be similarly located on each dollar bill.

Cluster zoning permits residential uses to be "clustered" more closely together than normally permitted, leaving substantial area to be devoted to open space in the form of parks, playgrounds, woods, and the like. The population density in the cluster zone remains essentially the same, and the only advantage to the developer may be the saving of some money on street construction. See Chrinko v. South Brunswick Township Planning Board, 77 N.J.Super. 594, 187 A.2d 221 (1963). The advantage to homeowners and to the public is the creation of an area which preserves many of the amenities of rural living within an urban environment. Property values are maintained (—and, in good developments, promoted—), and thus a basic aim of residential zoning is carried out in a nontraditional context.

The planned unit development (PUD) is broader in scope. It not only involves the clustering of residential uses but also permits commercial uses which are compatible and perhaps even light industry. Height variations may also be involved. See Orinda Homeowners Committee v. Board of Supervisors, 11 Cal.App.3d 768, 90 Cal.Rptr. 88 (1970). Once again, the relative population and use density of the total area is intended to remain stable while the amount of open space is increased. Implicit in the PUD is the requirement that varying uses blend harmoniously within the area and create an attractive, interrelating unit which should maintain both property values and the aesthetics of the area. The PUD obviously presents a greater potential for abuse than a cluster plan because it involves mixed uses. If it were utilized as a sham to permit commercial or industrial incursion into an area zoned residential, thereby failing to fulfill the underlying rationale for permitting a PUD, it would amount to an arbitrary and capricious abuse of the police power.

A PUD or a cluster zone which is in accord with the criteria previously described should also meet the requirement of being in accord with the master plan (or, if not, the master plan should be amended to permit such developments). *Euclid* sustained zoning at least partly on the basis that this exercise of the police power resulted in maintaining property values. A properly planned PUD or cluster zone does that and with considerably less monotony than the scheme approved in *Euclid*.

Moreover, the PUD has the planning value of allowing people to live closer to shopping areas and perhaps closer to where they work, which is a substantial factor in a time when the energy problem is important. The only danger in the PUD would be its potential abuse by greedy developers who were able to overcome the planners politically and create a monstrosity in the name of the PUD.

The PUD concept obviously goes beyond that of the floating zone in that it involves the harmonious integration of multiple uses. It is somewhat comparable to the new town concept on a smaller scale and is attached to an already developed urban area. Proper utilization of the PUD, however, readily lends itself to a comparison with new towns in the sense that both should have similar objectives. PUD ordinance provisions must be carefully drawn to require adequate open space and to achieve the objective of a successful blending of uses. In this regard it is important that adequate acreage be involved in a development, since otherwise the utilization of the PUD concept could result in a peculiar hodge-podge which could adversely affect property values both in the PUD area and in the surrounding area. If utilized properly, however, the PUD provides a new dimension particularly for suburban or fringe area development. It offers the potential for creating the equivalent of small, model towns around an urban core.

When employed properly, the PUD also offers considerable potential for alleviating the problems of commercial strip zoning and the unfortunate traffic situation which it usually creates.

In judicially evaluating challenges to local actions approving PUDs, the most important role of the courts is to determine whether they are dealing with a device which conforms to the intent behind and the criteria for a PUD or whether the particular action taken allows a large-scale developer to achieve indirectly what he could not achieve directly. Entering into this determination are questions as to population density, the architectural and engineering considerations involved in arranging and locating different uses within the PUD, the interrelationship or successful blending of the various uses, traffic patterns, and provisions for open space and recreational areas.

Similarly, in evaluating PUD ordinances, courts should be primarily concerned with whether the provisions of the ordinance are designed to achieve the purpose of the PUD (or of a cluster zone, if it is that type of ordinance).

§ 10.　Buffer or Transition Zones

An older device which was also intended to provide for compatibility of nearby disparate uses was the buffer or transition zone. Such a zone was employed, for example, to assure that in the area between a single-family residential zone and a commercial zone, a multi-family residential zone would smooth the transition or, more appropriately, provide a "buffer" for the single-family residential zone. Open space in the form of a park or playground area could provide for a similar transition and amount to a buffer. See, generally, Evanston Best & Co. v. Goodman, 369 Ill. 207, 16 N.E.2d 131 (1938).

Of course, the use of buffer zoning cannot destroy the value of the property thereby zoned. The use of the device must be reasonable and not confiscatory.

The interrelationship of the buffer zone with the PUD or cluster zone, both of which are of later lineage, is that these devices attempt to blend harmoniously the uses within an urban area, maintain property values, and on occasion provide open space which adds to the amenities of the urban environment. Transition zoning, or a buffer zone, may but does not necessarily involve open space and is an earlier recognition of the problem of reconciling different uses. The PUD is a more recent, more sophisticated device. Both have been upheld in situations not involving unreasonable or arbitrary classifications or applications.

§ 11. Judicial Review of Zoning

Some courts in fairly recent years have wrestled occasionally with the problem of the nature of the zoning process and the standards for review of zoning decisions. Traditionally, the process was viewed as legislative in nature, and this remains the predominant view today. Under this approach, the exercise of judgment by a zoning authority is not overturned unless it is shown to be arbitrary, capricious and unreasonable.

While courts seldom go beyond that statement, some have attempted to distinguish the original legislative enactment of the ordinance from situations in which an owner is petitioning for reclassification of his land or for administrative relief. See South Gwinnett Venture v. Pruitt, 482 F.2d 389 (5th Cir.1973), cert. denied 416 U.S. 901, cert. denied 419 U.S. 837 (1974). This case refers to the "adjudicative decision inherent in tract rezoning" which "requires the decision maker to adhere to concepts of minimal due process." In Kropf v. Sterling Heights, 391 Mich. 139, 215 N.W.2d 179 (1974), the Michigan Court stated that it could not "second guess the local governing bodies" unless the action taken was arbitrary or capricious, but the concurring opinion argued that zoning "represents particularized applications of administrative power, reflecting choices made over an extended period of time . . . *ad hoc, ad hominen.*" It argued that such actions were administrative and quasi-judicial in nature. Following this latter line of thought, the Oregon Court rejected the idea that review of zoning decisions by local governing bodies is limited to the question of whether the action was arbitrary or capricious. Fasano v. Board of County Commissioners, 264 Or. 574, 507 P.2d 23 (1973). The court recognized that most jurisdictions regard a zoning ordinance to be a legislative act and entitled to presumptive validity. But it held that zoning changes involve judicial rather than legislative actions. The opinion states that while it may be argued that planning authorities should be vested with the ability to change classifications due to changed conditions, account must also be taken of "the almost irresistible pressures that can be asserted by the private economic interests on local government."

This approach would allow a court to overturn a zoning change without having to find the action taken to be arbitrary, capricious and unreasonable. In affecting the presumption of validity, it would conceivably affect the result in cases in which the court finds that "reasonable minds might differ" and that the action taken would thus have to be sustained. The reason why some courts have challenged the old premise is expressed in part by one court's concern that in most of the rezoning cases "there actually has been spot zoning and the courts have upheld or invalidated the change according to how flagrant the violation of true zoning principles has been." Fritts v. Ashland, 348 S.W.2d 712 (Ky. App.1961).

It may be said in opposition to eliminating the presumption in situations involving zoning amendments or administrative relief that courts should not become super boards of adjustment actively involved in the zoning process. To the contrary, however, it is the widespread abuse of the process on the local level which has encouraged courts to rethink the traditional rule. The minority jurisdictions are correct in that it is too much of an ad hoc process and that zoning changes actually involve more of an administrative, quasi-judicial type of activity than a legislative one.

The reconsideration of what is actually taking place in the rezoning process is a recognition of the fact that a rezoning ordinance is not normally the end product of a comprehensive study by planners over a period of time culminating in proposed amendments. It is normally an ad hoc process which zeroes in on a relatively small parcel of land and which is heavily influenced by developers and other real estate interests of the type that are often predominant on planning commissions. The effect of the zoning request on the neighborhood involved is often submerged by the desire to let the project proceed and thereby satisfy the developer. The project may be approved at the commission or city council level over the opposition of the professional staff. Why then should such a basically administrative, and sometimes politically tainted, process be clothed with the finery of the legislative presumption of validity? It is not surprising to find courts, having become aware of what is actual-

[*161*]

ly happening, looking at this "legislation" with increased cynicism and recognizing it for what it actually is.

Finally, another phenomenon which was discussed in an earlier chapter is the increasing tendency of plaintiffs to resort to federal court relief for alleged violations of their constitutional rights. These cases include due process and equal protection allegations and suits involving alleged antitrust violations. Moreover, the use of 42 U.S.C.A. § 1983 to question zoning decisions has increased dramatically since Monell v. Department of Social Services, 436 U.S. 658 (1978) held that cities are subject to suit under that provision. The complaint must allege that a constitutional right has been infringed upon, but in zoning cases, the federal courts (unlike the state courts) have shown an increasing willingness to permit damages for "taking" property which accrue in between the time the city refuses to change an improper zoning classification and the time that the zoning classification is changed (after it has been declared invalid). This remedy of damages and the injection of the federal courts into what has traditionally been largely an area of state adjudication has been an area of substantial concern to many scholars but is in keeping with federal judicial activism over the past thirty years or more.

§ 12. Nonconforming Uses

While zoning traditionally intended to exclude disparate "lower" uses within a zone, it could not eliminate structures which were already in existence. Thus, when zoning came in, and when an area was zoned residential, the corner grocery store and neighborhood service station became nonconforming uses. The same problem reoccurs today with regard to municipal annexations. Zoning deals with these largely through a "control" approach, *i.e.,* a different form of nonconforming use cannot be permitted, the location cannot be changed, the use cannot be expanded, and a new product or service cannot be allowed. This approach has not been too successful. Interpretive problems arise in regard to repair of a structure as opposed to expansion or extension, in regard to whether new equipment or machinery is an extension or only a replacement, in regard to whether a new product is such an addition as to amount to an extension, and in regard to whether an increase in the use or volume of business is a violation. Generally speaking, significant changes which involve substantial alterations in the nature of the business, or equipment which is not a replacement but a subterfuge to expand the use, or new structures, amount to illegal expansion or extension.

Another problem arises in regard to the destruction or partial destruction of the nonconforming use by fire or similar occurrences. Can it be rebuilt? Ordinances generally provide that if it is destroyed beyond a certain percentage of the nonconforming structure (usually half or more), it cannot be rebuilt or repaired. These ordinances are valid, but in the absence of such a provision, the building could be repaired and the use resumed. Moreover, the ordinance could not be unduly restrictive—*i.e.,* it could not provide for discontinuance based upon minor fires.

There is a problem also with discontinuance of use not resulting from natural causes. Some courts have held that statutory provisions stating that a discontinuance for a specified period (such as a year) will terminate the nonconforming use refer to a purely mechanical interpretation of discontinuance (*i.e.,* it is the non-use that matters, not the intent of the user). But the general view is that the word "discontinuance" implies also an intent to abandon the use. Discontinuance due to repairs, acts of war or nature, government controls, foreclosure, condemnation, or injunctions are not regarded as manifesting an intent to abandon where the situation is beyond the control of the user, or even a discontinuance under statutes relating to a specific period of non-use. The underlying assumption is that the use would continue but for the outside interference.

The most active tool in dealing with nonconforming use situations is the amortization device. The idea is that the useful economic life of nonconforming structures can be estimated to the point that the use must cease within a district after a given number of years. Unless the time span is too short or the classification is arbitrary or discriminatory or the regulation is deemed unreasonable, such ordinances are normally upheld. However, such ordinances are usually limited to certain uses. Since it is difficult to justify the amortization period for fixed structures, and since the time span involved is usually too long to prove useful, this device is used most often in connection with billboards, junkyards or similar uses. See, *e.g.,* Grant v. Mayor & Council of Baltimore, 212 Md. 301, 129 A.2d 363 (1957). Even then, the device may on occasion be declared to be an unreasonable exercise of the police power. See, *e.g.,* Akron v. Chapman, 160 Ohio St. 382, 116 N.E.2d 697, 42 A.L.R.2d 1140 (1953). Obviously, in attacking an ordinance, the plaintiff will allege that it is confiscatory and amounts to a taking without just compensation, in addition to some of the allegations previously mentioned. Although the *Grant* case upholding such ordinances represents the majority view, and although many ordinances contain amortization provisions, the device has not proved very effective in eliminating nonconforming uses due to its rare application to buildings or structures representing a substantial capital investment. (But see City of Los Angeles v. Gage, 127 Cal.App.2d 442, 274 P.2d 34 (1954), which upheld a five-year amortization period causing the defendants to discontinue using property for a plumbing business in a situation in which they had had eight years to move and the property was suitable for residential purposes.)

While nonconforming uses could be eliminated through use of nuisance doctrines or through eminent domain, nuisance rules seldom can be successfully applied and condemnation costs normally exceed available funds.

Nuisance doctrines could be employed if the court followed the thinking of such cases as Hadacheck v. Sebastian, 239 U.S. 394 (1915), in which an ordinance forced a nonconforming brick kiln to cease operations and move. This approach, however, would be useful only in a situation in which the nonconforming use was noxious in some respect when compared to surrounding land uses.

Finally, one argument that can sometimes be asserted successfully against a nonconforming use is that it was not established or in place at the time of zoning. Often, the question of a good faith change of position by the landowner in making substantial expenditures on the improvement of the site will be dispositive. Had construction begun and how much of the work had been done are questions relating to this proposition.

The result of the foregoing is that most nonconforming uses remain in existence until the landowner finds it economically desirable to terminate them. This situation illustrates the need for regional planning and zoning.

§ 13. Popular Involvement: The Initiative and the Referendum and Consent by the Neighbors

Ordinances allowing property owners to establish zoning regulations are unlawful in the absence of a referendum submitted to public vote. Cases have, however, permitted modification or waiver of restrictions by concerned landowners. The former is regarded as a legislative delegation of authority, and thus unlawful, while the latter is viewed as valid if the police power is not abused and if there is no reasonable basis for denying the modification or waiver.

A case illustrating this distinction is Valkanet v. Chicago, 13 Ill.2d 268, 148 N.E.2d 767 (1958). The court upheld a consent provision in a situation involving location of a home for the aged in an apartment district but ruled that consent was not needed since no valid distinction could be made between an old folks' home and apartments or boarding houses. *Valkanet* applied the rules mentioned in the first paragraph of this subsection predicating its decision on Eubank v. Richmond, 226 U.S. 137 (1912), and Thomas Cusack Co. v. Chicago, 242 U.S. 526 (1916).

If zoning restrictions can be waived or modified by homeowners in the affected area, then may a city condition the granting of a variance on consent of abutting property owners? This was answered in the negative in Lugar v. City of Burnsville, 295 N.W.2d 609 (Minn.1980). There was no specific statutory authority permitting this, and unlike a referendum, this was not an exercise of power reserved to the people by themselves.

Referendums have been treated almost with holiness by the United States Supreme Court. James v. Valtierra, 402 U.S. 137 (1971), sustained a provision in the California Constitution which required approval by referendum within the community of any proposed low-rent public housing project. The thought that such an election might have racial overtones or involve economic discrimination did not appeal to the Court. A later case reversed the Ohio Supreme Court's conclusion that use of the referendum process, provided for in a city charter, in submitting zoning amendments to the voters constituted a delegation of power violative of federal constitutional guarantees and a violation of due process because the voters were given no standards to guide their decisions. Eastlake v. Forest City Enterprises, Inc., 426 U.S. 668 (1976). Relying on *James v. Valtierra, supra,* the hallowed town meeting concept, and its reverence for populistic democracy, the majority of the Court refused to recognize the chaos that such procedure would create in land use planning and the fact that such process is the antithesis of what the court approved in *Euclid v.*

Ambler Realty Co., supra (although the dissent does recognize the problem).

One theory in sustaining such referendums is that the referral to the voters only "stays the effect of the action . . . until the electorate has had an opportunity to approve or reject it" and "does not change zoning as an initiative would." Queen Creek Land & Cattle Corp. v. Yavapai County Board of Supervisors, 108 Ariz. 449, 501 P.2d 391 (1972). Such reasoning is nonsense. The submission of technical, planned decisions to a popular, generally uninformed, vote may be good populistic politics, but it is the antithesis of the use of zoning as a tool of comprehensive planning.

Since *Eastlake,* a growing number of state courts have held that a zoning amendment is not subject to the referendum process because it amounts to an administrative or quasi-judicial judgment instead of a legislative act. *E.g.*: Leonard v. Bothell, 87 Wash.2d 847, 557 P.2d 1306 (1976).

§ 14. Intergovernmental Zoning Conflicts

This problem arises in conflicts between city and county planning and zoning authority, or between cities and neighboring local governments, or between state and local instrumentalities of government.

City versus county problems are usually resolved on the basis of what the courts regard to be the

prerogative of each under the applicable state statutes if it is simply a matter of conflicting jurisdiction. But it is not all that simple. What if a city
wants to take some action inside the borders of a
neighboring instrumentality of local government?
Fargo v. Harwood Township, 256 N.W.2d 694
(N.D.1977) held that in seeking a site for a sanitary
landfill, a city had to comply with a neighboring
township's zoning ordinance. But in Kirkwood v.
Sunset Hills, 589 S.W.2d 31 (Mo.App.1979), it was
held that a city acquiring a municipal swimming
pool by eminent domain in a neighboring town was
not bound by the zoning ordinance. The courts
thus seem to be in conflict on what is required.
The latter case seems to reflect the eminent domain test for intergovernmental immunity, which
is subsequently discussed.

With regard to whether state agencies are required to comply with local zoning regulations,
various doctrines have been applied. One which a
good many states still adhere to is the "superior
sovereign" test, which provides a presumption of
state immunity in the absence of statutory provisions to the contrary. Another is the "governmental versus proprietary" test, which provides immunity if the agency is performing a governmental
function. Finally, there is the "eminent domain"
test, where immunity is presumed if the agency
possesses that power. Brown v. Kansas Forestry,
Fish and Game Commission, 2 Kan.App.2d 102,

576 P.2d 230 (1978). *Brown,* after reviewing and rejecting these tests, tended toward the "balancing of the interests" test applied in Rutgers v. Piluso, 60 N.J. 142, 286 A.2d 697 (1972), Pittsburgh v. Commonwealth, 468 Pa. 174, 360 A.2d 607 (1976), Oronoco v. Rochester, 293 Minn. 468, 197 N.W.2d 426 (1972), and other cases. Under this test, which seems to represent the trend, the "superior sovereign" test does not apply and the "eminent domain" test and "governmental versus proprietary" test are not conclusive of the issue. Instead, credence is given to the local zoning regulations, to the extent merited, and the court looks at various factors suggested as relevant by the *Rutgers* case, *supra,* and by *Brown,* which include (a) according deference to the needs and goals of the state agency, (b) examining the importance of the function to be performed by the agency when compared with public interest in maintaining the local zoning intact, (c) considering the interests and needs of the public with regard to the proposed project as compared to the impact on the locality by overturning its zoning to permit the project, (d) the convenience or inconvenience of relocating the project elsewhere, and (e) the impact on the land use plan and on the affected neighborhood if the project should be carried out. Obviously, these considerations are somewhat overlapping, but they illustrate the major considerations involved. Under the "balancing of interests" test, obviously, considerable credence and importance is attached to local

zoning and while the state may prevail, it must make its case. It does not win automatically as in the "superior sovereign" test or by flexing its power of eminent domain or by demonstrating that it is performing a governmental function.

These cases might be compared with Matter of Suntide Inn Motel, 563 P.2d 125 (Okl.1977), in which the court stated that as a general rule a state agency is not subject to local zoning, but that state agencies must establish that (a) the project is for a public use, (b) the public purpose is an essential governmental function, (c) the public need for it is urgent, (d) the public goal would be thwarted by local intervention, and (e) the statute is devoid of legislative intent that such a facility should be restricted by local zoning. These, in essence, are the same or similar considerations to those listed previously. This seems to be the trend in the case law, but some courts still accord to the state superiority and immunity from local zoning on the basis that to do otherwise would hamper the state unduly and would thwart state policy. *E.g.*: Dearden v. Detroit, 403 Mich. 257, 269 N.W.2d 139 (1978); New Orleans v. Louisiana, 364 So.2d 1020 (La. 1978).

As for the federal government, the "superior sovereign" rule still applies in the absence of congressional actions to the contrary. *E.g.*, see: U.S. v. Chester, 144 F.2d 415 (3d Cir.1944); and Groton v. Laird, 353 F.Supp. 344 (D.Conn.1972).

An additional problem is that of standing to sue. What are the rights of neighboring units of local government with regard to actions taken by an adjacent governmental unit? In the leading case of Borough of Cresskill v. Borough of Dumont, 15 N.J. 238, 104 A.2d 441 (1954) some Dumont landowners who joined neighboring boroughs in attacking zoning amendment clearly had standing to sue, but the court stated that Dumont owed a duty to her adjoining boroughs and nearby residents and consider their objections. In River Vale v. Orangetown, 403 F.2d 684 (2d Cir.1968), an allegation of depreciation of property values without due process and violation of its constitutional rights were sufficient to keep a New Jersey township in court against a New York town. A number of cases reach essentially the same result. However, in Rohnert Park v. Harris, 601 F.2d 1040 (9th Cir. 1979), cert. denied 445 U.S. 961, it was held that Rohnert Park lacked standing to assert a violation of the federal antitrust laws by a developer and a neighboring city because it had to show a threatened loss or injury cognizable in equity as the proximate result of the alleged violation. It also lacked standing to allege violations by HUD of federal housing statutes in approving the sale.

The state of the law on standing to sue seems directed toward the principle that if injury or deprivation of constitutional rights can be shown by the neighboring governmental unit, then it has standing to sue. Another issue, not fully explored however, is whether a unit of local government may act as parens patriae for its citizens. The *Rohnert Park* court answered in the negative and stated that the city's own proprietary interests were speculative. That case, however, involved a different issue than the adverse impact of nearby rezoning, as in *Creskill.* If proposed land use controls in one community adversely affect land use controls in a neighboring community, then clearly its governmental interest is affected. In that situation, standing to sue should be granted.

CHAPTER VII

ZONING AND DISCRIMINATION

§ 1. Exclusionary Zoning

Zoning ordinances segregate uses and make differentiations even within the use classifications. By their very nature they are exclusionary. "Exclusionary zoning" thus appears to be a somewhat redundant term. What is intended by the use of it, however, is to describe a form of economic segregation, with perhaps occasional racial overtones, which serves to keep out lower income groups. If large-lot minimums are prescribed, if a house must contain a certain minimum amount of square feet, or if no apartment houses or mobile homes or low-cost, government-sponsored apartments are permitted in an area or in a community, the result is to exclude what is often a substantial segment of the population. In recent years the issue has arisen in a variety of situations as to whether this form of exclusion is a valid exercise of the police power. How exclusive can a community be without raising constitutional problems relating to equal protection, due process, the right to travel from place to place, and similar issues?

Other issues relate to other types of land uses. Can certain types of commercial or industrial uses be excluded by local governments? To the contrary, must every type of land use be permitted within a particular township or unit of local government or can some be turned away?

We will attempt to develop this problem and the answers to it by proceeding through a variety of land uses, beginning with the most protected—the single-family home. In all of this, it must be kept in mind that just because an ordinance is exclusionary does not necessarily mean that it is invalid. We have to look for what is invalid in a particular context, keeping in mind that there is considerable disagreement among jurisdictions with respect to many of these issues.

A. The "Single-Family" Classification

Zoning, in its original form and before innovations such as the PUD, created a hierarchy of districts with the most protected being the single-family residential district. This district was protected from all other uses. In fact, Euclid v. Ambler Realty Co., 272 U.S. 365 (1926), the landmark case which approved comprehensive zoning, clearly has as its foundation the desire to protect single-family dwellings from incursions into the district by apartments. Justice Sutherland's opinion denounces apartments as being "mere parasites."

Zoning originally was cumulative in the sense that higher uses could exist in lower use districts—thus permitting someone to build a single-family house in an apartment or duplex zoning district. Today, most zoning ordinances are non-cumulative and make an effort to keep disparate land uses apart except in a carefully planned arrangement such as a cluster zone or planned unit development. This change, however, serves only to heighten the apparent importance placed on protecting single-family dwellings.

In more recent years, there have been attacks on the legitimacy of the single-family classification itself. In Des Plaines v. Trottner, 34 Ill.2d 432, 216 N.E.2d 116 (1966), the court struck down a definition of family as one or more persons each related to the other by blood, adoption, or marriage, together with the relatives' spouses, including domestic servants and not more than one gratuitous guest, living together in a single dwelling and constituting a common household. The court found the ordinance objectionable because it was not based on a specific type of use but sought to inquire into the relationship of the occupants.

But the United States Supreme Court in Belle Terre v. Boraas, 416 U.S. 1 (1974), upheld a definition which limited the application to persons related by blood, adoption or marriage (excluding servants) or to two unmarried and unrelated people. This case upheld the exclusion of a number of unrelated people living together in a communal arrangement over allegations that the ordinance interfered with the right to travel, with persons

traveling in interstate commerce, with social preferences, with the right of privacy, and with our
open and egalitarian society.   Justice Douglas,
speaking for the majority, regarded a "quiet place
where yards are wide, people few, and motor vehicles restricted" as "legitimate guidelines in a land
use project addressed to family needs."

Belle Terre v. Boraas was in effect reinforced by
the difficulty the Supreme Court had in striking
down a patently ridiculous ordinance in Moore v.
East Cleveland, 431 U.S. 494 (1977).   The people
involved were all related by blood and yet it had
the effect of making the occupancy of a dwelling by
a mother, her son, and her two grandsons (who
were first cousins) illegal.   The Court distinguished
Boraas as involving only unrelated persons and
regarded this ordinance as an intrusive regulation
of the family which violated the due process clause.

Despite the emphasis placed on protection of the
single-family classification by the Supreme Court,
state courts are free to disagree based on their own
interpretations of their state constitutions.   This
was the result in Santa Barbara v. Adamson, 27
Cal.3d 123, 164 Cal.Rptr. 539, 610 P.2d 436 (1980),
in which an ordinance's definition of family included groups of no more than five unrelated people.
The court relied in part on the right of privacy but
also said that the city's goals could be met by the
use of less restrictive means.   Other cases involving foster homes, nuns, and similar non-traditional

families also illustrate situations in which either the ordinance has been invalidated or the courts have considered such unrelated individuals to be the equivalent of a single family. See, *e.g.,* State v. Baker, 81 N.J. 99, 405 A.2d 368 (1979).

Although most state courts probably have no quarrel with the traditional single-family definition, the trend seems to be to liberalize it to include certain non-traditional living arrangements and to place emphasis on the type of structure, its appearance, its surroundings, its basic use and the way the "family" operates—*i.e.,* if they act like a family with a common kitchen and dining facilities and if the house looks like a traditional single-family dwelling and functions largely in that way, then it is a single-family dwelling. Courts thus have tended in these recent cases to look to whether there is "a legitimate aim of maintaining a family style of living" or whether the "group bears the generic character of a family unit as a relatively permanent household" or whether the unit involves "a reasonable number of persons who constitute a bona fide single housekeeping unit."

On the other hand, courts which wish to retain a more traditional definition of family will find comfort in the *Belle Terre* and *East Cleveland* cases.

B. Large Lot Zoning Requirements

Provisions in the ordinance specifying a minimum area for a particular use have health, fire control and traffic control benefits, but also may affect tax revenues, promote aesthetics, and preserve property values. These provisions are most controversial where they are applied so as to require large residential lots. A leading case from Massachusetts, upholding a one-acre minimum, held that a city is justified in asserting the police power for such purposes where the public interest is involved and the devices and means employed are reasonable. Simon v. Needham, 311 Mass. 560, 42 N.E.2d 516, 141 A.L.R. 688 (1943). That case also stated, however, that such a regulation cannot be used to exclude respectable people who want to come in and build on lots of fair and reasonable size.

What is reasonable and not exclusionary in nature cannot be defined with mathematical precision. Five-acre, four-acre, and three-acre lot sizes have been upheld. See, *e.g.*, County Comm'rs. of Queen Anne's County v. Miles, 246 Md. 355, 228 A.2d 450 (1967); Flora Realty & Inv. Co. v. Ladue, 362 Mo. 1025, 246 S.W.2d 771 (1952), appeal dismissed 344 U.S. 802 (1952). Lot sizes of four acres and 100,000 square feet have been invalidated. National Land & Inv. Co. v. Kohn, 419 Pa. 504, 215 A.2d 597 (1965); Aronson v. Sharon, 346 Mass. 598, 195 N.E.2d 341 (1964).

In order to understand these decisions, consideration must be given to the factors which courts utilize. Factors which courts use to support the upholding of large-lot zoning include overcrowding and undue concentration of people, the burden on public facilities (including schools, fire and police stations, streets, water and sewer systems), the fact that there are other zones with smaller minima, the rural and occasionally historic character of the area, the desire to promote tourism, and compatibility with the socio-economic situation and existing uses prevailing in the community. Factors which courts cite in invalidating large-lot zoning include the lack of reasonable relationship to the police power, a size which is so large and reduces the overall value of the land so much that the court regards it as confiscatory, a tendency for the lot sizes to be exclusionary and to serve private interests, the fact that the town is in the onward path of suburban development, and the fact that the result would be to exclude low-income people from living there. These latter factors, relating to exclusion, were the primary factors in the leading *National Land* case, *supra.* See also Appeal of Kit-Mar Builders, 439 Pa. 466, 268 A.2d 765 (1970).

This problem of exclusion is the basic concern relating to large lot zoning today. The rule expressed by the Pennsylvania Court in *National Land* that Easttown Township could not "stand in the way of natural forces which send out growing population into hitherto undeveloped areas in search of a comfortable place to live" is essentially the same as the thinking of the New Jersey Court in the oft-heralded, sometimes criticized and much discussed case of Southern Burlington County NAACP v. Mount Laurel, 67 N.J. 151, 336 A.2d 713 (1975), discussed *infra,* in which a zoning regulation was invalidated on the basis that low and moderate income families were unlawfully excluded by it. Unlike the later *Mount Laurel* case, in which the concern over exclusion was involved with low income people, *National Land* involved a suit by a developer concerned with the diminution in the value of his property as a result of the regulation. The thrust of the *National Land* opinion, however, as in *Mount Laurel,* is that the police power cannot be employed to keep people out.

A key point in *National Land* is the fact that the township was in the path of population expansion outward from an urban area. The result might have been different (and some cases have produced different results) except for that circumstance.

Not every court, by any means, has shown a tendency to invalidate ordinances of this type on the basis that they discriminate against poor people. *Mount Laurel* was based on the New Jersey Constitution. *National Land* was based on the idea that people in general were being excluded. But in Ybarra v. Los Altos Hills, 503 F.2d 250 (9th Cir.1974), an ordinance was upheld which zoned only for single-family housing built on one-acre lots against an attack by Mexican-Americans alleging that it prevented construction of a multi-family housing project. The court held that the ordinance did discriminate against poor people, but found that to be valid because there was no showing that the plaintiffs were deprived of an opportunity to live in such housing elsewhere in the county.

Consequently, the validity of large-lot zoning is likely to vary depending on the size of the lot, the circumstances of the community or area involved, and the hostility or lack of it to large-lot zoning in a particular jurisdiction.

C. Minimum Building Size

This type of regulation has its counterpart in subdivision regulations. However, the requirement of a certain minimum square footage has been upheld in many cases, particularly in older ones. In recent years, particularly since the *Mount Laurel* decision, such regulations have increasingly been attacked as promoting economic segregation. However, the general rule remains in most jurisdictions that a minimum size requirement which can be reasonably related to health considerations is valid. Modern courts have shown a tendency to look with skepticism at such requirements, however, because substantial variations in the size of the family make such requirements less meaningful in terms of mental health considerations and because some ordinances provide for different minimum requirements in different districts.

Some courts have found regulations prescribing cubic foot content to be invalid (when all a person would have to do to comply would be to enlarge the attic). Frischkorn Construction Co. v. Lambert, 315 Mich. 556, 24 N.W.2d 209 (1946). Others have invalidated sliding scales as to floorspace requirements on the theory that what amounts to minimum requirements for one district ought to be the minimum for all districts if it is a reasonable use of the police power. Appeal of Medinger, 377 Pa. 217, 104 A.2d 118 (1954).

The fluctuation in the attitude of courts with respect to such requirements is somewhat illustrated by the New Jersey cases of Lionshead Lake, Inc. v. Township of Wayne, 10 N.J. 165, 89 A.2d 693, appeal dismissed 344 U.S. 919 (1953), and Home Builders League, Inc. v. Township of Berlin, 81 N.J. 127, 405 A.2d 381 (1979). *Lionshead Lake* was a leading case for the proposition that minimum square footage could be required. The case was debated pro and con at the time, and some scholars periodically returned to the attack. That ordinance only provided for a 768 square foot minimum. In *Home Builders League,* the court took another look at *Lionshead Lake* and agreed with its critics. How big an area is required for the mental well-being of a house's inhabitants will depend on how many occupants there are, said the court. Another problem in *Home Builders* was that the minimum floor area varied for similar housing in different zones. *Lionshead Lake* was thought to have rested its conclusion on the protection of land values and the character of the community. The ordinance in Berlin Township was thought to be directed toward economic segregation and not related to a valid police power concern. Although the court did not reverse *Lionshead Lake,* it severely reduced its value as precedent. *Lionshead Lake* related to preserving the character of the area as against small vacation homes and might remain as a precedent in that limited situation. Moreover, the court stated that the earlier case had been erroneously characterized by scholars as based on "public health grounds" (presumably because it would have to overturn it if that were so), but the decision in *Lionshead* is by its own words based in part on such grounds.

These New Jersey decisions should not mislead those who live and work in other jurisdictions, however. Despite these recent questions about the validity of such requirements, most jurisdictions have upheld regulations as to minimum size. Also, unlike New Jersey, most jurisdictions do not hold (as New Jersey did in *Mount Laurel*) that economic discrimination is invalid. It is fair to say, however, that the rational relationship of such a regulation to health considerations is increasingly being questioned because how much space is required is based on how many occupants there will be.

If public health is a legitimate concern of the
police power, which it is, then reasonable minimums as to living space are and should be valid.
Arguments as to exclusion should only form a basis
for invalidating the unreasonable. Moreover,
courts should uphold reasonable variations within
a city from district to district. Cities and their
inhabitants are not monolithic, and reasonable variations should be permitted even within prescribed
minima. The contrary theory potentially diminishes health considerations without diminishing
the exclusionary effects of minimums.

D. Exclusion of Commerce and Industry

The area of zoning law involving exclusion of
apartments, commerce and industry is still developing, and the cases present conflicts. Cases have
held that a suburb may restrict the use of all land
to single-family dwellings, thereby excluding all
other residential uses and all office, commercial
and industrial uses. McDermott v. Calverton
Park, 454 S.W.2d 577 (Mo.1970). But other courts
have held to the contrary. Gundersen v. Bingham
Farms, 372 Mich. 352, 126 N.W.2d 715 (1964). The
theory of courts which uphold one-use zoning is
that some suburban or "bedroom" communities are
best suited for such uses considering the character
of the area and the police power is not abused by
such a limitation. Decisions to the contrary vary
from those concerned with the exclusion of other
residential uses, such as apartments, to those con-

cerned with exclusion of non-residential uses. The cases dealing with multi-family uses hold that these cannot be entirely excluded because suburbs which are logical areas for development and population growth cannot close their doors to people who seek or can only afford this type of housing. Appeal of Girsh, 437 Pa. 237, 263 A.2d 395 (1970). These cases will be considered at greater length, *infra*.

Other cases, particularly Pennsylvania cases, hold in effect that a unit of local government must provide adequately for all types of uses within its confines. Thus, each community must accept its "fair share" of commercial growth. *E.g.:* Beaver Gasoline Co. v. Zoning Hearing Board, 445 Pa. 571, 285 A.2d 501 (1971); Sullivan v. Board of Supervisors, 22 Pa.Cmwlth. 318, 348 A.2d 464 (1975). Where some land is allocated for commercial use, the burden is on the developer to show that the allocation is inadequate in relation to the needs of the citizens. A total ban on otherwise legitimate commercial uses places the burden on the municipality to justify the ban. The Pennsylvania cases have carried this to an extreme—even to the point of forcing townships to permit waste disposal facilities and quarrying operations. Exton Quarries v. Zoning Board of Adjustment, 425 Pa. 43, 228 A.2d 169 (1967); General Battery Corp. v. Zoning Hearing Board, 29 Pa.Cmwlth. 498, 371 A.2d 1030 (1977).

Most jurisdictions which are concerned about single use zoning at all are not concerned about exclusion of certain commercial and industrial activities. These cases usually focus on housing and hold such zoning invalid on the basis that it excludes housing for people of low and moderate incomes. Such zoning usually also excludes a disproportionate number of non-whites. But most jurisdictions would not deny municipalities the ability to exclude all or certain types of industrial activities or limit commercial acreage.

The argument to the contrary is based in part on the idea that since zoning is local, rather than area-wide, in most jurisdictions, the exclusion of such uses by one body of local government could lead to exclusion of such uses from the entire area. Thus, each governmental unit (Pennsylvania says) must absorb its "fair share."

But most courts which are concerned about exclusionary zoning have limited their concerns to housing considerations and "keeping people out" as opposed to keeping out commercial or industrial operations. Regional or area-wide planning and zoning obviously could relieve most of these problems and concerns.

E. Exclusion of Apartments

As stated, the concerns of the courts are largely with exclusion of various forms of residential use. Thus, zoning which excludes apartments, although it has been approved in some jurisdictions, is looked upon with disfavor in others. *Appeal of Girsh, supra.* Courts which disapprove of such exclusion commonly state that zoning cannot be used to keep people out or to stand as a barrier to outward population expansion from a central metropolitan area. These cases follow the same theory as *National Land, supra,* which invalidated a large-lot zoning requirement because of such considerations. Moreover, in the *Mount Laurel* case, to be discussed *infra,* and other cases, we see instances in which courts have taken an affirmative action approach to force communities to create a situation which will encourage development of housing for people of low and moderate incomes.

Clearly, the attitude of the courts has shifted since the 1920's when Justice Sutherland, writing for the majority in *Euclid v. Ambler Realty Co., supra,* sought to protect single-family uses at the expense of all others and referred to apartment houses as mere parasites.

As we have seen in *McDermott v. Calverton Park, supra,* all courts do not agree that exclusionary residential zoning is a matter of concern. There is a split of authority on this in the state courts. In the federal courts, as we shall see, local zoning regulations cannot operate so as to exclude federally subsidized housing for low and moderate income people. With that exception, however, unless there is proof of an intent to discriminate racially, single use zoning is an issue to be decided by each particular jurisdiction. The trend of recent years would seem in the long run to augur against ordinances which exclude multi-family and other residential uses.

F. Exclusion of Mobile Homes

If Justice Sutherland viewed apartment houses as mere parasites, as he stated in *Euclid,* then mobile homes have taken the place of apartment houses in recent years with respect to how they are viewed by many courts. Thus, the Supreme Court of New Jersey in the 1960's could uphold an ordinance which permitted a rural township to exclude mobile homes entirely from its 23 square miles. Vickers v. Township Committee of Gloucester Township, 37 N.J. 232, 181 A.2d 129, cert. denied 371 U.S. 233 (1962). The dissenting judge argued that localities should not be able to erect exclusionary walls around their borders and keep people out. He later wrote the majority opinion in *Mount Laurel, infra,* which effectively overruled *Vickers* in that it required local governments to accept their "fair share" of population growth and make accommodation for low and moderate income housing.

But this attitude has begun to change. Limitations on mobile homes which are regarded as unreasonable have been struck down as unconstitutional, and courts are increasingly recognizing the

need by many people for housing of this type.
Glocester v. Olivo's Mobile Home Court, Inc., 111
R.I. 120, 300 A.2d 465 (1973). Most efforts to
exclude mobile homes totally from a multi-use
community have been held unconstitutional; but
courts generally permit the separate classification
of mobile homes and the restriction of them to
certain zones because of their adverse impact on
neighborhood development and property values,
their minimum storage capacity for items of personal property, and the fact that aesthetically they
are less pleasing. See, *e.g.,* Duckworth v. Bonney
Lake, 91 Wash.2d 19, 586 P.2d 860 (1978).

There has been an increasing pressure in the
United States during the 1980's for affordable
housing. Spiraling interest rates have placed
much of traditional housing, whether single-family
homes or condominiums, beyond the financial
reach of many citizens. This has led to a reassess-
ment of attitudes toward the mobile home market
in general and particularly toward prefabricated or
modular housing which is manufactured off of the
site and is assembled on the site from the component units. These manufactured houses look much
the same as on-site or "stick built" single-family
homes. The same change in attitudes, to a lesser
degree, is true with regard to "double wide" mobile
homes which look more like a traditional house
than an elongated, narrow trailer. Probably, we
will see an increase in ordinances which permit

prefabricated homes to be trucked to the site in segments and assembled on the site, at least in some residential classifications. But as far as the mobile home, including the "double wides," is concerned, substantial public resistance remains because of the ill effect on property values and neighborhood development and because of aesthetic considerations. Mobile homes will likely continue to have separate zoning classifications or be permitted as conditional uses in some, not highly restricted, residential zones.

As a general rule, mobile homes have not been successful in seeking to be classified as single-family dwellings and have not been able to avoid separate treatment. However, mobile homes generally cannot escape the ban of a properly worded restrictive covenant excluding them from a development.

G. Institutional Uses and Group Homes

The problem here normally arises from the question of whether an institutional or "group" home constitutes a single-family residence under the terms of the zoning ordinance. When such homes are operated in essentially the same manner as a single-family home, they can quite often avoid exclusion. Thus, a home for foster children who live with a married couple in a family atmosphere or type of arrangement has been held to be a family for purposes of the single family classification.

White Plains v. Ferraioli, 34 N.Y.2d 300, 357 N.Y.S.2d 449, 313 N.E.2d 756 (1974).

The same holding would probably result in most cases involving restrictive covenants which limit the use to "single family," although the definition of family could be written in such a way as to exclude group or institutional homes. If it were so written, courts would have to enforce the restrictive covenant since these private rights would outweigh the general public policy favoring such facilities and there is no constitutional violation with respect to race, religion or the like. Where there is no definition of "family," then if the group home functions as a family does, courts will usually permit the use to continue. Thus, the result in interpreting restrictive covenants has, in the absence of specific words of exclusion, been much the same as in most of the zoning cases. There are, of course, cases to the contrary.

Some of the cases involving group homes for mental patients, the mentally retarded or wayward children have arisen in the context of homeowners seeking an injunction against them based on nuisance allegations. An injunction generally will not be granted in such circumstances based on fear of anticipated injury. Moreover, some of these cases involve state-operated facilities which raises the issue of whether the state is immune from local zoning. On this latter point, most courts today do not hold the state totally immune but apply a balancing of the interests test. In zoning cases, however, some courts will give priority to state policy.

A different definition of the single family requirement may be employed if the group home is supervised by a professional staff as opposed to a live-in couple operating the house as a family would. This may be said to be the operation of an institution in a non-family setting as opposed to the family situation provided by a resident married couple. See, *e.g.,* Culp v. Seattle, 22 Wash.App. 618, 590 P.2d 1288 (1979).

The more controversial group homes involve "halfway houses" for convicted felons or parolees whom the state is gradually attempting to return to society or institutional homes for delinquents. Such rehabilitation facilities are often excluded from single family districts. The decisions upholding this are predicated on the reasonableness of such classifications, although the root of the matter is the fear of the nearby populace.

As in some other zoning considerations, an analogy can be drawn to nuisance doctrine. In fact, courts have held that the operation of a halfway house for parolees and prisoners constitutes a nuisance in fact. See, *e.g.,* Arkansas Release Guidance Foundation v. Needler, 252 Ark. 194, 477 S.W.2d 821 (1972); but compare Nicholson v. Connecticut Halfway House, 153 Conn. 507, 218 A.2d 383 (1958), which arrived at a different result where suit was instituted prior to the beginning of operations by the halfway house.

H. Religious Institutions and Private Schools

Opinions of courts vary as to the exclusion of churches from areas zoned single-family. A number of courts have invalidated ordinances excluding churches entirely from single-family districts on the basis that this does not relate to the police power or that it is an infringement on religion. Some courts, however, have said that the question should be whether it is an *undue* infringement— *i.e.,* whether exclusion of the church will promote the general welfare or whether the exclusion is a burden which is not commensurate with the general welfare. See, *e.g.,* State ex rel. Lake Drive Baptist Church v. Bayside, 12 Wis.2d 585, 108 N.W. 2d 288 (1961). If there are other available sites, as was held in *Bayside,* then the zoning would not be invalid (although the church won in that case for other reasons).

In many zoning ordinances, churches are permitted as special or conditional uses in single-family districts. This would seem not to be unconstitutional because modern churches usually meet or have functions during the week and sometimes have a recreational or educational component. If a church could locate anywhere in a residential district as a matter of right, it might choose a site which from a traffic and safety standpoint was wholly unsuited and harmful to the neighborhood. There *are*, therefore, police power considerations which apply to churches, and courts which hold that such regulation is a per se violation of freedom of worship are not taking such factors into account. It is likely, however, that the conditional use procedure could be successfully defended in most courts (except those which permit no regulation of churches at all). But when this procedure is employed, the criteria for granting or denying the permit must be specified, or the ordinance may be invalidated on that ground.

It is well to observe, in connection with churches, that some courts appear to reverse the usual presumption in favor of police power regulations and to place the burden upon the municipality of showing a lack of impairment or insubstantial impairment of religious freedom.

This separate standard manifests itself in connection with ancillary religious institutions such as convents, monasteries or use of a dwelling by members of a religious society. Some cases have held that unrelated members of a religious society living together as a single housekeeping unit constitutes a "family" within the meaning of the ordinance. But this is not applied to college fraternities, sororities or clubs even where they have kitchen and dining facilities and operate as something similar to a large "family." An extreme example of this is a holding which considered sixty student members of a religious order to constitute a single-family group. Laporte v. New Rochelle, 2 N.Y.2d 921, 161 N.Y.S.2d 886, 141 N.E.2d 917 (1956), affirming Application of LaPorte, 2 A.D.2d 710, 152 N.Y.S.2d 916. A fraternity or sorority house would have lost. Thus, the true nature of the "use" is ignored. This is clearly a double standard because it is the nature of the use that is at issue under the police power and not the nature of the organization.

The fact that it is the use that should be at issue is also illustrated by an occasional double standard as between public schools and private schools. Sometimes a distinction is made between public schools, which are permitted, and private schools, which are prohibited, on the basis that public education is a governmental function. Private schools, it is argued, discriminate and impose all of the burdens of a public school without the same benefit to the public. State ex rel. Wisconsin Lutheran High School Conference v. Sinar, 267 Wis. 91, 65 N.W.2d 43, appeal dismissed, 349 U.S. 913 (1954). But in terms of land use controls, it can hardly matter to the people around the school as to whether it is public or private since the impact on the neighborhood is the same in terms of noise, traffic and congestion. Moreover, if the contention of the court in the above case were relevant, it might be pointed out that private or parochial schools do serve the public indirectly by relieving the public schools of the burden that would be added if they were non-existent. Since the tax base remains the same, it might be said that the public is indirectly subsidized by private and parochial schools. See Roman Catholic Welfare Corp. v. Piedmont, 45 Cal.2d 325, 289 P.2d 438 (1955).

A sounder approach from a land use standpoint is illustrated by cases which require that classifications in zoning ordinances must bear a reasonable relationship to the police power. Thus, governmental attempts to distinguish between a permitted grade school or high school and a non-permitted prekindergarten or nursery school have been invalidated on the basis that the latter is no more of an impact on land use in the neighborhood than the former. Chicago v. Sachs, 1 Ill.2d 342, 115 N.E.2d 762 (1953). There must be reasonable distinctions made between classes of uses, and like uses should not be excluded from a particular class.

I. Housing Discrimination

(1) *Racial Exclusion*

The Civil Rights Act of 1866, passed pursuant to congressional authority under the Thirteenth Amendment to eliminate the badges and incidents of slavery, was followed over a century later by the Civil Rights Act of 1968 which included provisions designed to assure fair housing practices in the

United States. 42 U.S.C.A. §§ 3601 et seq. In that same year, in Jones v. Alfred H. Mayer Co., 392 U.S. 409 (1968), the Supreme Court held that private persons could not discriminate on the basis of race in the sale of houses.

The Fair Housing Act of 1968, however, gave rise in the 1970's to cases which focused on the legality of zoning practices in the light of the requirements of this act and of equal protection and due process in general. This development extended the "badge of slavery" basis of *Jones, supra,* into the area of exclusion by zoning of certain types of housing.

A prime example of this litigation is U.S. v. Black Jack, 508 F.2d 1179 (8th Cir.1974), cert. denied 422 U.S. 1042 (1974), in which the prohibition of multi-family housing by a suburb of St. Louis was invalidated under Title VIII of the 1968 Civil Rights Act. Black Jack is one of the suburbs which ring St. Louis on its western border. Statistics were employed by the court to show that such zoning had the effect of locking in the large black population in the central city by preventing erection of public housing for low and moderate income families. Thus, the ordinance was deemed to have a discriminatory effect in that it denied availability of housing on the basis of race and could not be justified by any compelling governmental interest. (This case was followed by a $450,000 award of damages under a consent decree in the district court and, some years later, by a holding that the city was under a continuing duty to take affirmative action to promote the development of moderately priced, interracial housing. Park View Heights Corp. v. City of Black Jack, 605 F.2d 1033 (8th Cir.1979).)

Other cases, however, held that a negative zoning decision on such housing could be defended by the city's demonstration of its adherence to a good faith use of basic zoning principles and an absence of discriminatory intent coupled with other nearby opportunities for housing for low income families. Ybarra v. Los Altos Hills, 503 F.2d 250 (9th Cir. 1974).

The question of "discriminatory effect" as opposed to "discriminatory intent" was addressed by the Supreme Court in Arlington Heights v. Metropolitan Housing Development Corp., 429 U.S. 252 (1977). This case was interrelated with Hills v. Gautreaux, 425 U.S. 284 (1976), which required the Chicago Housing Authority and HUD to utilize the entire Chicago metropolitan area, including the suburbs, to disperse publicly financed housing throughout the area. Arlington Heights is a Chicago suburb, and considered in a racial context, the result of *Gautreaux* was somewhat similar to the desegregation cases mandating the busing of school children. In fact, the Seventh Circuit opinion in *Gautreaux* was largely predicated upon such cases.

Arlington Heights held that a "discriminatory effect" was insufficient under the Fourteenth

Amendment to invalidate a zoning regulation and
that, under normal circumstances, a "discriminatory purpose" or intent would be required. As far as
due process and equal protection were concerned,
an exclusionary zoning ordinance of a suburban
community would be permitted. However, the
case was remanded to determine whether the requirements of the Fair Housing Act might necessi-
tate a different standard as to public housing.
That was answered in the affirmative by the Seventh Circuit upon remand. The circuit court addressed four critical factors to be considered and
stated, in essence: (1) "Discriminatory effect" is
relevant when it has a greater adverse impact on
one racial group than on another or when it serves
to perpetuate racial segregation in a community;
(2) while of lesser importance, the question of discriminatory intent is relevant if there is some
evidence of such intent, even though inconclusive;
(3) the interest of the defendant in taking such
action as produces a discriminatory impact is perti-
nent if it is a governmental body acting within the
scope of legitimate authority; and (4) courts should
be more reluctant to grant relief when affirmative
action to compel construction of integrated housing
is requested than when a plaintiff simply seeks
relief from being prevented by a defendant from
building integrated housing. Applying the foregoing to Arlington Heights, the court held that it had
a statutory obligation under the Fair Housing Act
to refrain from zoning policies which effectively

foreclosed construction of publicly financed housing for low income families within its borders. Metropolitan Housing Development Corp. v. Village of Arlington Heights, 558 F.2d 1283 (7th Cir. 1977), cert. denied 434 U.S. 1025 (1978).

These cases need to be distinguished from Southern Burlington County NAACP v. Mount Laurel, 67 N.J. 151, 336 A.2d 713, appeal dismissed 423 U.S. 808 (1975), discussed *infra,* which was based on the New Jersey Constitution and which invalidated zoning regulations that had the effect of excluding low and moderate income families. That decision, decided on economic rather than racial grounds, was based on state law rather than on the federal Constitution or federal statutes.

The upshot of these cases would seem to be: (1) states remain free, as in *Mount Laurel, supra,* to override exclusionary zoning based upon state law, or as in *Calverton Park, supra,* to uphold exclusionary zoning based upon state law, except insofar as such practices are racially motivated or would violate the Fair Housing Act; (2) absent a discriminatory purpose or intent, cities do not violate the federal Constitution through exclusionary zoning practices as a general rule; (3) but, in the case of the Fair Housing Act and public housing, a more extensive examination may result and such factors as those delineated by the Seventh Circuit upon remand of *Arlington Heights* will quite possibly be considered. (See generally, Wright, Constitutional

Rights and Land Use Planning: The New and the Old Reality, 1977 *Duke L.J.* 841 (1978).) It would be an over-simplification, however, to say that the developer of racially integrated housing for low and moderate income people has clear sailing under the Fair Housing Act and the more stringent requirements suggested by the Seventh Circuit. Not every denial of a building permit or refusal to rezone can be shown to be racially exclusionary, particularly in cities with many different types of zoning classifications including high density multifamily.

(2) *The Problem of Standing*

Those seeking to challenge allegedly exclusionary zoning ordinances must comply with the procedural limitations imposed by Warth v. Seldin, 422 U.S. 490 (1975), which held that certain individual taxpayers and organizations interested in providing housing for low and moderate income persons lacked standing to sue. The petitioners lived in Rochester, N.Y., and the suit was against Penfield, a suburb. The Supreme Court affirmed the Second Circuit's decision that they lacked standing to press a claim that Penfield excluded low income persons from living there. The petitioners would have to show that they purported to represent a class. It was held that the associations in the suit had no standing because the interests of their members were not directly affected.

This decision was a severe deterrent to suits by organizations representing racial minorities or poor people. Plaintiffs must be able to establish a connection between the zoning and the denial of their constitutional or statutory rights. An owner of property who could not develop it for low-cost housing would have standing. A housing authority thwarted by such regulations would normally have standing. Someone with a property interest such as an option to buy affected land, contingent on rezoning, would have standing. Someone prevented by the zoning from buying land for a public housing project would presumably have standing. But outsiders who could not show some deprivation to themselves would not have standing.

Some state courts have shown a tendency not to be so strict. Some have permitted a showing that the zoning practices excluded them from residing in the city in question. See *e.g.,* Home Builders League v. Township of Berlin, 81 N.J. 127, 405 A.2d 381 (1979).

(3) *Age Discrimination*

Can one discriminate based on age? In Taxpayers Association v. Weymouth Township, 80 N.J. 6, 364 A.2d 1016, appeal dismissed 430 U.S. 977 (1976), a mobile home park classification which limited occupants to those of 52 years old and above was upheld because of the special housing needs of the elderly. The township in this case had a general ban on mobile homes, but this exception in favor of older people was deemed to be reasonable.

Unless other land in the area was zoned for mobile homes, without age restrictions, it is difficult to say that this was not exclusionary. Also, one might question the arbitrariness of the age 52 and older requirement, since there is not much difference between ages 50 and 52, for example. It might be contended that the real reason was to eliminate young people who might more greatly burden the need for more schools and public facilities.

Other cases have held to the contrary on the subject of age discrimination on the basis that creating such a category would be ultra vires under the enabling act. Hinman v. Planning and Zoning Commission, 26 Conn.Sup. 125, 214 A.2d 131 (1965).

In the absence of the ultra vires question, the key to this would seem to be whether the zoning based on age does or does not exclude young people when you consider other housing opportunities for them in the community or in the immediate area. If there were no other similar housing opportunities, it would appear that such zoning would be invalid under federal decisions protecting the right of citizens to travel freely from place to place.

§ 2. Inclusionary Zoning

A. Providing Low-Cost Housing Opportunities

The leading case on this is Southern Burlington County NAACP v. Township of Mount Laurel, 67 N.J. 151, 336 A.2d 713, appeal dismissed 423 U.S. 808 (1975), otherwise known as *Mount Laurel* (or as *Mount Laurel I*, to distinguish it from a later opinion). In this case, the New Jersey Supreme Court held that townships must absorb their "fair share" of the housing needs of their particular geographical areas. A township could not be wholly or largely single-family and would have to provide for all types of housing. Mount Laurel was held to be unlawfully exclusionary by not making it possible to provide for housing for low and moderate income persons. This economic exclusion was held unconstitutional under the state constitution. The court indicated that if zoning and planning were conducted on a regional basis, the situation would be different; but since zoning and planning are local, then each local unit must absorb its fair share.

Mount Laurel I did not require affirmative action by the township. The township was only required to provide the opportunity for such low income housing developments through its zoning regulations. It was suggested, however, that the township might be required to take further action in the future.

This decision left a number of unanswered questions, such as what is the "fair share" of a particular township, what is a township's particular area or region, and how much zoning for multi-family units is required to meet the "fair share" requirements. Further litigation was bound to ensue, and it did. In Oakwood at Madison, Inc. v. Township of Madison, 72 N.J. 481, 371 A.2d 1192 (1977), it was stated that a lower court need not define the region and set the number of low-cost housing units to be allowed as a township's fair share; it required zoning for "least cost" housing but did not require precise formulae for estimating the fair share and did not require governmental aid to private developers of such housing; it did provide certain minimal criteria which had to be met to provide for the township's fair share.

Eventually, in Township of Mount Laurel, 92 N.J. 158, 456 A.2d 390 (1983), a very long opus, the court developed new burdens of proof, procedures and standards intended to lead to faster and more effective remedies. The test would not be whether good faith attempts had been made by a community to meet such needs, but whether a real opportunity had been provided for "least cost" housing. Plaintiffs would not have to prove what a "fair share" amounted to in a locality, but only would have to show that the zoning is substantially affected by restrictive devices—which would apparently then create a rebuttable presumption that

such zoning was unfair. Exclusionary zoning cases
would be assigned to one of three judges, each of
whom would have responsibility for a certain area
of the state, and who could make use of masters.
Implementation of new policies would be phased
in. Local governments found in compliance would
be protected from such suits for six years thereafter.

Obviously, the judicial activism manifested by
the *Mount Laurel I* decision and its progeny has
provided some cause for concern, and the case has
been criticized by some scholars. It might be questioned whether low income persons have actually
benefited from such efforts. An underlying assumption of these cases is that it is economically
feasible to build new housing for lower income
families, and that may be seriously questioned in
today's market situation and in consideration of
sources of available funds. *Mount Laurel* may be
simply an idealistic attempt to solve a problem
which is heavily rooted in economics.

The *Mount Laurel* decision had an impact primarily on other northeastern jurisdictions, and it met
with a somewhat mixed acceptance. Berenson v.
New Castle, 38 N.Y.2d 102, 378 N.Y.S.2d 672, 341
N.E.2d 236 (1975) held that zoning ordinances must
give consideration to regional housing needs. After the trial court, upon remand, ordered the town
to provide for 3,500 units of multi-family housing
over approximately the next decade, the Appellate

Division held that this order went too far and simply directed the town board to remedy its zoning deficiency and to rezone the plaintiff's property multi-family. Berenson v. New Castle, 67 A.D.2d 506, 415 N.Y.S.2d 669 (1979). In Pennsylvania, Surrick v. Zoning Hearing Board, 476 Pa. 182, 382 A.2d 105 (1978), provided that state's version of the adoption of the "fair share" concept. A concurring opinion disagreed with the "fair share" approach, stating that it would impose an unnecessary burden on the courts and should not be imposed on localities or regions.

Judicially mandated inclusionary zoning has also been employed in some federal courts in such a way that the orders issued parallel the desegregation cases mandating school busing. Such a case is U.S. v. Parma, Ohio, 494 F.Supp. 1049 (N.D.Ohio 1980), subsequently affirmed, which went so far as to mandate numerous affirmative acts which had to be undertaken by the city governing body. The New Jersey experience and the experience of the federal courts in school desegregation cases would seem to suggest that this process would engage the courts in a constant case-by-case approval and general review process, in which, aside from new cases, the old cases would continually go from the trial courts to the appellate courts and back again. This is no doubt the reason why such judges as the concurring judge in *Surrick* are hesitant about venturing into such a milieu. Perhaps this is also

the reason why, despite the applause which originally greeted *Mount Laurel,* there have been numerous second thoughts about it and more critical
observations. *E.g.:* Rose, The Mount Laurel II
Decision: Is It Based on Wishful Thinking?, 12
Real Estate L.J. 115 (1983).

Mount Laurel differs from *Arlington Heights* in
that it holds that the state constitution prohibits
economic discrimination while the U.S. Supreme
Court opinion holds that the Fourteenth Amendment only prohibits discrimination based on race
or religion. Most state courts have not gone beyond *Arlington Heights,* and it seems doubtful that
they will.

The answer to the problem lies in regional planning and zoning of a type that would adequately
provide for the various types of housing within a
reasonable geographical area.

B. Legislative Approaches

Some states have passed statutes which confer
on boards of appeals or agencies concerned with
urban development the power to override local
zoning, generally for the purpose of promoting
housing for low and moderate income families.
These laws have withstood objections that such
legislation violated the home rule amendment to
the state constitution, amounted to spot zoning,
and were void for vagueness of standards. *E.g.:*
Board of Appeals of Hanover v. Housing Appeals

Committee, 363 Mass. 339, 294 N.E.2d 393 (1973). Such decisions view special efforts to provide housing for low and moderate income people as promoting the general welfare.

There are non-judicial approaches which seem preferable to the judicial process. The latter almost inevitably lapses into some form of court-supervised affirmative action. Such legislation may be politically unrealistic in most jurisdictions because local control of zoning is highly entrenched, and there is usually legislative opposition to state control or to special agencies fulfilling a social function and exercising a veto power over local actions.

C. Inclusionary Zoning Ordinances

What then of local ordinances themselves? In Board of Supervisors v. DeGroff Enterprises, Inc., 214 Va. 235, 198 S.E.2d 600 (1973), a zoning amendment requiring a developer of fifty or more dwelling units to agree to build at least fifteen percent of such units as low and moderate income housing was invalidated as being ultra vires with respect to the power granted local governments by the enabling act. The county viewed the ordinance as attempting to promote a public purpose, but the court viewed it as "socio-economic zoning" which attempted to control the compensation for the use of the land. It was also held to be a taking in that it compelled the sale or rental of property to low or moderate income persons at prices not fixed by the market.

It should be noted, however, that a dissenting opinion in *Oakwood at Madison* spoke approvingly of mandatory inclusionary ordinances as remedial measures, pointing out that ordinances similar to that invalidated in *DeGroff Enterprises* have been implemented in several parts of the country. The opinion criticizes *DeGroff* for its "excessively narrow" view of the zoning power, and asserts that the taking argument can be avoided by making certain that developers receive a fair and reasonable return on their investment.

However, perhaps because of the ultra vires and taking arguments and perhaps also due to the opposition from developers, these inclusionary ordinances do not appear to have been adopted on a widespread basis.

CHAPTER VIII

AESTHETICS AND PRESERVATION OF HISTORICAL AND CULTURAL RESOURCES

§ 1. Introduction

Zoning, as previously discussed, is predicated on the police power. This relates to such tangibles as health and safety, but it also relates to the general welfare. Is it within the "general welfare" to regulate land use based upon aesthetic considerations alone? Can you measure what is aesthetically acceptable when beauty, in the old cliche, lies in the eyes of the beholder? Is it valid to regulate land use for the purpose of preserving our historical and cultural heritage? This brief chapter deals with these issues.

§ 2. Sign and Billboard Regulations

The amortization device is often employed in regard to signs. However, some ordinances limiting the size of signs, without utilizing amortization provisions, have been upheld. State v. Diamond Motors, 50 Haw. 33, 429 P.2d 825 (1967), predicated such a decision on the acceptance of "beauty as a proper community objective, attainable through the use of the police power." But the majority of courts have found it necessary to uphold such

[*213*]

ordinances on the basis of traditional considerations such as health, safety or morals, to accept
aesthetic considerations only as a side benefit, and
to strike down ordinances which solely achieve
aesthetic objectives. See, *e.g.,* Thomas Cusack Co.
v. Chicago, 242 U.S. 526 (1917); Baltimore v. Mano
Swartz, Inc., 268 Md. 79, 299 A.2d 828 (1973). The
trend, however, seems to be in favor of viewing
aesthetics alone as a valid basis for exercising the
police power to preserve the appearance of the
community. (See, *e.g.,* People v. Goodman, 31
N.Y.2d 262, 338 N.Y.S.2d 97, 290 N.E.2d 139 (1972);
Fayetteville v. McIlroy Bank, 278 Ark. 500, 647
S.W.2d 439 (1983).)

The *Goodman* case upheld an ordinance limiting
the size of signs on buildings (although allowing
nonconforming signs to exist for a period of two
years unless destroyed or changed). The court
pointed out that the state and local governments
could regulate outdoor advertising under the police
power and that communities had statutory power
to regulate various kinds of signs. Although this
ordinance was predicated upon aesthetic considerations, promotion of the appearance of the community was viewed as a valid police power objective.
An ordinance regulating "off-site" signs or billboards was upheld in California with regard to
signs which had been fully amortized; but as to a
few signs not fully amortized, the court ruled that
a reasonable amortization period would have to be

allowed. National Advertising Co. v. County of
Monterey, 1 Cal.3d 875, 83 Cal.Rptr. 577, 464 P.2d
33, cert. denied 398 U.S. 946 (1970). This decision
obviously depended upon the amortization approach. This is more common, and sign regulation
ordinances without some traditional police power
considerations and without reasonable amortization periods will normally fail.

The principal argument against the "aesthetics
alone" rule, as suggested in the introduction, is
that since beauty is in large measure in the eye of
the beholder, then decisions based on aesthetic
considerations would be subjective determinations
governed by personal feelings and attitudes. The
answer to that may be that if such attitudes result
in capricious use of the police power, such decisions
can be invalidated in the same manner as arbitrary zoning classifications. The problem is the lack
of objective criteria and, in that respect, it might
be compared to the obscenity cases.

An important United States Supreme Court decision which bears upon this problem was Me-
tromedia, Inc. v. San Diego, 453 U.S. 490 (1981),
which involved a ban on off-site billboards while
permitting on-site signs. The ordinance was challenged on the basis that it prohibited noncommercial speech and violated the First Amendment.
Political campaign signs had been specifically ex-
empted from the ordinance's application. The plu-
rality of four justices stated that the ordinance's

purpose of promoting aesthetics and traffic safety were valid goals, but it did not regard the ban on off-site, noncommercial advertising as valid because such speech is afforded greater protection than commercial speech, and the city could not choose permissible subjects of noncommercial discourse. The ordinance was thought to reach "too far into the realm of protected speech." A concurring opinion of two justices stated that the city had failed to justify its substantial restriction on protected activity and had also, due to the partial ban, failed to show a sufficient governmental interest in promoting aesthetics in this manner.

Federal and state efforts to beautify the highways by control of billboards has produced mixed results. The 1958 Federal act relied on the state police power to control outdoor advertising. Most of the states which passed upon these acts upheld the state legislation as being within the general welfare in promoting natural beauty. The 1965 Federal act contained just compensation provisions based on use of the power of eminent domain. The enforcement of the just compensation requirement was attacked in a lawsuit by a state legislator who wanted to rely on police power controls. His suit was dismissed due to his lack of standing to sue. Lamm v. Volpe, 449 F.2d 1202 (10th Cir.1971). Either compensation or reasonable amortization provisions are obviously "safer" in terms of legality, but the earlier decisions based on preservation of scenic beauty provide a basis for arguing that these largely aesthetic considerations should suffice for regulation and removal.

§ 3. The Appearance of Structures: Architectural Considerations

Cases have upheld ordinances which regulate architectural "appeal" and functions on the theory that protection of property values is a legitimate concern of the police power in that such regulations promote the general welfare. State ex rel. Saveland Park Holding Corp. v. Wieland, 269 Wis. 262, 69 N.W.2d 217, cert. denied 350 U.S. 841 (1955). That case stated that it was immaterial whether the sole objective was to protect property values. Such decisions are not predicated upon aesthetics alone, although Berman v. Parker, 348 U.S. 26 (1954), contained dictum suggesting that aesthetic considerations alone were a sufficient basis for the exercise of zoning powers. *Berman v. Parker* stated that the public welfare concept was broad enough to include aesthetics. In a Missouri case involving the much-protected St. Louis suburb of Ladue, an ordinance required that a board approve plans and specifications for structures in order to promote conformity to "minimal architectural standards" and prevent "unsightly, grotesque and unsuitable structures." When the ordinance was challenged by someone whose proposed residence was described by the city as "a monstrosity of grotesque design," on the basis that the state statutes did not authorize such an ordinance, the ordinance was upheld as being within the general welfare and promoting property values. State ex rel. Stoyanoff v. Berkeley, 458 S.W.2d 305 (Mo. 1970). But other cases have overturned such ordinances on the basis of lack of authorization under state enabling legislation, vagueness of provisions contained in the ordinance, and disapproval of the function of the architectural review board. *E.g.:* Piscatelli v. Township Committee of Scotch Plains, 103 N.J.Super. 589, 248 A.2d 274 (1968); West Palm Beach v. State ex rel. Duffey, 158 Fla. 863, 30 So.2d 491 (1947); Pacesetter Homes v. Olympia Fields, 104 Ill.App.2d 218, 244 N.E.2d 369 (1968).

One of the leading cases sustaining land use controls based on aesthetic considerations alone is People v. Stover, 12 N.Y.2d 462, 240 N.Y.S.2d 734, 191 N.E.2d 272, appeal dismissed 375 U.S. 42 (1963), in which an ordinance prohibiting clotheslines in front or side yards was sustained in a situation in which the Stovers erected and continually added to clotheslines of rags and unsightly apparel in their front yard to protest against high taxes. Nonetheless, the majority of courts sustain these ordinances, if at all, based on some more traditional ground in addition to aesthetic considerations.

A case subsequent to *Stover,* Cromwell v. Ferrier, 19 N.Y.2d 263, 279 N.Y.S.2d 22, 225 N.E.2d 749

(1967), made it clear that ordinances enacted for aesthetic reasons alone were permissible in New York (if there was any doubt about it). It cited *Stover* as "now the leading case" on the "aesthetics only" rule and rejected prior holdings that required some other valid police power objective.

§ 4. Junkyards

Before leaving amortization of signs and billboards, it should be pointed out that junkyards can sometimes be the target of valid amortization ordinances also—and indeed, amortization ordinances are usually aimed either at signs and billboards or at junkyards. Ordinances excluding junkyards or wrecking yards from the city have been upheld as a valid police power exercise based solely upon aesthetics. Oregon City v. Hartke, 240 Or. 35, 400 P.2d 255 (1965). Again, this is the minority view, as the majority of courts require the more traditional police power basis which, when established, may be combined with aesthetic considerations.

§ 5. Historic Districts

Akin to and yet apart from aesthetics is the preservation of historic districts. Purchase or condemnation by the government for historic preservation purposes is valid. More importantly, acts establishing historic districts have been upheld as promoting the public welfare. See, *e.g.,* Opinion of the Justices, 333 Mass. 773, 128 N.E.2d 557 (1955).

And zoning to preserve historic architectural patterns has been upheld. Sante Fe v. Gamble-Skogmo, 73 N.M. 410, 389 P.2d 13 (1964). The only problem seems to be one of proof with regard to the historic or cultural nature of the area.

The reasoning of courts in these situations is illustrated by the thinking of the Massachusetts Court in approving preservation of Beacon Hill in Boston. The court noted the historic nature of the area, the uniformity in design and structure, and held that the prevention of inappropriate forms of construction from coming into this area was for the educational, cultural, and economic advantage of the public and was within the general welfare. Opinion of the Justices, 333 Mass. 773, 128 N.E.2d 563 (1955). Obviously, there are some aesthetic considerations involved in such cases, but the courts generally view these as secondary to the main object of preserving the historic and cultural structures of the past and, in so doing by preventing commercial intrusion, maintain the property values of the area.

In addition to Boston and the New Mexico decision preserving "Old Santa Fe Style" architecture, Louisiana has a long history of attempting to preserve the character of the French Quarter. New Orleans' "Vieux Carre Ordinance" was based on constitutional authorization and was upheld as not being just for sentimental purposes but for preserving the commercial value of the area. In Williamsburg, Virginia, zoning was employed to preserve a restored area rather than an existing historic area. In Illinois, a historic district regulation was upheld which served to protect only one historic structure within the district—Lincoln's home. Rebman v. Springfield, 111 Ill.App.2d 430, 250 N.E.2d 282 (1969).

Such ordinances have come into widespread use and have generally been accepted by the courts. They exemplify the blending of aesthetic, historic and cultural concerns. They have been bolstered by such legislation as the National Historic Preservation Act of 1966 and by statutes in such states as Arkansas and New Mexico designating or creating commissions or committees with functions and duties on the subject.

§ 6. Landmark Preservation

Landmark preservation interrelates with historic preservation except that it normally involves a structure rather than an area. Landmark preservation ordinances, such as that in New York City, prevent demolition of buildings designated by a commission as landmarks. Such ordinances have, at times, run into the difficulty of being declared confiscatory as to the particular situation. See Lutheran Church v. City of New York, 35 N.Y.2d 121, 359 N.Y.S.2d 7, 316 N.E.2d 305 (1974). Solutions include authorizing acquisition of an easement in the facade of the structure rather than the entire fee and transfer of development rights permitting more intense development than allowed by zoning regulations as compensation to the landmark owner for not demolishing it. Fee title acquisition, through condemnation, presents the problem of acquiring property in prohibitively expensive locations.

The National Historic Preservation Act of 1966, 16 U.S.C.A. § 470 et seq., established a national register of historic sites. It was aimed at federal agencies and imposed no duties on state or local governments. It provided for protection and restoration of historic sites and districts. Any federal agency must take into account the effect of any project which might demolish an historic site, but preservation is not guaranteed even if the site is listed in the National Register. The standing of citizens to sue under this act to protect historic landmarks has presented a hurdle to relief in some cases. See Kent County Council v. Romney, 304 F.Supp. 885 (W.D.Mich.1969).

§ 7. Transfer of Development Rights

As mentioned, this device has been proposed for use in connection with landmark preservation, as well as open space acquisition. Referred to occasionally as "TDR," it is a relatively recent land use control device. The device has even been advanced as a substitute for zoning.

What TDR essentially involves is separation of
the right to develop property from other property
rights. A landowner may have his property limited to open space or may agree not to demolish a
landmark in return for issuance of certificates of
development rights which will allow him to develop elsewhere. He may also be allowed a tax reduction. The question arises as to whether this satisfies the just compensation requirement for a taking
under the power of eminent domain. The owners
may contend that the designation amounts to inverse condemnation and that the development
rights certificates represent only a potential for
future development elsewhere and do not amount
to just compensation. The contrary argument is
that by transferring development rights the landowner had received his equivalent elsewhere.

In Fred F. French Investing Co., Inc. v. City of
New York, 39 N.Y.2d 587, 385 N.Y.S.2d 5, 350
N.E.2d 381 (1976), the New York Court of Appeals
held that "floating development rights" which
could be used elsewhere within a certain area of
Manhattan could not be evaluated until such
rights were applied to a specific piece of property.
The award of such rights as compensation for rezoning two private parks as public parks was held
to amount to a deprivation of substantive due
process because such rights were an "abstraction,"
the value of which could not be determined until
some uncertain later date.

But in Penn Central Transportation Co. v. City of New York, 42 N.Y.2d 324, 397 N.Y.S.2d 914, 366 N.E.2d 1271, affirmed 438 U.S. 104 (1977), the court sustained the city's landmark preservation provisions and a denial of Penn Central's request to develop the airspace over the Grand Central terminal—one of the main reasons being that Penn Central would be allowed transferable development rights at some other location. These rights were viewed in that case as "valuable" and as providing "significant, perhaps 'fair' compensation." The court went to some lengths to distinguish a contrary holding involving ownership of an historic structure by the Lutheran Church, in which the ordinance had been declared unconstitutional because economic conditions did not permit the building to be maintained in its present form and the church was a charitable institution which did not reap the same pecuniary benefits of massive governmental investment enjoyed by the railroads and Grand Central Terminal.

French and *Penn Central* appear to be in conflict, but a factor in *Penn Central* that was not present in *French* was the landmark preservation provisions of the city code. Since landmark preservation generally has received favorable treatment in the courts and since the Penn Central railroad could continue to be benefited by use of the landmark terminal, then the transfer of development rights sweetened the pot, so to speak, with regard to the action taken. Moreover, these rights could be attached to specific parcels of property, some of which were already owned by Penn Central or its affiliates. In this context, the rights were viewed as being of value.

CHAPTER IX
NATURAL RESOURCES

§ 1. Introduction

The preservation of natural resources interrelates with preservation of historic and cultural districts and sites; and both bear a relationship to the preservation of aesthetics and of the environment. The interlocking effect of such problems and activities should be kept in mind.

§ 2. Restrictions on Removal of Earth

Many cases have upheld zoning ordinances which prohibit the removal of natural resources from property lying in specified zones. Problems arise when the question is whether it is reasonable and not arbitrary to do so under certain circumstances. In one case, it was demonstrated that the plaintiff's property had no real economic value for anything other than excavation of rock, sand and gravel, but an ordinance restricting the land to agricultural and residential uses was upheld. (Nearby communities housed people suffering from respiratory ailments.) Consolidated Rock Products v. Los Angeles, 57 Cal.2d 515, 20 Cal.Rptr. 638, 370 P.2d 342, appeal dismissed 371 U.S. 36 (1962). While the court found that many other uses might be made of the land, it was conceded that the value of these other uses was small in comparison to excavation of natural resources. But the court reasoned that if the classification was reasonably justified, it would be the antithesis of zoning theory to permit private benefits to override public welfare considerations. On the other hand, such ordinances may be declared to be unreasonable and confiscatory in situations in which adjacent lands are being used in a similar manner or in which there are no standards to govern determination of the grant or denial of a permit to excavate. Lyon Sand & Gravel v. Township of Oakland, 33 Mich. App. 614, 190 N.W.2d 354 (1971). The nuisance cases, such as *Hadacheck v. Sebastian*, illustrate the importance of surrounding uses in upholding or overturning such regulations.

Restriction on excavation in Pennsylvania might run afoul of that state's rule that all lawful uses must, in general, be accommodated within each township. Thus, a complete ban on quarrying was invalidated in Exton Quarries, Inc. v. Zoning Board of Adjustment, 425 Pa. 43, 228 A.2d 169 (1967), which stated that a total ban must receive greater scrutiny than regulations confining such use to a particular location. The court rejected contentions that quarrying operations interfere with the public welfare due to dust, noise, vibration and excessive truck traffic, interfere with the water supply, and create conditions which would endanger children.

§ 3. Agriculture

Zoning sometimes classifies land lying outside of urban areas as agricultural and limits the use either to pure agricultural uses or a variety of rural uses bearing some similarity or interrelationship. As the urban fringe extends outward and subdividers appear on the scene, the ordinance is amended to accommodate residential development within the agricultural zone.

Agricultural zoning has real estate tax implications. Those whose land is zoned exclusively for agriculture (with farm-related structures permitted) receive a tax break. This usually extends until reclassification of the land as residential.

Some problems have arisen from loosely drafted ordinances involving the urban fringe, in which farming has been treated as a permitted use. Expansion or development of operations involving animals, such as cattle, pigs or chickens, has led to litigation based on whether such operations or the expansion of same are permissible. The result often hinges (in the absence of specific wording in the ordinance) on whether the court views the raising of animals as farming.

Occasional agricultural designations have limited land uses over a substantial area. This is usually for the purpose of preventing nonconforming uses of land which may shortly become urban or semi-urban in nature. Courts have to be alert to prevent abuse of the ordinance through the establishment of "pre-existing" nonconforming uses which are not really pre-existing. Mang v. County of Santa Barbara, 182 Cal.App.2d 93, 5 Cal. Rptr. 724 (1960).

§ 4. Forests

Regulations restricting or prohibiting the wasteful or unnecessary cutting of timber have been upheld as falling within the police power and as not constituting a taking. Opinion of the Justices, 103 Me. 506, 69 A. 627 (1908). Similarly, statutes requiring private forest landowners to patrol their woods during dry seasons or pay for such patrols have been upheld. Destruction of trees to eliminate Dutch elm disease, cedar rust in cedar trees, orchard pests or other types of diseases has been upheld. Preservation of timber and the food supply is considered to be a valid objective of the police power. Thus, it is valid either to enact legislation to conserve trees or to destroy diseased ones.

Some subdivision exactions require landscaping in the form of tree planting as a condition to approval. In England, tree planting is required in connection with land development.

§ 5. Coastlines and Beaches

The Coastal Zone Management Act of 1972, 16 U.S.C.A. § 1451 et seq., arose from concern about industrial complexes (particularly oil refineries) in coastal waters, rapid shoreline urbanization, the threat to the wildly beautiful Pacific coastline produced by residential growth, commercial fishing activities, waste disposal and related problems. This act did not involve direct federal regulation of coastal areas but provided encouragement and money for the states to develop coastal management plans. All affected states and territories have moved toward development and implementation of coastal zone plans. California voters by initiative adopted a commission possessing the power to require on an interim basis a development permit for land extending 1000 yards inward from the mean high tide line. The Commission was charged with submitting a coastal zone plan to the legislature for its adoption and implementation. The validity of the California act was upheld when challenged as a violation of substantive and procedural due process, a taking, a violation of the right to travel, an invalid delegation of legislative power, and the like. See CEEED v. California Coastal Zone Conservation Commission, 43 Cal. App.3d 306, 118 Cal.Rptr. 315 (1974).

Regulation of beaches has been upheld on two theories: custom and prescriptive rights. The issue may arise as to the power of the state to prevent landowners from enclosing the dry sand area of ocean-front property. This power to regulate use was upheld in Oregon, Florida and Hawaii under the custom doctrine, *i.e.*, the custom of the public to use the beaches for recreational purposes joined with the relative inadequacy of such areas for erection of permanent facilities. State ex rel. Thornton v. Hay, 254 Or. 584, 462 P.2d 671 (1969); *Daytona Beach v. Tona-Rama*, 294 So.2d 73 (Fla. 1974); In re Ashford, 50 Haw. 314, 400 P.2d 76 (1968). In the Oregon case, the state had passed a statute maintaining state sovereignty over ocean beaches. While it was admitted that the legislation could not divest a landowner of his rights, the court (without rejecting the doctrine of prescriptive rights) held that long-standing customary use of the beach by the public as a recreational area resulted in vesting in the public a right to use the beaches. Relying on Blackstone, the court found that all requirements of the custom doctrine had been met—antiquity of use, without interruption, reasonable and peaceable use, certainty as to the boundaries, obligatory upon all landowners, and not inconsistent with other customs or other law.

Since use by the public of the dry sand area of beaches based upon custom does not create any rights in the beach, Florida upheld the right of a landowner to construct a tower in an area near a pier because this did not interfere with customary use. *Daytona Beach v. Tona-Rama, supra.*

Obviously, the custom doctrine bears some relationship to the prescriptive rights doctrine, which involves prescriptive use by the public for the statutory period of time. The problem with that doctrine is that it must be proved in each case, whereas a decision which follows the custom doctrine easily applies to all the beaches. But two states with long shorelines, California and Texas, have adopted the prescriptive rights approach. See, *e.g.,* Gion v. Santa Cruz, 2 Cal.3d 29, 84 Cal. Rptr. 162, 465 P.2d 50 (1970).

Controls relating to beach or shorefront areas have presented other problems. Michigan rejected the argument that public rights in Lake Michigan created an implied easement of access to the lake across private lands. Pigorsh v. Fahner, 386 Mich. 508, 194 N.W.2d 343 (1972). A New Jersey decision involved whether a city could charge nonresidents higher fees than residents for use of the beach. The court construed the public trust doctrine (which derives from the English principle that the land covered by tidal waters is held by the sovereign for the common use of all the people) as extending to recreational uses and as permitting municipalities to charge reasonable fees for use of their beaches but as not permitting discrimination between residents and nonresidents. Neptune City v. Avon-by-the-Sea, 61 N.J. 296, 294 A.2d 47 (1972). Wisconsin has held that the public trust doctrine extends to all public uses of water. Hixon v. Public Service Commission, 32 Wis.2d 608, 146 N.W.2d 577 (1966).

While the above doctrines and statutes based on them are more common forms of regulating beach-

es, zoning has been used to prevent beachfront
development. McCarthy v. Manhattan Beach, 41
Cal.2d 879, 264 P.2d 932 (1953).

Certain asserted rights of public use have been
held to be outweighed by other considerations as
where the Secretary of the Interior successfully
banned public nude bathing due to environmental
harm being caused due to increase of people and
traffic in the area. Williams v. Hathaway, 400
F.Supp. 122 (D.Mass.1975).

§ 6. Rivers and Streams

Generally speaking, the state is the owner of the
bed of a navigable river or stream, and the owners
of land along its banks own only to the high water
mark (or low water mark, depending on the jurisdiction). In the case of a non-navigable stream,
adjoining landowners own the stream itself out to
the center or thread of the stream. But this ownership relates to the definition of navigability.
Traditionally, a stream is viewed as non-navigable
if it is not subject to commercial use. Some recent
cases, however, have extended the definition to
encompass recreational use. *E.g.,* State v. McIlroy,
268 Ark. 227, 595 S.W.2d 659 (1980). A better
approach would seem to be the passage of a statute
creating a public easement for recreation in all
waters of the state, subject to the right of the state
and local governments to enact reasonable police
power regulations and subject to other statutory

and common law rights of landowners. Otherwise, it would seem that by changing the definition, riparian landowners are deprived of a valuable property right. Support for this contention may be found in Kaiser Aetna v. U.S., 444 U.S. 164 (1979), in which the water was found to have been made navigable by its private owners, and the public was held to be excluded until just compensation had been paid to the owners.

Another way to acquire the right to navigate non-navigable waters is through prescriptive use by the public for the period of time necessary to establish prescriptive rights.

§ 7. Other Regulatory Activities

The situation with regard to regulation of agriculture, forests, coastal areas and the like extends to similar subjects of regulation. Requirements that farmers dip cattle or sheep to destroy ticks or disease, statutes requiring destruction of weeds, regulation aimed at preserving fish and wildlife, legislation to assure drainage of farmlands, statutes prohibiting the waste of natural gas and crude oil, acts aimed at conserving the water supply, and the establishment of conservancy districts to prevent floods, have all been upheld under the police power. The courts have over the years shown a strong tendency to approve reasonable legislation intended to preserve and protect our natural resources.

CHAPTER X

ENVIRONMENTAL CONTROLS

§ 1. Introduction

As earlier mentioned, there is an interrelationship between regulation of aesthetics, historic preservation, controls on exploitation of natural resources, and environmental concerns. When the environment is regulated, or when historic and cultural districts or landmarks are preserved, aesthetics enters in. It is aesthetically pleasing to have clean air in a city or clean water in a lake or stream. Similarly, it is aesthetically pleasing to preserve our coastlines and beaches for public use and protect them against unsightly exploitation. All of these activities involve aesthetic considerations and all of them have environmental ramifications. Thus, the two preceding chapters have particular relevance to the material covered here.

This chapter does not purport to come even close to covering the subject of environmental law. It provides some basic information and considers situations in which environmental controls have particular effect upon land use development or other land use controls. Of course, all environmental controls are, in some measure, controls on the use of land, but we will deal here only with some of the more basic and direct ways in which land use is affected by environmental regulations.

§ 2. National Environmental Policy Act

Whatever may have gone before, and much did, the National Environmental Policy Act of 1969 (NEPA), 42 U.S.C.A. § 4321 et seq., made both the public and private sector conform to certain environmental standards and involved the federal courts in the review process. The interrelationship of the objectives of NEPA and more traditional forms of land use control under the police power are illustrated by its stated objectives, which relate not only to the environment, but also to assuring aesthetically pleasing surroundings, protecting health and safety, preserving our historic and cultural heritage, and preserving our national resources.

Probably the most significant effect of NEPA pertained to federal agencies. Not only were they required to undertake certain specific acts related to environmental policy and make information available on the subject, but they also had to include a detailed statement on the environmental impact of any proposal involving major federal activity. There were requirements as to consultation on the statement with federal agencies having expertise on the subject as well as to circulation of the statement to interested agencies of government at all levels. Agencies were also required to pro-

pose policies and measures to bring themselves
into conformity with NEPA. NEPA was intended
to supplement and not supersede the mission of the
federal agencies. Nonetheless, it clearly placed an
additional burden upon the various agencies as
well as supplementing their powers.

The goals or objectives of NEPA are fulfilled
principally through the Council on Environmental
Quality (CEQ), which was created under Title II of
the Act, and through the work of the Environmental Protection Agency (EPA). The Council was
given powers relating to examination of the quality
of the environment, review of federal programs
and activities, and preparation of environmental
quality reports. Subsequent acts or orders added
functions permitting the Council to gather information and coordinate the activities of different
agencies. The Council advises the President, but
its greatest impact is probably felt in the guidelines it prepares for environmental impact statements. Its studies on various topics have influenced national policies affecting the environment.

The CEQ guidelines are treated somewhat like
agency regulations by the courts. These guidelines
are influential and are employed by the courts, but
they are not invariably followed. Cases have varied on whether the guidelines should be viewed as
advisory or should be applied in all or practically
all instances. *Cf.:* Greene County Planning Board
v. Federal Power Commission, 455 F.2d 412 (2d Cir.

1972), cert. denied 409 U.S. 849 (1972); Trout Unlimited v. Morton, 509 F.2d 1276 (9th Cir.1974);
and Environmental Defense Fund, Inc. v. Corps of
Engineers, 325 F.Supp. 728 (E.D.Ark.1971).

CEQ does not control or veto procedure or policies of agencies or pass upon impact statements.
But the Environmental Protection Agency (EPA) is
more active. Under one section of the Clean Air
Act, 42 U.S.C.A. § 1857h–7, EPA is directed to
review and comment in writing on the environmental impact of matters relating to the subject of
that act contained in any federally proposed legislation, newly authorized Federal project, major federal agency action, and proposed agency regulations. This gives EPA a powerful check on other
agencies of the federal government. Moreover,
criticism by EPA of federal projects or proposed
regulations has a substantial effect on the courts.

NEPA amounted to a policy decision that federal
agencies would have to conform to environmental
standards and that their actions would be subjected to careful scrutiny. After a great deal of litigation and the enforcement of environmental standards by the courts, the agencies seemed to realize
that environmental concerns would have to be met.
Judicial admonition along that line no doubt led to
this realization. See, *e.g.,* Calvert Cliffs' Coordinat-
ing Comm. v. Atomic Energy Commission, 449 F.2d
1109 (D.C.Cir.1971), cert. denied 404 U.S. 942
(1972).

Calvert Cliffs was the first court of appeals case to apply NEPA, and it was a strong affirmation of the congressional intention that federal agencies comply with the requirements of the act. In this case the Atomic Energy Commission had adopted rules on environmental matters which were held not to comply. The AEC was compelled to adopt rules which took environmental concerns into account and which would lead to a "systematic balancing analysis" in evaluating projects and activities of the agency. Looking specifically at the AEC rules, the court found them to be a "crabbed interpretation of NEPA" that "makes a mockery of the Act." The court viewed the agency as reluctant to meet its obligations, and it refused to condone such footdragging.

§ 3. Judicial Review

Judicial review of agency actions has been a careful and thorough process involving rather close scrutiny. This is in line with the decision in Citizens to Preserve Overton Park, Inc. v. Volpe, 401 U.S. 402 (1971), which required that judicial review involve "substantial inquiry" and be searching, probing, and complete. Thus, administrative decisions must be carefully contrived and subject to reasonable explanation.

In the *Overton Park* case, the agency had attempted to rely upon a provision in the Administrative Procedure Act, 5 U.S.C.A. § 701(a)(2), which eliminated judicial review where action by the agency was by law made dependent upon agency discretion. But the Supreme Court held that this was true only where there was no applicable law affecting the situation. Although courts were held not empowered to substitute their views for those of the agency, the inquiry should be searching and careful and the reviewing court should determine whether relevant factors were considered and whether there was a clear error of judgment.

In this process, agencies may be called upon to explain how decisions were arrived at and what formed the basis for such decisions. See Kennecott Copper Corp. v. Environmental Protection Agency, 462 F.2d 846 (D.C.Cir.1972). The matter may also be remanded for further hearings on questions not considered.

§ 4. Federal Pollution Legislation

Although there were federal laws pertaining to air pollution prior to the 1970's, the present law on air pollution largely stems from the Clean Air Act. See 42 U.S.C.A. § 1857 et seq. This act deals with fixed sources of air pollution, emissions from motor vehicles and airplanes, as well as provisions pertaining to administrative and judicial review. Among other things, this Act contemplates a national program to prevent and control air pollution, establishes air quality control regions and criteria, and makes provision for ambient air quality standards, standards of performance by manufacturing plants and similar sources, and national emission standards for hazardous pollutants.

The counterpart to the Clean Air Act is the Federal Water Pollution Control Act, 33 U.S.C.A. § 1251 et seq. It too was preceded by other federal laws dealing with the subject. After providing in two titles for research and demonstration projects and grants for sewage treatment plants, it provides for imposition of standards and for rules relating to enforcement. It also provides for permits and creates the National Pollutant Discharge Elimination System.

Of less importance than the air and water pollution legislation in terms of its scope and the volume of cases it produces is the Noise Control Act of 1972, 42 U.S.C.A. § 4901 et seq. Noise pollution is simply excessive noise, and this act attempts to control noise on a federal basis. The act emulates many of the provisions of the earlier pollution control laws. EPA is authorized to conduct or contract for research on the subject. Technical assistance to local governments and studies are provided for. Most importantly, however, federal regulations are authorized in the establishment of noise emission standards for various sources and aircraft noise can be regulated. The enforcement provisions of the act, however, are relatively weak. Although the act gave EPA important duties, substantial power was retained in the Federal Aviation Administration and the Civil Aeronautics Board. This included authority over noise emitted by jet aircraft.

Other federal legislation includes the Federal Environmental Pesticide Control Act of 1972, 7 U.S.C.A. § 135 et seq., which involves various registration provisions prior to sale of pesticides. A pesticide can be classified for restricted use, which means that the environmental or personal risk in using it is substantial.

§ 5. Recent Legislative Concerns

Recent concerns involving legislation have centered in large measure around hazardous waste. A 1981 EPA study arrived at the conclusion that five to six times more hazardous waste was being generated than the agency believed even a year before to be the case. The Resource Conservation and Recovery Act, 42 U.S.C.A. §§ 6901 *et seq.* provides for granting permits for 8,500 waste facility sites. The cleaning up of known hazardous sites is the objective of the so-called "Superfund" or Comprehensive Environmental Response, Compensation and Liability Act, 42 U.S.C.A. §§ 9601 *et seq.,* adopted in 1980. Reports suggest that progress is slow under both. There are an estimated 2,200 dangerous sites, and by 1984, work had begun on less than 300 of them and only a handful had actually been cleaned up.

Other recent concerns which may ultimately be the subject of federal legislation include acid rain, groundwater loss and pollution, and what is sometimes referred to as cross-media pollution. Although the problem is still being studied, somewhat incessantly, industrial air pollutants which produce acid rain many hundreds of miles from the source appear to be damaging American forests in addition to polluting the atmosphere and offering water pollution problems. This is an example of cross-media pollution, as is the apparent fact that most metal deposits in the Great Lakes come from air pollution rather than water pollution, according to one report.

With respect to groundwater, there are already serious problem areas of the United States because of the exhaustion of underground aquifers by excessive agricultural or industrial use requiring large quantities of water. This is rapidly becoming an acute problem, for example, in the fertile high plains area of West Texas. Competition for groundwater in the West is an increasing problem, and the decision in Sporhase v. Nebraska ex rel. Douglas, 458 U.S. 941 (1982), holding unconstitutional state restrictions on the transfer of interstate groundwater, could lead to new conflicts and increasing litigation over groundwater, including suits between states. The *Sporhase* decision, joined with increasing groundwater shortages and pollution problems, would seem to call for a national initiative. But the Water Resources Council was disbanded in the early 1980's, and water resource policy or management from the federal level is largely absent.

§ 6. State Legislation

The states have adopted various and sundry statutes which emulate the federal legislation. These laws are usually more general in nature and less powerful in terms of enforcement. They create state and sometimes local air and water pollution control agencies.

Enforcement of state laws is generally weak and less consistent than at the federal level. Many or most states have probably come to depend upon federal control over the abuse of the environment. Whatever the cause, the center for imposition and enforcement of standards has largely resided in the federal courts and with EPA.

There are state and local environmental policy acts (SEPA's) which provide some assistance. Most of the states now have requirements relative to environmental impact statements, and a number of states have comprehensive legislation. An example of a rather extensive law is the California Environmental Quality Act of 1970. Cal.Public Resources Code § 21000 et seq.

§ 7. The Impact of Environmental Considerations

The impact on federal activities of environmental impact considerations has been quite substantial. In Hanly v. Kleindienst, 471 F.2d 823 (2d Cir. 1972), by way of illustration, the situation involved construction of a jail and related facilities by the General Services Administration. The case had twice been before the district court, and this was its second trip to the court of appeals. The case was again remanded due to the failure of the GSA to make certain required findings. Earlier, the court of appeals had found GSA's environmental impact statement to be insufficient in that it did not take into account the effect of the detention center on its neighbors with respect to noise, the danger of crime from the out-patient treatment center, certain traffic problems, and the need for parking. This time, the court was concerned with the standard of review to be applied and the determination of whether there would be a "significantly" adverse environmental impact as a result of the project. After adopting the "arbitrary, capricious" standard of the Administrative Procedure Act, the court decided that every major federal action had some adverse effect on the environment. But in considering whether a specific activity affected it "significantly," the proposed action would have to be considered in the light of the extent to which the adverse environmental effects exceed

those created by existing uses and the quantitative
adverse environmental effects of the action including resulting cumulative harm. Although the
GSA had submitted a new 25-page environmental
assessment, the court of appeals did not feel that it
had dealt adequately with the question of the effect
of a drug maintenance program and whether crime
in the area would be increased, and it also felt that
GSA had failed to comply with certain procedural
requirements. For one thing, it had not given
notice to the public of its proposed action and
allowed relevant facts to be presented prior to
making its "threshold decision." The GSA was
directed to consider the two questions and permit
further evidence to be submitted by those opposing
the project.

The thought of the Second Circuit that every
major activity affects the environment in some
way is illustrated by Aberdeen & Rockfish Ry. Co.
v. Students Challenging Regulatory Agency Procedures (SCRAP), 409 U.S. 1207 (1972). The railroads had filed for a rate increase, and SCRAP
argued that this would further discourage the
movement of recyclable goods in commerce and in
turn lead to increased degradation of the environment by discarded, unrecycled goods. SCRAP objected to the ICC's failure to issue an impact statement evaluating the effect of the rate increase on
shipments of recyclable materials. A three-judge
district court held that the ICC decision not to

suspend the rate increase while it looked into the environmental effect was a major federal action that would require an impact statement. On appeal, Chief Justice Burger, sitting as Circuit Justice, denied a stay of that order pending appeal.

It should be obvious from the foregoing that almost any federal project or important federal activity has environmental ramifications. In Anaconda Co. v. Ruckelshaus, 352 F.Supp. 697 (D.Colo. 1972), reversed 482 F.2d 1301 (9th Cir.1974), EPA itself was required to file an environmental impact statement with regard to a proposed emission limitation on a copper smelter. The court held that when Congress said all federal agencies had to comply, they intended no exceptions.

§ 8. Environmental Concerns in the Context of the 1980's

The crisis of the environment, which was seen so clearly in the late 1960's and most of the 1970's, has been in large measure put on a back-burner in the 1980's. In 1981, the staff and budget of the Council on Environmental Quality was reduced by about sixty percent, and since that time, the sparsity of environmental information has had to be supplemented by private foundations in large measure. Problems with toxic waste sites, acid rain, and pollution in general have taken a backseat to concerns over government spending, the tax struc-

[247]

ture, the federal tax deficit, and relations with the Soviet Union.

This seems to have come about for a variety of reasons. One is the national desire, manifested by individuals and corporations alike, to remove the national government as much as possible from regulative involvement in the lives of the people. This desire served well the aims of businesses engaged in pollution causing activities. But it cut across a wide front—from heavy industry to the agricultural use of pesticides. A second reason, interrelated with the first, was the perception that government spending was too high and government programs too extensive, expensive and wasteful. A further reason seems to have been the thought that federal taxes were overly burdensome and should be reduced. Again, this interrelated with the prior two concerns. Environmental programs thus became a visible, outward sign of what was perceived to be an inward, spiritual evil. They were involved with the lives of the people—private individuals and farmers as well as large corporations; they cost money (although a drop in the bucket compared to either national defense or entitlements); and they were supported by tax dollars. Such programs offended the powerful elite of the industrial establishment; and through such devices as an automobile emission control apparatus which necessitated more expensive gasoline, offended many ordinary citizens. The movement

also occasionally bogged down in silliness, such as
an over-concern for the possible extinction of the
Tennessee snail darter, a problem which does not
touch 99% of the public with the same concern as
that over hazardous waste sites.

In this way, the great movement for a clean
environment was substantially blunted. Aside
from cutting funds and toning down the aggressive-
ness of EPA, there have been reductions in technical assistance to the states and local governments
and a softening of regulations in numerous areas of
concern, including surface mining and protection
of wetlands ecology.

The environmental movement, however, is probably only in remission. The problems mentioned
previously will not go away and indeed are building up. Some day they will have to be addressed
on a more forceful national scale.

CHAPTER XI

HOUSING AND URBAN RENEWAL

§ 1. Urban Redevelopment: Legislative Background

The renovation of our urban environment received its first great boost with the enactment of the National Housing Act of 1949. This Act provided for the clearing of slum areas and for their redevelopment for new purposes. In 1953, an advisory commission appointed by President Eisenhower recommended that the slum clearance program include the conservation and rehabilitation of neighborhoods. The term "urban renewal" was employed as descriptive of the aims and objectives of the program, and the federal statute was amended accordingly.

The urban renewal program has been said to be the first federal program to require comprehensive planning. The program itself is carried on through local agencies which acquire deteriorated areas of the urban complex, demolish and remove the obsolete buildings, and sell the land under a redevelopment plan for the area, or under which the property owners themselves rehabilitate the structures in an area, accompanied by the improvement of community facilities by the local government and thereby resulting in urban conservation. Not all of these programs emanated from federal thinking or federal programs. Even before the Housing Act of 1949, a number of states had adopted slum clearance legislation based on model acts which had been prepared. But it was the federal legislation, activity and financial support which gave the real impetus to urban renewal in the United States.

Requirements in relation to slum clearance projects and the action and methodology available to urban planners have varied as new legislation has been enacted and new regulations and guidelines adopted pursuant to such legislation. The Housing Act of 1954 broadened the provisions of the 1949 Act to include federal assistance for the prevention of the spread of slums and urban blight through rehabilitation as well as through conservation of deteriorating areas. It was based in large measure on the 1953 advisory commission report to the President, the recommendations of which were aimed primarily at greater involvement of private enterprise in the elimination and prevention of urban blight through rehabilitation of existing buildings, the requiring of cities to assume greater responsibility in the program, and the increase in private residential development with particular attention being given to providing low-cost private housing for displaced families. It sought to provide a more comprehensive approach which would strike at blight before demolition was the only answer.

The Housing Act of 1956 once again broadened the original act by authorizing relocation payments to individuals, families, and businesses for moving expenses and property losses resulting from displacement due to urban renewal projects. It also permitted federal funds to be expended for preparation of "general neighborhood renewal plans." The authorized amount of capital grants and a new alternative capital grant formula were provided in the Housing Act of 1957.

The authorization for federal assistance to urban renewal was again increased in the Housing Act of 1959, which enacted new provisions for grants to "community renewal programs" designed to be long-range plans with regard to all of the renewal needs of an urban area.

The Housing Act of 1961 again increased federal grants and increased from two-thirds to three-fourths the contribution by the federal government for cities of 50,000 or less (or for cities of 150,000 or less in an "economically distressed" area).

Legislation in the 1960's in the urban renewal field was directed toward a general broadening of the program and the providing of additional funds to carry it on. It focused attention on problems relating to rehabilitation and relocation. Title III of the Housing Act of 1964 contained a number of provisions designed to improve the operation of the program, such as an additional authorization of $600,000,000 for grants, requirements encouraging greater rehabilitation and code enforcement, a new program of three percent rehabilitation loans for homeowners and businessmen in urban renewal areas for improvements to properties, and a strengthening of relocation requirements along with additional relocation benefits to businesses, families, and individuals who had been displaced as a result of urban renewal projects. In the Housing and Urban Development Act of 1965, an additional $2.9 billion was authorized to continue the program for four more years. This act also strengthened the project requirements to minimize relocation hardships and continued the three percent loan provisions for four years.

Some extensive revisions and amendments to the original 1949 Housing Act were made by the Housing and Urban Development Act of 1968, P.L. 90–448, 82 Stat. 476. Among the most significant of these were the provisions for the Neighborhood Development Program (NDP) and provisions for grants to be made for urban renewal open land projects, which had previously qualified only for loans. The 1968 Act also increased available grant funds by $1.4 billion, extended the areas eligible for three percent rehabilitation loans and grants, and authorized the Secretary of Housing and Urban Development to enter into contracts and to

make grants in amounts up to $15 million per year
to assist localities in alleviating harmful conditions
in slum and blighted areas where urban renewal
activities were planned but immediate action was
required.

By 1968, criticism of urban renewal and redevelopment programs had increased substantially.
The problem of relocation led to legal attacks by
displaced minorities as the *Norwalk* case, *infra,*
illustrates.   However, attacks also came from a
National Commission on Urban Problems, which
after stating some of the achievements of urban
renewal, criticized the process as being too time-
consuming and as not giving enough attention to
the problem of the displaced poor.   In connection
with the first criticism, their report showed that
the average project took $4\frac{1}{3}$ years to get the project
into contract form and that this was only the
beginning of the project.   The most common time
from beginning to end was six to nine years, and
over a third of the projects took longer than that.
With regard to the urban poor, the report found
that they had not been rehoused, for the most part,
in urban renewal sites, that public housing for
them had been inadequate, and that relocation had
had mixed results.

Criticism of this type led to an emphasis in the
1968 Act on projects intended to produce low and
moderate-income housing.   However, there also began to be a reduction in the amount of federal

funds allocated to urban renewal programs. This
was spurred on by increasing criticism of government involvement in projects involving misman-
agement or questionable management as well as by
the effects of inflation on the cost of such projects.
Finally, in 1973, funding was terminated for most
of the subsidized programs (except for existing
projects). The operation of the principal subsidized
housing programs was suspended, and a review
was initiated by HUD. The Housing and Community Development Act of 1974, P.L. 93-383, 88 Stat.
633, sought to consolidate urban renewal and other
community development programs into a "block
grant" approach which would provide aid to localities for community development. This was sup-
posed to supersede such programs as urban renewal, public housing, the Model Cities program and
the like. There was a focus on neighborhood assistance intended to conserve and rehabilitate older
areas. The financial underpinnings of the law
were such, however, that the development funding
would largely have to come from private sources.
From a political or socioeconomic standpoint, this
change in methodology began with the departure
of Lyndon B. Johnson from the presidency and the
beginning of the Nixon administration. Since that
time, it has remained essentially in that pattern.
The substantial infusion of federal funds into the
economy for these purposes is largely a matter of
the past.

Despite that situation, activity in the area of public housing and urban redevelopment has been a matter of considerable importance in this country since the period following World War II, and legal developments in that regard have been important. Therefore, substantial space is accorded this subject.

§ 2. The "Public Use" Requirement

As in other situations involving the state's power of eminent domain, urban renewal activities have been attacked on the ground that the power of eminent domain was exercised in violation of the requirement that it be employed only for a "public use." This requirement stems from state constitutional provisions (and implicitly from the United States Constitution) to the effect that no property is to be taken for a public use without just compensation. Where urban renewal projects are planned in such a way that the governmental body is to purchase the land through the power of eminent domain and is then to redistribute the property to private owners, the projects have been attacked on grounds that sales to private owners do not constitute a "public use."

State constitutions have differing provisions with regard to whether "public use" is to be judicially determined. For example, Arizona provides that the question is judicial "and determined . . . without regard to legislative assertion that the use is public." Ariz.Const. art. 2, § 17. Missouri has a similar constitutional provision. Mo.Const. art. I, § 28. However, the Virginia Constitution provides that the question is a legislative one. Va.Const. § 59.

The prevailing judicial rule regarding whether the resale to private owners constitutes a "public use" is that it constitutes such a use if it serves a public purpose or advantage, and a legislative determination that such projects are a public use will be given considerable weight by the court. In the landmark case of Berman v. Parker, 348 U.S. 26 (1954), the Supreme Court upheld the District of Columbia Redevelopment Act of 1945, which provided that "the acquisition and the assembly of real property and the leasing or sale thereof for redevelopment pursuant to a project area redevelopment plan . . . is hereby declared to be a public use." The court found that the judicial role in determining whether the project is for a public purpose is an extremely narrow one, because the basic determination of what is in the public interest is a legislative matter. Having found that the act was within the police power of Congress to legislate for the public health, safety, and welfare of the inhabitants of the District of Columbia, the Court also determined that the concept of the public welfare is sufficiently broad to include regulations regarding the aesthetics of the community. With regard to the provisions for resale of the

property to private interests, the Court concluded
that once the legislative object has been upheld,
the means for attaining the object is a legislative
determination and that private purchases of property for redevelopment within an overall plan is a
legitimate means of attaining a public purpose.

The Texas Supreme Court determined that
whether the taking is for a public use is properly a
judicial question, but it stated that the declaration
of the legislature was entitled to great weight and
upheld provisions in the Texas Urban Renewal
Law which permitted resale of land in the urban
renewal project area to private owners. The Court
found that the legislative intent was to fulfill a
public purpose relating to the clearance of slums
and blighted areas and was not intended to benefit
private individuals. Davis v. City of Lubbock, 160
Tex. 38, 326 S.W.2d 699 (1959).

The Illinois Neighborhood Redevelopment Corporation Law was upheld in Zurn v. City of Chicago,
389 Ill. 114, 59 N.E.2d 18 (1945), where the court
took the position that the clearance and redevelopment of slums and blighted areas "constitutes a
public use and a public purpose, regardless of the
use which may be made of the property after the
redevelopment has been achieved." This view disregards the ultimate use of the property and limits
the "public use" determination to whether a public
purpose has been achieved by the clearance and
redevelopment.

This line of cases, although the reasoning varies somewhat, reaches the sounder result and represents the better view.

A minority of jurisdictions take the position that the public use requirement is satisfied only when the land is to have public occupancy as its ultimate use. In Edens v. City of Columbia, 228 S.C. 563, 91 S.E.2d 280 (1956), the Housing Authority of the city had proceeded under the state's redevelopment law and had determined that an area was a blighted area principally occupied by slum dwellings. They proposed to take the property, clear it, and sell it partly to the University of South Carolina for expansion and partly to private parties for light industrial sites. The South Carolina Court had no problem in upholding the project as to the portion which was to go to the University, but it refused to go along with the rest of the scheme because of the plan to ultimately place a large part of the land in private hands. The court specifically refused to find that a public purpose is a public use for purposes of exercising the power of eminent domain. Similar positions have been taken by Georgia in Housing Authority of Atlanta v. Johnson, 209 Ga. 560, 74 S.E.2d 891 (1953), and by Arkansas in City of Little Rock v. Raines, 241 Ark. 1071, 411 S.W.2d 486 (1967). In the latter case the Arkansas Court declined to depart from its "public use" position and embrace the "public purpose" concept. The case involved the condemnation of land for

construction of port facilities, an industrial park,
and related uses. The court held the port facility
to be a public use, but the sale of the property to
private interests for industrial uses was not considered a valid exercise of the power of eminent
domain.

§ 3.   Permissible Scope of Redevelopment

Urban renewal acts generally contemplate the
redevelopment of an entire area, not merely the
condemnation and rebuilding or redevelopment of
structures that are below standard or structures
that are residential. Property owners whose structures within a project area do not qualify as deteriorated or slum-like in nature may not attack an
urban renewal project on grounds that their buildings are not substandard. In *Berman v. Parker,
supra*, the plaintiff's property was a department
store within the area, and the Court found that the
overall purpose of the redevelopment plan could
not be served if structures such as the plaintiff's
were immune from eminent domain because they
were not offensive or unhealthy per se. Likewise,
in *Davis v. City of Lubbock, supra*, one of the
plaintiff landowners was not successful in his argument that his building, which met the city's building code, should not be taken for the purpose of
eliminating a slum. As in the *Berman* case, the
court pointed out that the act provided for the city
to deal with an entire area, not individual struc-

tures, and that such a provision is not "manifestly unreasonable."

Even though these cases make it clear that individual structures within an urban renewal area may not be immune from the project because their conditions are not substandard, there have been questions raised from time to time with regard to what types of property may be taken pursuant to urban renewal laws. In a New York case the plaintiff, as a taxpayer, disputed the conclusion of the city planning commission and other public administrative bodies that a certain area in Manhattan was "substandard and insanitary." The area in question was primarily occupied by parking lots and nonresidential structures, with 20% of the area occupied by residential structures and 7% by hotels and rooming houses. One commercial building in the area was assessed at $1,500,000. The plaintiff contended that the reason this area had been designated for slum clearance was to acquire land for a coliseum. Upholding the administrative determinations, the court said that when such determinations are not made corruptly, irrationally or baselessly they are not subject to court revision and that under modern standards it was reasonable to find the area "substandard" and "insanitary." Kaskel v. Impellitteri, 306 N.Y. 73, 115 N.E.2d 659 (1953), cert. denied 347 U.S. 934 (1954).

With the aid of an adequate state enabling act and appropriate provisions in a local ordinance, a

city could create an inspection and elimination
program which would compel owners to repair or
tear down substandard structures without cost to
the municipality. Such provisions could save a
substantial amount of money by enabling the city
to avoid paying for substandard buildings in urban
renewal areas. Politically, of course, this would be
a hot potato. Moreover, from a legal standpoint,
there is the problem of determining where the line
can be drawn between a legitimate exercise of the
police power in this regard and the requirement of
compensation. California, however, upheld such
an approach in the demolition of antiquated, un-
safe structures located in the "Downtown Rehabilitation District" of Los Angeles. Takata v. Los
Angeles, 184 Cal.App.2d 154, 7 Cal.Rptr. 516
(1960); Yen Eng v. Board of Building and Safety
Commissioners, 184 Cal.App.2d 514, 7 Cal.Rptr.
564 (1960).

§ 4. Standing to Sue

One of the problems incident to challenging
these projects, which has undergone legal development over approximately the last fifteen years, is
the problem of standing to file suit. The owners of
property in the affected area have no problem in
that regard. The problem arises with regard to
slum tenants and groups or organizations which
are inclined to assist them but which possess no
property interests which have been affected. The

problem arose principally in the 1960's because these more recent attacks on urban renewal programs have come from the poor and minorities in large urban centers rather than from slum landlords.

A reasonably early, although somewhat differing, encounter came in Harrison-Halsted Community Group, Inc. v. Housing and Home Finance Agency, 310 F.2d 99 (7th Cir.1962), cert. denied 373 U.S. 914 (1963). Many of the plaintiffs did own property and businesses in the area, and they had originally favored the slum clearance program. They objected when they learned that the proposed use of the area was to form a part of the Chicago campus of the University of Illinois. The Seventh Circuit dismissed the case due to lack of standing, stating that citizens did not possess standing to challenge the choice made by public authorities between different competing but legitimate public interests. The court relied on *Berman v. Parker, supra,* and Zurn v. Chicago, 389 Ill. 114, 59 N.E.2d 18 (1945), in which the Illinois Court stated that the redevelopment of slum areas was a public use and purpose regardless of what use was later made of the redeveloped property.

The *Harrison-Halsted* case was later distinguished on the basis that it did not involve a right the courts would protect. This distinction was made in Norwalk CORE v. Norwalk Redevelopment Agency, 395 F.2d 920 (2d Cir.1968). There it

was alleged that the activities of the agency
amounted to a denial of equal protection, that the
activity complained of would have the effect of
forcing low-income Negro and Puerto Rican families outside of the city, and that a provision of the
federal statute on urban renewal had been violated. The Second Circuit, in upholding the standing
of the plaintiffs to sue, ruled in *Norwalk* that the
right not to be subjected to racial discrimination in
government programs was "immediate and personal" and one which the courts would protect. They
also undertook to distinguish Green Street Ass'n v.
Daley, 373 F.2d 1 (7th Cir.1967), cert. denied 387
U.S. 932 (1967), which did raise constitutional issues as to the legitimacy of the plan, on the basis
that the court "harbored some doubt as to the
justiciability of the issues" being raised because the
plaintiffs sought to force a prior review of an urban
renewal program before the exercise of the power
of eminent domain. In *Norwalk,* on the other
hand, the Second Circuit found that the complaint
was of a denial of equal protection in the implementation of the program. This may seem to be a
rather narrow distinction, but in any event, it
opened the door to a solution of the problem of
standing on the part of racial minorities affected
by urban renewal.

Whether a particular type of plaintiff has standing to sue is yet another question. In *Norwalk,* the
plaintiffs consisted of the local chapter of CORE,

two tenants' associations composed of low-income racial minority groups, and eight people representing four classes of individuals. The classes were those still in the project area, those whose homes had been demolished and who were occupying overcrowded rental units at excessive rentals outside of the area but within the city, and those who claimed they were now forced to occupy rental units outside of the city. The court stated that no one can bring suit who does not have some personal stake in the outcome. It then held that plaintiffs' stake in the outcome was immediate and personal. Whether this would be true as to all of the plaintiffs is rendered in some doubt at least by Warth v. Seldin, 422 U.S. 490 (1975), in which the Supreme Court held that individual taxpayers and organizations seeking to provide low-income housing opportunities lacked standing to challenge an ordinance of a Rochester, New York, suburb. While some or all of the individuals involved in *Norwalk* clearly had standing, a question necessarily arises as to the involvement of an outside organization which, as an organization, is not directly affected. With regard to this type of case, however, the problem of whether the plaintiffs are sufficiently affected is less likely to be a major concern than in the exclusionary zoning cases.

§ 5. The Relocation Problem

The *Norwalk* case has only been discussed as it relates to the problem of standing to sue. It had far greater ramifications, however. While urban renewal, slum clearance, and related programs were funded for the worthwhile societal purposes of revitalizing the core of cities and providing decent housing for low-income families, they engendered substantial distrust and distaste on the part of racial minorities because of problems stemming from the relocation of displaced families. These families lived in the slum areas for a variety of reasons, but the more salient ones were that they were too poor to afford better housing elsewhere and there was no benefit in exchanging a familiar slum for an unfamiliar one. While it was reasonable and desirable to attempt to eliminate or prevent slum conditions, the problem was one of where these people might go. Racial minorities are more difficult to relocate than displaced whites, and since minorities have a right not to be subjected to racial discrimination in government programs, this right extended to the relocation issue.

Norwalk involved Negroes and Puerto Ricans who had been displaced by urban renewal, and they alleged a denial of equal protection. Their cause of action was deemed valid because they had alleged that the housing authority and city officials had not assured or attempted to assure relocation for them to the same extent as they had for white people. They argued that the defendants, with knowledge of the discriminatory character of the private housing market, intended to drive many of them out of the city by contracting to build moderate-income housing which they could not afford. Moreover, it would be built on the only land available for construction of low-income housing. The congressional act had required that the agency provide housing in the same area, or in areas not less desirable, which would be within the financial means of the displaced families and would be essentially equal in number to the families and reasonably accessible to their jobs. The court concluded that if the allegations were proved, the result would be a violation of the 14th amendment as well as the provisions of the federal statute.

When this case is compared to *Harrison-Halsted* and *Green Street,* which it carefully distinguished, it is perhaps difficult not to arrive at the assumption that courts tend to elevate violations of individual rights above the invasion of property rights (which are, really, only another facet of individual rights). Property rights were at stake in *Harrison-Halsted,* but not in *Norwalk.* But this is overly simplistic, even as the Second Circuit's effort to distinguish the cases was painfully contrived. The basic factor in *Norwalk* was the recognition by the court of the necessity to provide for non-discriminatory relocation as the Congress had mandated.

The basic failure of the local agency was that it
apparently had not fulfilled that requirement.
But, in holding as it did, *Norwalk* had a substantial
impact on urban renewal and slum clearance
projects.

§ 6. Conservation and Rehabilitation

Conservation involves the prevention of further
deterioration of neighborhoods in order to prevent
slums.   Rehabilitation involves the restoration of
the deteriorating area.   Although these concepts
are old ones, they did not have widespread impact
until the 1954 amendments to the Federal Housing
Act.   Even then, projects developed slowly.   Possibly this was partly due to the fact that state
enabling legislation was required for cities to participate, although by the mid-1960's all but a handful of states had such legislation.   More likely the
process was hindered by normal bureaucratic de-
lays and complicated procedures.   To qualify for
federal aid, a "Local Public Agency" (LPA) had to
select a conservation locale, assess its problems,
and adopt a program for it (which was called a
"Workable Program").   To proceed further, the
city had to demonstrate that it had a comprehensive plan, that it had the money to go through with
the non-federally funded portion of the project,
that it had suitable zoning, housing and building
regulations, and that there were ample citizen par-
ticipation and administrative resources available.

Later housing legislation, such as that in 1964, lent new impetus to such projects. In terms of federal funding for these and other projects, however, the situation of the 1960's changed to a substantial degree in the early 1970's with the advent of revenue-sharing and the "block grant" approach of the Housing and Community Development Act of 1974.

Be that as it may, the conservation and rehabilitation approach was upheld in People ex rel. Gutknecht v. Chicago, 3 Ill.2d 539, 121 N.E.2d 791 (1954). An Illinois act aimed at slum prevention through creation of conservation areas in deteriorating neighborhoods was attacked on the grounds that this was a taking for a private use, an unconstitutional delegation of legislative power, and that it created arbitrary classifications of real estate and amounted to a taking without just compensation because necessary repairs became a lien on the property. On the first issue, the court pointed out that possessory use by the public is not required and that there is no constitutional requirement that an evil cannot be prevented before it has reached fruition. The delegation of powers argument centered on provisions allowing a board to designate conservation areas and formulate plans, but the court observed that the plan had to be approved by the city council before anything could be done. The court also found that no arbitrary classification scheme existed. The court did not

pass on the just compensation question relating to
liens for repairs, but held that that part of the act
was severable and would not affect the constitutionality of the remainder. A somewhat later case,
Cannata v. New York, 11 N.Y.2d 210, 227 N.Y.S.2d
903, 182 N.E.2d 395 (1962), upheld a provision
allowing cities to condemn largely vacant areas for
redevelopment and conservation purposes and to
prevent slums.

§ 7. Public Support for Housing

While in more recent years attention has focused
on government programs involving urban redevelopment and the elimination of slums, federal aid
for housing has a much older lineage. It extends
back, of course, into the depression years and the
creation of the Federal Housing Administration
(FHA). Under this program, the government
would underwrite private loans for people of moderate income to purchase houses with relatively
little collateral. FHA was buttressed by the Federal National Mortgage Association (FNMA), which
was established in 1938 to provide another market
for FHA mortgages in the event the private market weakened due to a rise in interest rates on
conventional loans. FNMA was followed by the
Government National Mortgage Association
(GNMA). The Housing Act of 1961, P.L. 87–70, 75
Stat. 149, permitted the government to buy certain
FHA mortgages which were part of a non-profit (or

largely non-profit) housing project and cover these mortgages through GNMA.

The Housing and Urban Development Act of 1965, P.L. 89–117, 79 Stat. 451, provided for rent supplements in non-profit housing projects. It provided for a limitation on maximum income of those who could receive the supplements. There were other limitations based on the rental price and similar factors. Legislation in 1966 eliminated the requirement that the housing be part of a public housing project.

The Housing and Urban Development Act of 1968, P.L. 90–448, 82 Stat. 476, made extensive changes. It authorized new programs to reduce mortgage interest rates, permitted a high-risk FHA insurance fund, authorized interest-free loans to cover preconstruction expenses of non-profit housing sponsors, required that over 50% of the housing in new urban renewal projects aimed at residential development be for low and moderate income families, and made various other provisions pertaining to housing and urban redevelopment.

But as mentioned in the first section of this chapter, the President suspended the operation of the main subsidized housing programs in 1973, and the Secretary of HUD undertook an extensive review of these programs. As has been mentioned, the Housing and Community Development Act of 1974, P.L. 93–383, 88 Stat. 633, followed a different perspective. Its consolidation provisions overhauled the FHA mortgage insurance programs and the low-rent public housing program, the latter of which also extended back into the depression era. HUD could deal with rental assistance to individuals under this act. It liberalized provisions allowing assistance to low-income occupants of rural housing. It also authorized experimental financing under which mortgages with varying rates of amortization corresponding to anticipated family income could be insured.

Under the 1977 Act, the mortgage limits were increased for FHA insurance purposes to $60,000 for a single-family dwelling. There were also increases on multi-family dwellings and other categories. The 1977 Act made mention of the need to deal with economic distress situations in areas involving a stagnating tax-base or areas with out-migration, although regulations to this effect were attacked in litigation over their validity.

As mentioned, public housing projects not involved with such devices as FHA extend back to congressional legislation in 1937. At that time, its purpose was to alleviate the problems of the middle class just as was FHA, and after World War II both helped the returning veterans. In more recent years, of course, public housing has related to the problems of the poor with some substantial emphasis being given to the elderly poor. Local housing authorities typically operate such projects with considerable federal aid being pumped in by

HUD. Problems of such projects include ever-increasing operating costs, the rapid deterioration and mistreatment of many of the structures, the occasional ill effects of vandalism and crime, delay in the planning and construction of such projects, a failure to consider cost reduction techniques in the construction process, a failure to coordinate public housing standards with FHA standards, a tendency to build high-rise and densely massed buildings, some disregard for the needs of children, omission of services essential to modern life, a neglect of aesthetic considerations, lack of adequate training for personnel, and the authoritarian exercise of control over such projects by public housing authorities. Suits by tenants associations have led to a liberalization of rules and increased procedural due process for tenants. The issue of tenants' rights persists in the public housing situation.

§ 8.   Constitutional Issues in Location of Public Housing

These problems have already been developed in a somewhat different way in the discussion of exclusionary zoning. Viewed principally from a housing context, however, a major problem in recent years has related to the site selection process for such projects. The leading case on the subject is Hills v. Gautreaux, 425 U.S. 284 (1976), which affirmed the Seventh Circuit decision in Gautreaux v. Chicago Housing Authority, 503 F.2d 930 (7th

Cir.1974). In the latter opinion, written by the
late retired Justice Tom C. Clark, a comprehensive
metropolitan area plan had been ordered by the
court of appeals with the objective of correcting the
segregated housing patterns in the Chicago metropolitan area. The allegations of the plaintiffs, who
were black tenants and applicants for public housing, were to the effect that, through their activities, the Chicago Housing Authority and HUD
were helping to maintain such segregated patterns
and thereby were violating the plaintiffs' civil
rights. They sought dispersal of public housing
throughout the entire area including the Chicago
suburbs. The opinion of Justice Clark devoted
considerable attention to Milliken v. Bradley, 418
U.S. 717 (1974), which was a school desegregation
case. *Milliken* had declined imposition of a metropolitan area solution but had suggested that metropolitan area solutions could be employed when
appropriate to do so. The Seventh Circuit concluded that such an approach was essential in remedy-
ing segregated housing patterns in the Chicago
area. Justice Stewart's Supreme Court opinion in
the case also dealt with *Milliken* and held that it
was consistent to order CHA and HUD to create
housing alternatives in the suburbs. It was stated
that HUD's power could be exercised without pre-
empting the power of local governments in the
suburbs. The nature and scope of the relief was
left up to the district court upon remand.

The *Gautreaux* result is affected by Village of
Arlington Heights v. Metropolitan Housing Development Corp., 429 U.S. 252 (1977). Arlington
Heights had refused to rezone a fifteen-acre parcel
to allow construction of subsidized housing by a
non-profit developer. The developer and some
blacks who wished to live there challenged the
action, and the Supreme Court ultimately held
that it was necessary to prove a racially discriminatory intent to establish a violation of the Fourteenth Amendment. The Court found no discriminatory purpose and viewed the discriminatory
effect as an insufficient basis for overturning the
local regulations. However, the case was remanded to determine the question of whether the Fair
Housing Act might have been violated. The Seventh Circuit, upon remand, determined that under
some limited circumstances, the Fair Housing Act
might be violated by a showing of discriminatory
effect without proving discriminatory intent.
(Metropolitan Housing Development Corp. v. Village of Arlington Heights, 558 F.2d 1283 (7th Cir.
1977).) The appeals court stated that the Fair
Housing Act is violated if there is no land other
than plaintiff's property within Arlington Heights
which is both properly zoned and suitable for federally subsidized public housing. This would seem to
leave the door open to carry out the *Gautreaux*
determination, although it left a relatively narrow
opening and one which conceivably could involve

litigation every time public housing wishes to enter a highly restricted suburb.

An earlier Supreme Court decision also is important in this regard. James v. Valtierra, 402 U.S. 137 (1971), involved a California constitutional provision which allowed local voters the power of initiative and referendum in connection with local laws. By amendment this had been extended to include public housing projects. When some local housing proposals were defeated in this manner, suit was brought alleging that this violated the equal protection clause, supremacy clause, and privileges and immunities clause of the U.S. Constitution. But the Supreme Court held that it did not. After discussing the long history of use of the initiative and referendum in California, the Court decided that the people of a community were entitled to a voice in decisions involving large expenditures of local governmental funds. This case would seem to open the door to a device whereby suburbs might prevent the intrusion of public housing projects involving local expenditures (if such a referendum procedure were permissible under state law). If it could be shown that the purpose of adopting a referendum procedure was to discriminate racially or if the vote on the issue was predicated on a racially discriminatory intent, it might be argued that the result would be different. This is suggested in Southern Alameda Spanish Speaking Organization v. City of Union City, 424

F.2d 291 (9th Cir.1970). Such proof might be quite difficult, of course. Moreover, the court in Ranjel v. City of Lansing, 417 F.2d 321 (6th Cir.1969), cert. denied 398 U.S. 980 (1970), stated that if the electors had the legal right to a referendum, their motives were immaterial.

Still another factor which enters the picture is that of environmental impact. HUD is required to consider a variety of alternatives, and if it does not, this may provide the basis for an attack upon its actions. This problem is illustrated by Trinity Episcopal School Corp. v. Romney, 523 F.2d 88 (2d Cir.1975), in which the court of appeals found that HUD had not adequately considered alternatives and the question of urban environmental factors.

Attempts to justify exclusion of low-income housing on the basis of overcrowding, burden upon the public schools, and the overburdening of recreational facilities and firefighting capacity have failed, however, where the courts find that the actions taken are motivated by a desire to exclude minorities. Dailey v. City of Lawton, 425 F.2d 1037 (10th Cir.1970). This is in keeping with the "discriminatory intent" test of *Arlington Heights*.

§ 9. Housing and Building Codes

Housing codes provide standards and serve as guidelines for habitability, generally focusing upon the safety and construction of buildings. The general rule is that it is within the police power to

establish minimum standards for the design and
materials used in the construction of buildings in
order to protect the occupants, their neighbors, and
the general public.   Horton v. Gulledge, 277 N.C.
353, 177 S.E.2d 885 (1970).

At present there is no nationwide or uniform
housing code or system of enforcement, and this is
viewed as unfortunate by some writers.   There is
also the problem of balancing the need for housing
in some communities with the strictness of the
code.   Federal grants to local communities for
housing create the necessity of compliance with
federal standards, and, of course, FHA standards
must be complied with to secure an FHA-insured
loan.

Problems may arise in the enforcement of building codes.   Camara v. Municipal Court of City and
County of San Francisco, 387 U.S. 523 (1966), required a building inspector to have either the consent of the property owner or a warrant in order to
seek housing code violations involving criminal
penalties unless there are "other satisfactory reasons" for entering.   Refusal by the owner of entry
or the lodging of a citizen complaint would establish probable cause for asserting the governmental
interest in protecting the health, safety and welfare of the public.   Alleged discrimination or sin-
gling out of a defendant may also present problems
in enforcement, as illustrated by People v. Walker,

14 N.Y.2d 901, 252 N.Y.S.2d 96, 200 N.E.2d 779 (1964).

When a city finds that a dwelling is unfit for habitation, but repairs are too costly, it has been held that it may not order demolition without compensation and then attach a lien on the vacated lot for the cost of demolition. Horton v. Gulledge, *supra.* The owner must be given a reasonable opportunity to conform to the housing code. Unless the cost of repairs exceeds the value of the building, that alternative is preferable. Injunctive relief, however, may be granted where a building offends the fire protection provisions of the building code. Such a violation has been construed as a public nuisance which affects safety and the general welfare. City of Bakersfield v. Miller, 64 Cal.2d 93, 48 Cal.Rptr. 889, 410 P.2d 393 (1966). Other sanctions for enforcing such codes include orders to vacate, criminal penalties, and various equitable remedies including receivership as well as injunctive relief. Moreover, a tenant may retaliate against a landlord who is in violation of housing codes through a rent strike or through such allegations as that of constructive eviction, construing the code violation as a breach or "illegality" of contract and negligence.

Activities of tenants' associations often produce relief in situations involving public housing. There is an increasing judicial recognition of the necessity of providing procedural due process in dealing with tenant complaints in such projects.

CHAPTER XII

EMINENT DOMAIN AND THE POLICE POWER

§ 1. Introduction

Land use controls put into effect by local governments involve the use of such tools as zoning and subdivision regulations which are based on the police power. The theory is that local governments can exercise such controls because they reasonably relate to the general welfare or to such public concerns as health, safety or morals. The police power, then, is for the benefit of all of us and supposedly does not impinge unduly on any one of us. Where it does pass the bounds of reason, becomes arbitrary or capricious, or where it is confiscatory in nature, the action is the equivalent of a taking of private property. Since no compensation has been paid in that situation for the deprivation of property rights for a public use or purpose, the use of the police power is unconstitutional.

Recent cases, particularly since 1978, have differed on the question of whether in addition to declaring unconstitutional an abuse of the police power, damages may be recovered for loss sustained by the landowner. This is discussed in some detail in Chapter V, Section 2, and will not be repeated here. However, this discussion relates to it in the sense that some scholars believe that such decisions illustrate a lack of understanding of the differing origin and nature of these doctrines.

There is obviously a fine line between what constitutes a reasonable exercise of the police power as opposed to what a court may deem to be an overextension of the power to the point that it is confiscatory—and thus, by being confiscatory may be described as amounting to a "taking." Since the police power cannot, unlike eminent domain, be used to acquire property rights, then use of the police power in such a manner is invalid. The police power, like eminent domain, is inherent in the sovereign; but, unlike the police power, the otherwise limitless power of eminent domain is limited by federal and state constitutions in that just compensation is required. Those who would blur this distinction hop-skip from Justice Holmes' statement in Pennsylvania Coal Co. v. Mahon, 260 U.S. 363 (1922), that if regulation goes too far it will constitute a "taking" to the conclusion that he meant that compensation could be awarded in that situation. That would expand the constitutional provisions to mean that in either the use of eminent domain or the police power, private property may be acquired for a public use and just compensation must be paid. If the distinction is blurred to that extent, then the difference between the police power and eminent domain simply relates to the type of activity or the procedure involved.

Running somewhat counter to this recent tendency to ignore the differences between eminent domain and the police power and to require compensation where regulation "goes too far" is the fact that in recent years there has been a liberalization of interpretation as to what actions may be validly taken under the police power. The trend seems to be toward liberal interpretation of what police power actions may be effectuated under state enabling legislation. But the "taking problem" is an ever-present one because the constitutional imperative of both the United States and state constitutions denies government action which takes away property without compensating for it.

Our purpose here will be to consider the power of eminent domain and relate its exercise to the police power.

§ 2. Historical Antecedents

Hugo Grotius, the great philosopher of the natural law, used the term "eminent domain" to describe the power of the state over private property. Only the state could be a taker, and the state was immune from liability. J. Beuscher & R. Wright, *Land Use* 709 (1st ed. 1969). But this was not the first reference to the power. While its origin is lost in obscurity, its lineage may be traced to references in the Bible and to use by the Romans. 1 Nichols, *Eminent Domain* §§ 1.2, 1.12 (1976). The power originated as an inherent right of the sovereign, under a common theory. The constitutional requirement of payment of just compensation is therefore a limitation on the power rather than a grant of the power.

The just compensation requirement in Anglo-American law may be traced back to the Magna Carta, which provided that "no freeman shall be . . . deprived of his freehold . . . unless by the lawful judgment of his peers and by the law of the land." Art. 39, *Magna Carta* (1215). But that provision does not provide for compensation. Also, over the centuries there remained friction as to what it meant. In 1352, the King agreed that proceedings to oust a freeholder would be dealt with by his peers and outside of the King and Council. F. Bosselman, D. Callies & J. Banta, *The Taking Issue* 59 (1973). Medieval disputes involved the King's practice of designating forests for his use for hunting and the ancient prerogative of the King to use land for defense purposes which was finally abolished statutorily during the reign of Charles II. It has been stated that eminent domain, as it presently exists, apparently grew out of the common law proceeding known as "inquest of office," by which jurors inquired into any matter that entitled the King to possession of property and which became the proper proceeding at common law to acquire land for public use. 1 Nichols, *supra* at § 1.21. Eminent domain was well-recognized in England by the time of the American

Revolution and was used in the colonies largely for roads. 1 Nichols, *supra* at § 1.22.

The absolute and unlimited form of the power which had been limited in England by the Magna Carta was limited even more by the United States Constitution in the Fifth Amendment and in many of the early state constitutions to require payment of just compensation. This was an extension of the Magna Carta, which did not refer to compensation. The first ratified constitution in this country to provide for reasonable compensation in the event of a taking was that adopted in Massachusetts in 1780. Bosselman, Callies & Banta, *supra* at 95. However, several of the first state constitutions did not provide for compensation, and in 1868 when the Fourteenth Amendment became effective, five of the oldest states still lacked such a provision. Possibly the influence of Blackstone's *Commentaries,* which were used extensively in America and in which Blackstone advocated compensation for takings, as well as controversial situations during the Revolutionary War and a desire to protect the propertied classes, led James Madison to insert the provision in the Fifth Amendment. Bosselman, Callies & Banta, *supra* at 101–104. In any event, in the states which did not have such a constitutional provision until some time later, natural law was relied upon, and the courts assumed the burden of requiring a taking for a public use to be contingent upon payment of just compensation. Beuscher & Wright, *supra* at 710.

§ 3. Public Use and Public Purpose

The basic rule is that private property can be taken only for a public use. However, only a few state constitutions specifically prohibit property from being taken for non-public uses. Early cases held that takings for private use were prohibited, first upon the ground that this was opposed to natural justice, beyond the power of the legislature and an act of spoliation, and later through interpretation of eminent domain and due process clauses of state constitutions.

There are two views of what a public use encompasses. The narrow view is that it means "use by the public," *i.e.,* to make a use public a duty devolves to furnish the public with the intended use and the public is entitled to such use. The broad view is that it means "public advantage," and that whatever tends to enlarge the resources, industrial potential, productive power, and growth of communities contributes to the general welfare. Generally today, private purposes can be served if the public is also served. Thus, private corporations performing a public function, such as utilities and railroads, may exercise the power under statutory authorization. This is viewed, however, as involving a public use under either interpretation.

The bifurcated interpretation of "public use" is almost identical to or essentially the same as judicial considerations of "public use" and "public purpose." In a South Carolina case involving urban

[*285*]

redevelopment of a blighted area, the court allowed part of the condemned property to go to the state university, but declined to permit part of it to pass to private parties for light industrial use. The state constitution used the term "public use," and the court did not view the seizure of slum property and its later disposition to private owners as meeting that requirement. Edens v. Columbia, 228 S.C. 563, 91 S.E.2d 280 (1956). See similarly, Little Rock v. Raines, 241 Ark. 1071, 411 S.W.2d 486 (1967). But in Davis v. Lubbock, 160 Tex. 38, 326 S.W.2d 699 (1959), the Texas constitutional provision on public use was interpreted to encompass a redevelopment plan on the basis that where the property is prevented from becoming a slum again in the foreseeable future, this involves "a public right or use." The redevelopment was to be carried on by private enterprise. Perhaps the most influential case on this is Berman v. Parker, 348 U.S. 26 (1954), in which the Court upheld a redevelopment program that would shift property to private hands and stated that public ownership is not the only way to promote public purposes.

The broad view of "public use" encompassing a public advantage or the fulfillment of a public purpose is essential to urban redevelopment projects which must necessarily either involve the private sector or ultimately lead to sales of redeveloped property to private purchasers. The weight of authority favors this interpretation.

§ 4. Determining "Just Compensation": The Fair Market Value Rule

The measure of compensation where all of a person's land is taken is the fair market value of the property as of the time of taking. Where only a part of the land is taken, the measure may be the fair market value of the portion taken plus damages to the part not taken less any special benefits to the land not taken. This is the "value plus damages" rule. Where part of the land is taken, the measure may also be the difference between the market value of the entire tract before the taking and the market value of the remainder after the taking. This is the "before and after" rule. Jurisdictions vary as to which test they follow, although the majority probably follow "value plus damages."

The Uniform Eminent Domain Code adopts but modifies the "before and after" rule in Section 1002 by stating that where there is a partial taking, "the measure of compensation is the *greater* of (1) the value of the property taken . . . or (2) the amount by which the fair market value of the entire property immediately before the taking exceeds the fair market value of the remainder immediately after the taking." This means that where the remainder not taken is so enhanced in value as a result of the taking that there would be a zero award, the condemnor must still pay the value of the land actually taken.

The fair market value of land is the amount that the property would be reasonably worth on the market in a cash sale to a willing buyer if offered for sale by a prudent willing seller. (The situation envisioned assumes that neither is obligated to buy or sell.) This is the "willing buyer-willing seller" test. Implicit in this is that the price offered must be what a reasonable buyer would pay for the highest and best use of the land. This is the "highest and best use" rule. If the highest and best use of the land is for a subdivision, even though it is at present used for some other purpose or is open or unimproved land, then the evaluation must be based on its value for subdivision purposes. The possibility of use of the land for all purposes, both present and prospective, for which it is adapted or might be applied in the reasonably foreseeable future, must be considered. When considered, the value of the land for the use to which reasonable men of adequate means would devote the premises is the ultimate test.

The highest and best use rule is commonly accepted in the United States, although these rules pertaining to valuation are usually not found in statutes. The Uniform Eminent Domain Code defines fair market value in Section 1004 by utilizing the willing buyer-willing seller test, but also provides that the value of property for which there is no relevant market is its value determined by just and equitable methods of valuation. The highest and best use requirement is implicit in Section 1007 of the Code. In the application of the highest and best use rule, a landowner should be required to show that the property is adaptable to the other use, that it is reasonably probable that it will be put to this use within a reasonable time, and that the market value has been enhanced by this other use for which it is adaptable.

The value of the land to the taker is generally rejected as having no relevance, and the value of the land to the owner bears consideration only in the sense that the market value should represent a rough approximation of its value to the owner. The problem with permitting the value to the owner to be considered is that any compensation for sentimental value would place an unfair burden on the condemning authority and cannot be accurately measured. The Uniform Eminent Domain Code rejects both the value to the owner and value to the taker approaches and follows the fair market value test which is almost universally employed. UEDC, Comment § 1004. Value to the owner should only be a factor when the market value is practically nil. 1 Orgel, *Valuation Under Eminent Domain* § 38, at 175–177 (1953).

§ 5. Determining Fair Market Value

Although there are many elements which enter into a determination of fair market value, the most commonly employed is the comparable sales approach. Appraisers make a determination of the price paid for similar land in the same general area sold voluntarily at a time not too distant from the time of the taking. The property sold must be comparable, and in determining that, consideration must be given to the location, size, sales price, date and character of the sale, commercial, industrial or residential advantages, the extent of improved or unimproved characteristics, and similar aspects. The comparable sales approach is the one most commonly employed by appraisers, but there are other approaches to valuation and other types of evidence. These other approaches include the capitalization of income method which is often used for industrial or commercial property and for rental property. (To be a valid approach the income must be closely related to the value of the land itself.) Another approach would be appraisal of the land value considered as vacant and available for improvement, plus the depreciated replacement cost of the improvements. These methods are resorted to only in special situations or when no comparable sales information can be produced.

The type of evidence most commonly employed is opinion testimony from experts or from persons having sufficient knowledge as to the value of the particular piece of property as well as other property in the area to offer a reliable opinion. The landowner himself is usually permitted to testify as to the market value if it is shown that he is familiar with the value of real estate in the area. Properly, all witnesses should be required to state the factors upon which their opinion is based, but some states do not require an expert witness to state the basis for his opinion.

As mentioned, a method occasionally employed to determine value is the actual rental value of the property, capitalized at the rate which local custom adopts for the purpose, if the property is then being rented for the use for which it is best suited. 4 Nichols, *supra* § 12.3122. Evidence of rent actually received at a time reasonably near the time of the taking should be admitted. However, it is generally held improper to consider profits from a business conducted on the property unless the profits are attributable to the character of the land. (There are some cases which admit evidence of profits from a farm.) The reason for not admitting evidence of business profits is that under the general rule the owner is not entitled to recover anticipated profits which are lost by reason of the taking. It would seem to be helpful to a court to have information on current profits which, although they are subject to change, could be considered as an element in determining value.

The cost of the property and the improvements may be admitted as an aid in determining market value where there is no readily ascertainable market value for the particular use. Evidence of the cost of improvements for restoration purposes, and evidence of relocation costs and removal costs are generally admitted.

The general rule is that the price paid by the condemnor for other land in the same area is not admissible. Such payments are not thought to be indicative of market value. While the price paid by the condemnor for similarly located lands may vary, it would seem difficult to segregate testimony of the comparable value of similarly situated property from evidence of the purchase price paid for it by the condemnor.

Unaccepted offers to purchase the property are generally excluded from evidence. Some states admit such evidence if the proponent can show that it was a bona fide offer for cash and was made by someone financially able to carry through with it. The danger of admitting unaccepted offers into evidence is that the offer might be an exorbitant offer not made in good faith. Compromise offers by the condemnor are also inadmissible. Although unaccepted offers are not admitted, the purchase price paid by the owner does have a bearing on the market value if the purchase is not too remote from the time of taking. Its usefulness must be weighed in the light of recent market fluctuations.

The Uniform Eminent Domain Code has an article which contains special rules for evidence in condemnation actions. It provides for a view of the property by the jury and judge for the purpose of understanding and weighing the valuation evidence offered. UEDC § 1102. This generally is in accord with the majority rule. It provides for opinion testimony from qualified witnesses, the landowner or shareholders, officers or employees of a corporation or partnership. UEDC § 1103. Evidence may be received on the extent of loss, the present use and highest and best use, loss of nonconforming uses, damage to crops, and zoning or other restrictions on the use and the possibility of a change in those restrictions. UEDC § 1104. Evidence as to the remainder value following a partial taking may be received on the increase or decrease in the productivity and convenience of use attributable to the taking, impairment or improvement of access to highways, benefit or detriment caused by a change in grade, enhancement or loss of appearance, view or light and air, benefit or damage from severance of the land, damage from the distance of the remainder or improvements on it to the project caused by such things as noise, fumes, vibration or the like, and cost of fencing necessary for the remainder. UEDC § 1105. Opinion evidence may be based on any nonconjectural matter ordinarily relied upon by experts whether it would be admissible in evidence or not. UEDC § 1106. A valuation witness may consider the price of any good faith sale or contract of sale regardless of when it was entered into. UEDC § 1107. The guidelines for consideration of comparable sales by opinion witnesses are in keeping

with the general rule earlier expressed. UEDC
§ 1108. Valuation witnesses may consider the
terms of leases, net rental income capitalized at a
fair interest rate, reproduction or replacement
costs, and the condition of property in the general
vicinity. UEDC §§ 1109–1112. Witnesses may not
base their opinions on the price of other property
acquired by condemnation, unaccepted offers, op-
tions or listings, the assessed value for tax purposes, an opinion as to the value of other property,
the terms of a trade or exchange, and in general
exercises of the police power or other noncompen-
sable damage. UEDC § 1113.

§ 6. Compensation and Compensable Inter- ests

Generally speaking, private property may not be
taken or damaged without payment of just compensation to the owner. 3 Nichols, *supra* § 8.1. Not
all state constitutions contain the provision that
compensation be paid for damaging as well as for
taking property. Damages, however, are generally
recoverable one way or another.

Obviously, compensation must be paid when all
or part of a piece of property is taken. There are
other compensable property rights, however, which
may be less apparent. A person holding a vested
or contingent remainder is entitled to compensation. Both the lessor and lessee are entitled to
compensation for their separate interests when

condemned property is subject to a lease. The holder of an easement is entitled to compensation for impairment or elimination of it. Mineral interests are compensable unless the severed mineral ownership and use remains unaffected by the condemnation. Under the better view, compensation should be paid for impairment or destruction of restrictive covenants creating equitable servitudes. All rights in property, including reversionary interests, possibilities of reverter, powers of termination, executory interests, charges upon the land, and prescriptive or adverse rights which can be established, should be compensated.

Other compensable elements are less distinct. The removal of earth from property is a compensable injury to land. Interference with an existing easement is compensable, as is interference reducing the value of property not physically taken. Loss of access or of ingress and egress or a change in the grade of a highway or street amounts to a taking of a property right, although the mere alteration of traffic flow does not go that far. Obstruction of the free flow of light and air to abutting property is an element of damage. The pollution of air and water is an interference with a property right which should be compensated. The taking or damaging of land includes interruption of the common, necessary use of the property which is so serious that it interferes with the rights of the owner to an extent greater than mere temporary inconvenience.

On the other hand, there are many "consequential damages" or side effects of condemnation actions which are not ordinarily compensable. These include loss of business income, goodwill, temporary interruption of business, temporary interference with the use of abutting property, losses resulting from relocation of a highway, and losses or inconvenience produced by noise, dust or fumes from projects. The Uniform Eminent Domain Code contains a provision allowing recovery for loss of goodwill (UEDC § 1016), but the traditional view is that this is too speculative to permit evaluation. Moreover, although state courts have traditionally not allowed compensation for moving expenses, the Code in Article XIV contains provisions allowing compensation for moving expenses, replacement housing and other relocation losses. This satisfies the provisions of Title II of the Federal Uniform Relocation Assistance and Real Property Acquisitions Policies Act of 1970 (P.L. 91–646), with which state and local agencies presently must comply in order to secure federal financial assistance.

It is difficult to catalogue compensable and non-compensable interests or elements of damage. The law is in a state of flux, tending toward a wider spectrum of compensability. The evolution of the idea that if a person's property is taken or his property rights damaged or destroyed, then he should be made whole, continues to broaden the concept of what relief should be awarded. For example, contrary to the traditional approach, the Uniform Eminent Domain Code makes provision for award of litigation expenses, including attorney's fees, upon dismissal of the action by the condemnor and under certain circumstances as part of the judgment. UEDC §§ 1205, 1303.

§ 7. Consequential Damages

In the preceding section, mention was made of such elements as loss of goodwill, moving expenses, interruption of business, and inconveniences of various kinds. These are forms of "consequential damages" for which recovery traditionally was denied. We have seen, however, that the trend of the law is toward a broadening of permissible recovery.

There are several difficulties in awarding damages of this type. The major problem is that they cannot properly be assessed. Loss of goodwill and loss of profits due to interruption of business activity are obviously speculative. Appraisers have to pluck at rainbows to arrive at a dollar figure. Also, some of these values continue—as in the case of goodwill in the event the condemnee sets up shop at some other reasonably suitable location. Moreover, aside from a condemnation suit, some portion of loss in this regard might result in any sale.

As indicated in the last section, courts have historically not permitted recovery for inconveniences or losses occasioned by noise, dust, fumes and the like from condemnation projects. The law on this subject may be in the process of changing. Temporary inconveniences of this type would probably still not lead to a recovery in most states, but permanent changes accompanied by these side effects have led to recovery in a substantial minority of jurisdictions. Noise, dust, fumes, lights and the like have in some instances transcended the traditional nuisance doctrine and have resulted in a taking. See, *e.g.,* U.S. v. Certain Parcels of Land in Kent County, 252 F.Supp. 319 (D.C.Mich.1966); Thornburg v. Port of Portland, 233 Or. 178, 376 P.2d 100 (1962); Martin v. Port of Seattle, 64 Wash.2d 309, 391 P.2d 540, cert. denied 379 U.S. 989 (1964). In *Thornburg* these nuisance-like qualities of an adjoining airport were held to constitute a taking even though there were no overflights and thus no trespass to the plaintiff's airspace.

As stated previously, there seems to be a broadening of concepts of compensability, and this trend is nowhere more apparent than in situations involving consequential damages and inverse condemnation.

§ 8. Inverse Condemnation

Actions brought by landowners alleging that a taking of their property has resulted from activities of public agencies or private bodies vested with authority to condemn are referred to as inverse condemnation actions. This is essentially "reverse condemnation" in that the landowner is the party bringing the suit and alleging a deprivation of property rights. No condemnation proceedings have been commenced by a condemning authority.

Inverse condemnation actions have been a fertile field for litigation in recent years. They have resulted from governmental activity which physically or indirectly invades the land or airspace of a landowner. Trespass can result, for example, from low-flying aircraft which interfere with the use of land or from the flooding of land through nearby governmental activity or, as we have seen, from excessive noise, fumes, dust and the like in some jurisdictions. Situations involving a change of grade or a loss of access in highway situations lead to such lawsuits. Extinguishment of certain private rights, such as restrictive covenants or easements, may lead to such actions. Substantial impairment of the exercise of private rights in property provide the potential for suits of this type. In addition, zoning itself, as we have seen, provides a major basis for allegations of a taking resulting from the use of the police power.

These cases, of course, result in payment by the government of the amount it would have been required to pay had there been formal condemnation proceedings if the landowner is successful. The basic arguments are about the same in every case: the defendant agency contends that it took no land and did not affect compensable property rights; and the plaintiff landowner argues that the action complained of was such an interference with or invasion of his property rights as to amount to a compensable taking. Over the past several decades, there has been a marked increase in inverse condemnation actions and a broadening of the bases for recovery which corresponds in large measure to the situation of the law of torts.

The aviation cases in particular have spawned a great many inverse condemnation actions. The *Thornburg* case mentioned in the previous section is an example, and it is a minority view only in the sense that it did not involve trespasses produced by continuous overflights. The landmark case, U.S. v. Causby, 328 U.S. 256 (1946), did involve overflights which trespassed in the airspace of the plaintiff landowner and produced interference with the use of his land. Later in Griggs v. Allegheny County, 369 U.S. 84 (1962), the Court held that flights in FAA-defined navigable airspace on landings and take-offs constituted a taking of an air easement when there was substantial interference with the rights of the landowner. An interesting "cross" between these cases and the highway loss of access cases is Bydlon v. U.S., 146 Ct.Cl. 764, 175 F.Supp. 891 (1959), in which compensation was allowed to resort operators in a national forest because a flight ceiling kept aircraft from flying in to the resorts and attempts to establish a land route were

unsuccessful. Their right of access by air (which
was the best means of transit) had been taken.
Inverse condemnation actions involving loss of access or easements of light, air and view are related—there is no direct invasion, no physical change
or improvement except on property which is already publicly owned, but in some situations the
action taken is sufficient to amount to a deprivation necessitating compensation. Thus the loss of
somewhat intangible property interests may form
a basis for recovery.

As the Supreme Court stated in Armstrong v.
U.S., 364 U.S. 40, 49 (1960): "The Fifth Amendment's guarantee that private property shall not
be taken for a public use without just compensation was designed to bar Government from forcing
some people alone to bear public burdens which, in
all fairness and justice, should be borne by the
public as a whole."

§ 9. Police Power or a Taking?

Whenever the use of the police power is arbitrary, capricious and unreasonable or is confiscatory
or both, the result is to deprive a landowner of
rights which can only be extracted by condemnation actions requiring payment of just compensation. Abuse of the police power, therefore, has
been compared to or described as a "taking"—in
other words, as being akin to inverse condemnation. The traditional difference in the two has

been that when zoning or a police power regulation is arbitrary or confiscatory, the landowner's remedy has been to have the regulation invalidated whereas in the inverse condemnation situation, property rights have been permanently damaged or lost and the usual remedy is a suit for damages. In the police power situation, the owner is seeking to alleviate the regulation, but in the inverse condemnation situation it is generally too late for injunctive relief to suffice. Of course, the owner may seek both damages and an injunction if it is a situation in which an injunction can be granted.

However, as mentioned in the introduction and as earlier discussed in Chapter V, a number of federal circuits have either awarded damages in situations involving unconstitutional land use regulations or have indicated that damages may be awarded in such situations. The tendency of the Supreme Court, as reflected in the *San Diego Gas & Electric* case cited in that chapter, appears to be in that direction. It seems quite possible and perhaps probable that the Supreme Court will ultimately allow damages to be awarded at least for the period between the time the ordinance was challenged and the time that the regulation was removed, assuming damages can be proved. This trend seems to ignore the historic difference between the nature of the police power and that of eminent domain, as discussed in the introduction to this chapter.

Another obvious problem, wrestled with to some extent in earlier material, is where to draw the line between valid regulation and a police power taking.

The difficulty is that there are no rules so specific that a particular situation can always be accurately identified as falling on one side of the line or the other. These cases will normally not involve activities which are obviously arbitrary or confiscatory nor activities which have been clearly established as valid. The discussion which follows attempts to provide guidelines and insights, but with the realization that there is no litmus paper test that can be applied and no precise dividing line delineating the point at which the exercise of the police power ceases to be valid and becomes a taking. See Van Alstyne, Taking or Damaging by Police Power: The Search for Inverse Condemnation Criteria, 44 *S.Cal.L.Rev.* 1, 14 (1971). Holmes did not attempt to provide criteria when confronted with the problem and contented himself with stating that it was a matter of degree as to whether a regulation amounted to a taking. Pennsylvania Coal Co. v. Mahon, 260 U.S. 393, 415–416 (1922).

Commentators before and since have wrestled with the problem and have attempted to develop the general propositions which Holmes avoided. Opinions in cases have largely been of little help, with most courts being satisfied with saying that the regulation goes too far in the specific situation under consideration. How the matter is viewed is dependent in large measure on how a particular commentator or court views private property rights as opposed to rights of society as a whole. The courts have rejected the two extremes—that an individual's land may never be regulated or his rights diminished no matter what the social necessity, and to the contrary, that the state has an absolute right to regulate no matter what the effect on a particular landowner. However, the outcome in a particular case may depend upon which of these polar positions a particular court generally leans toward.

In that regard, one group of writers propounded the suggestion that the United States Supreme Court should overrule the rather general balancing test which Holmes enunciated in *Pennsylvania Coal* and declare that a land use regulation would *never constitute a taking* if it were reasonably related to a valid public purpose. F. Bosselman, D. Callies & J. Banta, *The Taking Issue* 238 (1973). They viewed Holmes' statement as historically inaccurate, unnecessary, and disastrous from an environmental standpoint. It seems almost certain that federal courts will never move to such an absolutist position in view of these recent decisions allowing damages, and although state courts have generally been reluctant to award damages in police power situations, it also seems highly unlikely that state courts will move in that direction. State and federal courts have gone to great lengths over the past fifteen or more years to uphold environmental regulations, but the courts have not departed from the proposition that if a regulation renders the land valueless or nearly so, the magic line has been crossed and the regulation is invalid. The flood plain cases illustrate this point. If the award of damages in federal courts (and, potentially, state courts) continues, however, the courts may be less inclined to strike down a regulation because of potential liability for damages on the part of already overburdened local governments.

The opposite side of the coin may be found in Blackstone's statement that the institution of private property is so greatly regarded that law "will not authorize the lease violation of it; no, not even for the general good of the whole community." Blackstone, *Commentaries* 139 (1782). The same underlying philosophy is embodied in Article 2, Section 22 of the Arkansas Constitution of 1874 which states that "the right of private property is before and higher than any constitutional sanction"—a rather extreme expression which the Arkansas Court tends to quote when striking down regulatory measures.

Courts today have largely moved away from this latter type of thinking. But modern support for the argument that a regulation should not be a taking if related to a valid public purpose can be

drawn by inference from recent environmental decisions. (Historically, probably the leading case
supporting or allowing the inference of such a
theory would be Harlan's opinion for the Court in
Mugler v. Kansas, 123 U.S. 623, 667–669 (1887).)
Just v. Marinette County, 56 Wis.2d 7, 201 N.W.2d
761 (1972) is a prime example of the impact of
environmentally related decisions on this subject.
In upholding a shoreland zoning ordinance providing protection of wetlands, the Wisconsin Court
stated that there is a taking only when the restriction is so great that the landowner should not have
to bear the burden on behalf of the public and not
when the damage is incidental. It reasoned that if
the potential use for the prohibited purpose would
produce "public harm," it could be validly banned
without compensation, while if the intention was
to produce a public benefit, compensation would be
required. The Wisconsin Court opined that the
flood plain cases place too much emphasis on the
commercial value of the land if its condition is
changed to make it usable. The depreciation in
the *Just* case was not based on use of the land in
its natural state. But the Court sought to distinguish the *Pennsylvania Coal* case by stating that
the ordinance in question did not seek to improve
the public condition but only to preserve the natural condition of the land based on environmental
concerns. Consequently, it cannot be said that
Just goes so far as to uphold any regulation which

promotes a valid public purpose since it would be a valid public purpose to attempt to improve the public condition. Related to *Just* are such cases as In re Spring Valley Development, 300 A.2d 736 (Me.1973).

Although environmental cases seem to go a long way toward upholding police power controls, they contain several factors which render them distinguishable: (1) The general recognition of the importance of the value sought to be protected led the courts to deal more liberally with the means employed; (2) the courts were able to rationalize that they were not preventing use of the land except in a particular way which if permitted would be harmful to the public; and (3) the "public harm" concept permitted the situation to be viewed as something related to preventing a public nuisance. While much of this may be viewed as sophistry since the end result of the *Just* case, for example, was to deny any alteration (and commercial exploitation) of the land, the fact remains that the court went to substantial lengths to avoid the appearance of changing the rule requiring compensation.

The more common approach to the problem is to accept the general balancing test of *Pennsylvania Coal* and attempt to develop principles or propositions from the cases which provide insight into what the courts are likely to do in a particular situation. This means that diminution in value, even if substantial, would not necessarily give rise to compensation but would only be a factor to be weighed. It also means that the importance of the regulation in terms of promoting the general welfare would be a major consideration but not the sole determinant. In short, both of the extremes would enter into the equation but both would be rejected as sole determinants in favor of considering all of the factors which lead to the result—factors which may be weighed differently under differing circumstances.

Many courts, in looking at the diminution of value of the landowner's property, follow the theory that if the owner's ability to profit from the property has been severely diminished as a result of governmental action (as in some zoning cases), the landowner is entitled to compensation. The assumption is that the government regulation vests in the public certain rights which were not previously possessed at the expense, in terms of profit capacity, of the private landowner. It has been suggested by a leading scholar that this is a denial of the existence of public rights. See Sax, Takings, Private Property and Public Rights, 81 *Yale L.J.* 149, 160–162 (1971). This process, it is argued, may deter government regulation and adversely affect resource allocation because it discriminates against public rights. But we have seen from the cases that although severe diminution of value resulting from use limitations does at times lead to recovery, cases have also upheld some rather substantial diminutions of value where the public interest being preserved was viewed as very important or where the effect on other landowners in the area would have been particularly harmful. The public interest considerations can be seen in environmental litigation, and the latter situation can be seen in the spot zoning cases and in cases involving nuisance-like commercial or industrial uses. Therefore, diminution in value is tempered by public interest considerations and by the interests of other nearby landowners. If the proposed use can be viewed as a public harm requiring prevention, as opposed to some public benefit to be derived from the restriction, compensation for the limitation is much less likely to be awarded.

Consequently, while we cannot develop an equation, we can clearly identify certain factors with the recognition that their quantitative effect will differ from situation to situation: How great is the public interest in a particular restriction and how essential is it to the general welfare in terms of societal values? Is the restriction intended to procure a public benefit or to prevent a public harm? What is the overall effect on other landowners in comparison to the aggrieved landowner and as opposed to the interests of the public in general? How substantial and how severe is the loss to the landowner as a result of the restriction when compared to the public interest? Where does the particular public value involved rank on the scale of values which are being affected in the particular jurisdiction considering the issue?

The equation which cannot be developed comes out, imprecisely, like this: Public interest (weighed on the jurisdictional scale of values) + public harm (to be prevented, if any) +interest of other landowners (not the public generally) – severity of loss to complaining landowner and – public benefits unrelated to preventing harm or to neutral public interests = either a valid exercise of the police power or a taking.

Having performed this illusory exercise, one cannot help but agree with the observation of a prominent land use scholar that the search for the answer to this problem "may be the lawyer's equivalent of the physicist's hunt for the quark." C. Haar, *Land-Use Planning* 766 (3d ed. 1977).

CHAPTER XIII

TAXATION AND THE CONTROL OF LAND USE

§ 1. Introduction

All of us know that taxation is not an isolated process having only the effect of raising revenue. Tax policy goes beyond that and affects the risk of investment through its benefits and burdens. It affects who will invest money in a particular venture and under what circumstances. As such, the taxing power becomes an extension of the police power in the sense that it becomes regulatory "for the general welfare."

It is obvious, then, that taxation can encourage or discourage the use of land. The difficulty in using it as a control on land development is that if it is focused on a particular parcel of land or seeks to promote or discourage a particular use, it is likely to be held invalid due to lack of uniformity of application or for related reasons. The power can be utilized for broader purposes, however, than simply taxation.

§ 2. The Property Tax in General

Property taxes are ad valorem taxes, which means that they are based on the value of the property. Some states have classification schemes which allow property to be placed in different rational classifications for tax purposes. This leads to variations with regard to the tax burden, but where such schemes are constitutionally permissible, the courts have upheld rational classifications and have held them not to be a violation of the requirement of uniformity.

In addition to the general property tax, land may be subject to other taxation in the form of special assessments for the benefit of improvement districts, schools, and the like. This situation creates an uneven tax base within a community, and the variation within a metropolitan area may be even greater due to differences among the various suburban areas and the central city.

Differentiations are also produced by assessment ratios, particularly in jurisdictions in which the property can be assessed at less than 100% of value. Even in situations in which it is purportedly assessed at 100% of value, the recognition of what the true value is may vary among assessors. State tax equalization laws help in this regard, but deviations among neighboring cities or counties remain.

Obviously, this form of system leads to variations among communities in the quality of services and public facilities even within the same metropolitan area.

§ 3. The Effect of Zoning and Subdivision Restrictions

There are substantial variations in the tax treatment of land depending upon whether it is within an urban area or is rural and whether it is developed or undeveloped. Developers quite often follow the practice of subdividing and developing land on the fringe of a community and then petition to have the land annexed. This allows them to operate within a minimal tax structure for the maximum period of time, carry out the development with fewer controls being imposed, and still gain the benefit of city services following annexation. It also encourages land speculation. Moreover, this affords an opportunity to avoid subdivision exactions and other controls during the development process (although some exactions may later be imposed as a condition of annexation). This problem is controlled in some areas by extraterritorial zoning and subdivision regulations or by regional planning.

Aside from the foregoing situation, however, zoning and subdivision restrictions still have a major effect on taxes and on services. Large lots may result either from restrictive covenants or from zoning. Aside from the economic exclusion aspect, large-lot suburban areas mean that water and sewer lines and other utilities will have to be extended over substantial distances, that arterial streets into the subdivision may have to be widened, that schools will have to be provided, and that police and fire protection will have to be extended. Since there is not likely to be much commercial activity in the immediate vicinity and since many of these people work in the central city, the traffic problem is exacerbated by travel to and from shopping areas and places of business. All of these situations result in an increased economic burden, and even if the area in question is a separate municipal corporation, a portion of its burden (as, for example, the traffic problem) will fall upon the taxpayers of the central city. Even aside from the tax problem, the situation often leads to rezoning of lands on the periphery of the central city to accommodate the suburbs—sometimes leading to strip zoning for commercial purposes.

Of course, the situation cuts both ways in that a separate suburban community may elect to buy water and sewer services from the central city and thereby bear the cost of extending the lines into the area. This will likely result in a water and sewer district with the landowners paying for the services. Because the density of people in the area is relatively sparse, the cost to each landowner will be greater. On the other hand, if the subdivision is one which exists within the municipality or has been annexed and has its own water and sewer lines, the entire municipality will have to pay for extension of water and sewer lines into the area or for their enlargement unless a special improvement district is created.

Large lot restrictions have other effects as well. For one thing, it is doubtful even with relatively high property taxes being assessed in affluent subdivisions that those lots will bear their fair share of the community tax burden. Every time a new subdivision is created, a portion of the increased costs of services and facilities is passed off on the existing community. In addition, if the city is strapped for money (and most of them are), there is a tendency to zone for industry or commercial activities in order to increase the tax base in situations in which the land might be better devoted to some other activity. There is a similar tendency to take substantially less interest in government-financed low-income housing projects.

The property tax itself, of course, is an inhibitor. It discourages rehabilitation of existing structures which are deteriorating or have collectively become slums. If the landlord spends substantial sums renovating these structures, his property assessment goes up and his lower income tenants cannot afford to pay increased rent to cover the cost of renovation plus the increased taxes. If the owner of the structure is also its resident, he is usually unable to afford either the cost of renovation or the higher taxes.

Consequently, there is a certain interaction between zoning, restrictive covenants, and the property tax which serves to make planning more difficult and to place increased burdens on the cost of municipal services.

§ 4. Regional Taxation

In 1971, Minnesota adopted a "Metropolitan Fiscal Disparities Act," Ex.Sess.L.1971, c. 24, Minn. Stat. 473F. This statute sought, in essence, to "even out" any disparities which might exist in taxation and tax expenditures in the seven-county area in which Minneapolis and St. Paul are located. In considering this statute, in Burnsville v. Onischuk, 301 Minn. 137, 222 N.W.2d 523 (1974), the Minnesota Supreme Court found the formulas in the law to be extremely complex but the objectives fairly simple. The act would avoid a "competitive scramble" by local governmental units for commercial and industrial development to improve their tax base. The units would instead pool 40% of the area-wide increase in commercial-industrial valuation subsequent to January 2, 1971. All units of local government would receive some distribution of the area-wide tax base, although some units would contribute more to the pool than they would receive. This amounted to a partial reallocation according to need in inverse ratio to fiscal capacity. The trial court relied on the uniformity clause in the Minnesota Constitution to invalidate this law, but the state supreme court reversed. The court believed that units of local government which contributed more to the pool than they

[*316*]

received were sufficiently benefited to meet the constitutional requirement. Thus, the benefits conferred on residents of communities which were the site of commercial-industrial development might exceed the burdens imposed on it. They enjoyed direct benefits from the existence of adjacent governmental units which provide open space, public facilities, low-density housing, and the like.

It should be noted, as a dissenting judge did, that the Minnesota act results in a diversion of funds from commercial-industrial areas of the region to support bedroom communities which exclude such property. In effect, then, this law provided relief for the suburbs rather than coping with the need for providing relief for the central city. Nonetheless, the merit in the law was its regional approach, which recognized the regional effect of taxation on land use and the interlocking nature of the metropolitan area. What would probably be more desirable would be to utilize regional planning to locate industries within the metropolitan area and adjust the tax base throughout the region in such a way that it was fair to all of its component parts and was expended on a region-wide basis. This concept would probably not be legally feasible in many states, however, without changes in the taxation provisions of the state constitution.

What this amounts to is regional tax-sharing, a concept which is increasingly being considered. In Meadowlands Regional Redevelopment Agency v.

State, 63 N.J. 35, 304 A.2d 545, appeal dismissed
414 U.S. 991 (1973), the New Jersey Court had
under consideration a meadowlands reclamation
and development act which involved regional activity and a pooling of the tax benefit and burdens
among municipalities. One major issue involved
the tax-sharing provisions. The sharing envisioned creation of an "intermunicipal account,"
into which municipalities would pay and from
which they would receive benefits based on a statutory formula. The court stated that the tax-sharing provisions appeared to be rational and fair and
did not appear arbitrary. The argument that some
municipalities would be providing tax revenues for
other municipalities was rejected on the basis that
this was simply a cost of government imposed on
all of the constituent municipalities.

A property tax involving Atlanta and its suburbs, which was specifically directed toward bene-
fiting education in the county, was upheld in Mc-
Lennan v. Aldredge, 223 Ga. 879, 159 S.E.2d 682
(1968). It was argued that this was invalid because
it was based on having a large city in the county
and could only apply to Fulton County, because it
discriminated against Atlanta taxpayers by requiring them to pay both this tax and city school taxes,
and because a classification based on population
does not bear a substantial relation to the taxing
power. In rejecting these arguments, the Georgia
Court stated that it was not unreasonable to im-

pose some county school burdens on cities because cities are wealthier and that Atlanta would ultimately benefit from having good county schools in the areas it would eventually annex.

Despite these cases, many jurisdictions would probably find such schemes to be unconstitutional under either the uniformity clause of the state constitution or because tax revenue was being diverted from one municipality or one part of the region to another.

§ 5. Taxation Which Regulates Urban Growth

Taxes have not been used extensively for this purpose. In fact, as earlier mentioned, present property tax systems usually tend to spur land speculation and urban growth by encouraging subdivision development on the urban fringe. This is due to low, preferential assessment of agricultural or unimproved land.

Vermont did use the tax power to deter land speculation. It adopted a land gains tax to be imposed on the gain derived from the sale or exchange of land held for less than six years. The rate was high for property held a short time and sold at a high gain, but it went down significantly as the time during which the property was held increased and the gain itself diminished. Because this tax had been enacted to deter land speculation, it was argued that it was arbitrary, capricious and unconstitutional under the equal protection clause. In upholding the statute, the Vermont Court stated that legislation could serve more than one objective, that the aims of the legislature were a valid basis for acting, and that the tax scheme itself was reasonable. Andrews v. Lathrop, 132 Vt. 256, 315 A.2d 860 (1974).

The end result of the Vermont act was not only to deter land speculation, but also to reduce subdivision of land without construction taking place. This tended to preserve land for agricultural uses. Essentially the same act was introduced in several legislatures. At the moment, however, most states have not attempted this scheme or some other plan which might reduce the proliferation of subdivisions immediately outside the boundaries of the municipality. In fact, tax preference for agricultural land or open space may be defended on the ground that it helps to preserve open space. If land value taxation, under which only raw land is taxed rather than improvements, came into widespread use, the high taxes would likely make it too expensive to maintain privately owned urban land in open space and would lead to increased construction and more intensive use. Moreover, the substantial increase in taxes in the central business area based on the land value of the area would likely deter new business construction.

Thus while developers benefit from low taxes on open land in the urban area or around the urban fringe, and while higher taxes might deter land speculation, higher taxes also could spur more sub-division and fringe-area commercial development rather than limit it. There is some benefit, therefore, to be derived from this form of preferential taxation.

Other forms of preferential taxation or exemptions may be employed to encourage certain types of new construction. While some of these laws have fallen prey to strict interpretation of uniformity clauses, many of them have been sustained. See, *e.g.,* Opinion of the Justices, 341 Mass. 760, 168 N.E.2d 858 (1960), which upheld a statutory exemption from taxation of urban renewal structures in Boston for a period of time.

Other ways which have been put forward to handle open land or farm land include deferred taxation and agreements limiting use of the land. Under the first method, agricultural land is valued only for agricultural use (as under the preferential method), but when it is sold for development there is an increased tax for that year and for a certain number of years prior to that time. Under the agreement method, the land is limited to agricultural use or open space by agreement between the owner and the local government for a specified number of years and, in return, the owner receives a low tax rate. Both of these methods tend to hold down land speculation and land development around the urban fringe, and the second method would obviously permit land use planning of a more meaningful nature.

§ 6. Integration of Land Use and Tax Policies

Hawaii has attempted to utilize tax policies and practices to a substantial extent to promote certain types of land use. The state land use commission establishes certain use classifications, and the director of taxation must consider those classifications in assigning land to one of the statutory categories. He also gives consideration to the districting established by the county in its zoning ordinance and to use classifications contained in the State's general plan. Various tax breaks result in certain situations. For example, if an owner makes improvements under an urban redevelopment project, his taxes do not increase for seven years. Repairs or improvements made to meet state health, sanitation or safety requirements do not increase taxes for a certain time period. Under certain situations, land may be dedicated to agricultural or ranching use and be assessed at that rate. The owner cannot change the use for a ten-year period. Low and moderate-income housing projects are exempt from taxes. The Hawaii statutes contain various other provisions integrating tax and land use policies.

No other state has gone to the extent of Hawaii in interrelating property taxes with controls on land use. In most of the mainland states, the uniformity provisions of the state constitution would make it difficult to emulate the Hawaii provisions to any substantial degree.

§ 7. A Summary of Problems with the Property Tax

Since the interrelationship of land development and the property tax is clear, but since few states have attempted to interrelate the two from a legal standpoint, it is useful to summarize some of the problems stemming from the property tax. With regard to urban development and housing generally, the tax reduces consumer demand for housing in less affluent neighborhoods, reduces demand for heavily taxed commercial property in the central city thereby encouraging its deterioration, discourages owners of low cost housing from making improvements, affects land use planning due to fiscal considerations, leads to land speculation and uncontrolled growth on the urban fringe, and results in wide variations in the quality of public services due to tax variations among communities in the same general area. Moreover, it is essentially a regressive tax up to a certain income level. With regard to utilities, disproportionately high property taxes lead to increased rates for consumers.

Solutions to this problem vary. One suggestion is to rely less on the property tax to support local funding and rely more on state sources. Some functions might be transferred to state government. The land value or "Henry George" tax, previously discussed, has been mentioned as a possibility. Greater reliance on other local sources of revenue also is a possibility. Taxation of increases in land values based upon unearned increment resulting from external activities of other landowners or from such governmental action as new highways, rezoning, and the like has been suggested. This latter possibility will be discussed briefly.

§ 8. Recapture of Unearned Increment

The underlying thesis in this regard is that land gains in value because governmental activities enhance it or because the land nearby is developed for subdivision purposes or for similar reasons. One way to recapture benefits to the land is through the special assessment device. Certain types of public facilities in an area enhance the value of the surrounding land. A special assessment would reduce or even eliminate the cost of a facility to the government and recover some of the unearned enhanced value. In Weitz v. Davis, 4 Ariz.App. 209, 419 P.2d 113, aff'd 102 Ariz. 40, 424 P.2d 168 (1966), a formula for assessments for street improvements based upon the front footage and other considerations was upheld. By statute in California, land which receives special benefit from being adjacent to a transit or rapid transit district may be placed in a "special benefit district," if the voters approve, in situations involving acquisition, construction or repair of the facilities of the transit district. A scheme to pay for placing electric lines underground, to be financed by special assessments, was upheld in Citizens for Underground Equality v. Seattle, 6 Wash.App. 338, 492 P.2d 1071 (1972).

In addition to special assessments, an unearned increment tax has been suggested for application to situations involving rezoning or granting a permit for a development, or to the transfer of property which has greatly appreciated in value, or to persons who hold land for long time spans. It seems unlikely that such a tax would gain political favor, although the device of subdivision exactions bears a relationship to the unearned increment tax on development permits.

§ 9. Federal Taxing and Spending

It requires no detailed discussion to illustrate the fact that federal taxing and spending policies also affect land use. The capital gains feature of federal income taxation leads to speculative investment in land around the urban fringe. Deduction of mortgage interest and property taxes by homeowners is an indirect subsidy to the building industry. Although the effectiveness of the real estate tax shelter as a tax avoidance device has been diminished, it still remains. Favored tax treatment is available to landlords who rehabilitate substandard housing occupied by low income tenants.

These are only some of the ways federal tax policies affect urban development.

That they do have an effect is quite obvious. The fact that someone occupying rental housing cannot deduct his payments while a homeowner can deduct his mortgage interest and property taxes obviously leads most renters to purchase housing when they are able to do so. This in turn spurs subdivision development. While this is good for the economy, it obviously affects land use planning and the problem of urban growth. Moreover, while there should be tax incentives relative to repair of substandard housing, since most of these occupants will not be able to afford a house, there is a neglected class of individuals in between the low income group and the middle or upper middle income group. They do not usually live in true substandard housing, but they may not earn enough to eventually afford a house. In the 1980's this group of people has been helped somewhat by low interest rate bond issues aimed at permitting first-time home buyers or persons earning less than a certain income to purchase a home with "bond money" at affordable monthly payments. But even then, there is a group of people just above the low income level who cannot qualify for such loans. Thus, federal tax and subsidy policies do not apply entirely evenly, just as the property tax fails in that regard also.

CHAPTER XIV

NEW INFLUENCING CONSID-
ERATIONS: ENERGY AND
SPACE

§ 1. Introduction

Controls on the use of land continually take on
new forms, and new problems continue to emerge.
Devices utilized as tools of the planning process,
such as planned unit developments, new forms of
subdivision exactions, transfer of development
rights, and other such concepts will either become
staples or provide the basis for new planning concepts or both. The ramifications of such cases as
Mount Laurel and its progeny, now being more
critically assessed, remain to be further explored in
those jurisdictions which have adopted or may
adopt that approach. The problem of exclusionary
zoning, particularly with regard to racial and economic implications, will likely be developed more
fully by case law in the years ahead. Perhaps the
difficulty of zoning which relates to mobile homes
and affordable housing in general will form an
important part of that development. Perhaps
most importantly, for local governments which
have to assess the cost effects of zoning, the question of damages for unconstitutional land use regulations is likely to be determined and that area of

the law will likely expand in the years ahead. The use of 42 U.S.C.A. § 1983 could increasingly involve the federal courts in such situations, just as the federal courts have become involved in cases involving federally financed housing and the exclusionary effects of local ordinances.

The nature of future planning and whether it will be on more of a regional or statewide scale than is the present norm remains a major issue. Local planning and zoning has been at least partly the reason that many state courts have intervened in the process in an affirmative or coercive way, as witness *Arlington Heights, Gautreaux, Mount Laurel* and *Black Jack,* to name only a few. But the shortsightedness of most states in failing to go beyond purely local planning and land use controls in the light of increasing urbanization and the interlocking nature and complexity of metropolitan areas and surrounding satellite suburbs remains with us. The quality of life in the next century is being established now, and much of it is already fixed; but the planning process remains in most jurisdictions essentially as it was thirty or forty years ago.

The energy crisis of the 1970's came and passed with only a relatively minor ripple as far as law is concerned. Highway maximum speeds were reduced and more fuel efficient cars were produced. But when energy prices stabilized and gasoline shortages ended, people went back to business as

[*328*]

usual. Many experts, however, predict more energy shortages in the late 1980's or early 1990's as the current oil glut diminishes and as consumption catches up with the supply. This impacts to some extent on land use planning, particularly in cities without rapid transit systems and limited bus capacities. In considering how the city of the future might be restructured to respond to this problem, let us consider the allocation and utilization of space in American cities and how cities might develop in the future.

§ 2. Airspace Utilization in American Cities

Many large American cities in all areas as well as smaller towns in the midwest and beyond were affected in their development by the railroad. By the latter part of the 19th century, the railroads had become essential to American commerce in the transport of goods and people. They ran into the heart of the downtown areas of all of the large cities, and their tracks and rail yards occupied large quantities of downtown land. As the cities grew outward from the core, as the value of commercial property grew, and as the property tax on such land increased, it became apparent that the tracks and rail yards were occupying valuable land which otherwise could be utilized for construction of business buildings.

The solution of the problem lay in the old common law maxim enunciated by Lord Coke, *cujus est*

solum, ejus est usque ad coelum et ad inferos, which
meant that the owner of the land surface owned
the space above it up "to the sky" and the space
below it down to the center of the earth. While
the advent of aviation had provided reasonable
limitations upon upward ownership, there seemed
to be no question (as the cases later established)
that the surface owner owned whatever airspace
he might utilize. Airspace was a commodity which
could be sold, leased, subdivided, and generally
dealt with in the same manner as the surface.
Thus, a way to create the modern condominium,
which came to us from civil law sources, already
existed in the common law.

Interestingly enough, an early environmental
law lent impetus to the utilization of airspace over
railroad facilities. Shortly after the turn of the
century, the New York legislature passed an act
requiring the railroads to operate on electricity in
the Park Avenue area. There was also a need for
larger facilities, and this gave rise to the construction of a two-level terminal yard which enlarged
Grand Central Station and utilized the space over
the tracks. This was followed in the same area of
midtown Manhattan by the construction of the
Biltmore Hotel and other hotels and public buildings over the tracks. Gradually, the tracks in the
area of midtown Manhattan began to disappear
and what appeared to be surface structures often
had tracks running beneath them and involved

ownership of the airspace with easements of support extending up from newly subterranean rights of way. Chicago pursued the same path in the late 1920's with the construction of the Merchandise Mart and the Chicago Daily News building. Numerous well-known buildings, such as the Pan Am building, the Seagram's building, the Union Carbide building and many others in New York City, and the Prudential building, the Chicago Sun-Times building, Marina Towers and many others in Chicago, are constructed in airspace. The same pattern has been followed to a lesser degree in other large cities. (See generally, R. Wright, *The Law of Airspace* 224–229, 261–271 (1968).)

The situation offers a potential for similar adaptation today in the case of large areas of urban space occupied by multi-lane highways. This has already occurred in a number of cities, although to a lesser degree than in the railroad situation, as buildings of various kinds extend across or occupy space over, below or along the side of major highways. This utilization was encouraged in the middle or late 1960's by the Bureau of Public Roads (now part of the Department of Transportation). This "joint development" concept was incorporated as federal policy in the Highway Assistance Act of 1968, P.L. 90–238, 81 Stat. 772, and it ultimately led to the promulgation of a Model Airspace Act by the American Bar Association. (See 60 Okla.Stat. Ann. §§ 801–816 (1984–85); and see Final Draft of

Model Airspace Act, 7 *Real Prop.Prob. & Tr.L.J.*
353 et seq. (1972).)

Airspace over or around transportation rights of
way offers potential use for various purposes. To
planners, it offers the possibility of combining different kinds of commercial, recreational and residential uses in a location which would permit
ready access to an individual's place of employment and permit most of his other needs to be
satisfied without extensive travel. Such utilization
might also alleviate the problem of displacement of
large numbers of people due to public projects and
permit the construction of new housing projects in
approximately the same area of displacement.
Through careful planning, in place of highway
corridors becoming the sole occupant of otherwise
wasted land, a carefully planned area of multi-
family housing, parks, recreational facilities and
shopping areas could develop. Some attention has
already been given to such multi-use plans, and the
potential of such plans in a time of shortage of
fossil fuels should not be overlooked.

§ 3. Utilization of Underground Space

Separate and apart from the possibility of airspace utilization in downtown urban areas to reduce dependence upon automobiles is the use of
underground space to minimize energy consumption wherever the building may be located. Buildings in some areas have already gone to window-

less arrangements and the use of earth berms against the sides. The design of such buildings necessitates some refinement, since these buildings often provide the appearance of huge bunkers of the World War II variety. Nonetheless, there is no question but that energy consumption can be reduced in this manner. It is known that substantially less energy is required to heat and cool an underground facility than is required for the equivalent facility above the surface. Underground temperatures vary much less from the average yearly temperatures than do surface temperatures.

Be that as it may, there are obviously certain amenities to be considered. People lived in caves during the Stone Age or occasionally occupied underground facilities in Europe during World War II out of necessity, but people prefer light and air. Therefore, it seems more likely that architects and planners may develop structures in which a portion of the building is subsurface (bearing a relationship to our split-level housing of today) or in which portions of the house are earth-covered and some parts are exposed to sources of light and air. Properly designed, and perhaps designed in conjunction with the use of solar energy, such structures could retain the necessary amenities at very substantial savings in energy. While perhaps most useful in relation to residential housing, non-high rise commercial and industrial structures could also make use of such devices, as could public buildings such as schools and hospitals. Multi-family structures, grouped closely together to maximize energy-saving and to provide substantial open space for use by the residents, could also be adapted in this manner.

§ 4. Public Controls on Use of Space

The use of either airspace or underground areas should not present problems substantially different from those involving the land surface. In regard to airspace, there is no reason why zoning, for example, could not regulate the upward extension of space on the same basis as the surface, or for that matter, provide appropriate zones for different spatial levels. A parallel to this can be seen in condominiums, which are composed of cubicles of space sold to individual owners and which have certain common areas. The Merchandise Mart, which was developed under the common law rules pertaining to airspace, was segmented on a multidimensional basis as well.

§ 5. Energy Consumption and Land Planning

The foregoing has provided some insight into new architectural and planning concepts which may have a role to play in helping to alleviate the energy crisis. But these are only devices which may result in one way or another in reduction of energy consumption. Utilization of airspace reduces reliance upon the automobile for transportation over long distances as well as offers the energy-saving potential which results from a clustering of uses. Utilization of underground space offers direct reduction in consumption for heating and cooling purposes through innovative design processes. But solar energy offers even greater potential for reduced consumption whether used alone or in conjunction with these other devices. The problem as to solar energy is twofold: (1) designing efficient, low-cost systems for all types of new construction, and (2) designing efficient, low-cost systems for existing structures. The latter, once designed, will require tax benefits or government loans (or the underwriting of private lending) in order to come into widespread use.

None of these or other devices can be effective, however, until recognition of the energy problem translates itself into federal, state and local legislation having an impact upon the planning process. To be specific:

(1) The movement to save the downtown area of cities is desirable, but if the people who work there must travel many miles each day from their residences by automobiles, the result is highly wasteful from the energy standpoint. Planning, therefore, must provide for rapid transit systems for the surburbanite and must consider (a) renewal and revitalization of residential areas closer to the central core, and (b) provisions for multi-family housing of some at-

tractiveness, including condominiums, close to the central city or to outlying business districts.

(2) The not-so-new concept of a multiplicity of business and commercial centers forming a core, with housing of various kinds close by, should be encouraged in order to reduce travel distances. Some aspects of this can be found in younger cities. This provides a number of commercial centers, rather than one, and permits people to live closer to where they work. The same can be done with light industrial centers. Open space, parks and playgrounds can be interspersed at appropriate points in between.

(3) Zoning, building and subdivision ordinances should encourage and in some instances require or give priority to structures which utilize energy-saving devices of the type discussed. This should reflect itself in something more than added thickness of insulation in the walls and ceilings of houses and apartments.

(4) Through regional and state planning, impetus can be given to promoting the development of new communities, new suburbs, or model neighborhoods which are planned for and intended to encourage energy conservation and which represent a mixture of residential, office and commercial components. This will require an entirely different approach for most states, however, and is unlikely to occur in many states very soon or with much effectiveness in the absence of

a national land use policy mandating or offering incentives for state and regional planning.

(5) In addition to the development of rapid transit systems, more attention should be given to the efficiency of traditional highway, road and street travel in moving traffic at peak hours in congested areas.

These are obviously only a few of the major considerations which planners must face in this regard.

§ 6. The Energy Problem and the Environmentalists

There have already been heated clashes between those concerned about the environment and those wishing to provide additional quantities of fossil fuels.   To save the environment was an overwhelming issue of the early 1970's with the result that environmental impact statements must now be filed and assessed in many situations in which boards administering traditional forms of land use ,controls have approved the proposed use.   These clashes present the problem of weighing competing values which vary depending on the situation involved: the need to preserve and protect the environment; the need to proceed with land development projects which fall within the acceptability of the comprehensive plan and zoning and subdivision standards; and the need to create more energy sources or preserve existing ones.   The standards of NEPA and related laws have generally been enforced or have prevailed or have, in some way, been satisfied. The result almost invariably has been delay.

It is safe to say that these conflicts may reoccur with a second energy crisis. People who are not used to being cold in the winter and hot in the summer when they are in their own homes or offices, and people who do not want to be laid off from work because an industry or business has had its energy source curtailed or reduced, are less likely to be sympathetic with environmental goals. The situation will increasingly cease to become a confrontation of environmentalists (the "good guys") with oil and utility companies (the "bad guys"), and will gradually develop into a situation involving the hard core environmentalists against average working people. Factory and business shut-downs would lead not only to reduced income for workers, but also to reduced profits for industries and businesses of all kinds, and in turn all of this would lead to a heightening of inflation and a reduction in living standards.

It seems safe to assume, therefore, that federal legislation and national policy will necessarily move, as it already has somewhat in the early 1980's, toward increased accommodation of energy needs at the expense of environmental values. It seems unlikely that we will ever again ignore our environment or permit it to dissipate to the extent that we did in the period preceding the 1960's.

Only a pending national catastrophe could lead to the repeal of basic environmental policies. It does seem likely, however, that the immediacy of environmental needs will become less immediate with the heightening of energy needs. It would, therefore, be in the best interest of the environmentalists to promote the development of safe, new forms of energy, such as solar energy and, for that matter, nuclear energy. This is perhaps an accommodation which demands too much of a seemingly passionate righteousness of Calvinistic proportions. Until the crisis of energy is solved, the nation's courts and governmental bodies will necessarily wade into the swamps and lower reaches of this conflict.

§ 7. Control of Land and the Equitable Balance

In the last analysis, the control of land under the police power and all of the peripheral considerations which enter into a reconciliation of the legality or illegality of particular controls in specific situations come down to a single set of factors—reasonableness, or the lack of it; arbitrariness, or the lack of it; or doubt as between the two, which generally sustains the governmental determination. But more than any other factor, cases quite often come down to the simple principle of "balancing the equities." It is a judgment of values, and how those values fall on a particular scale in a specific situation and in a given moment will often determine the outcome. Patent or obvious deviations will not be tolerated on the part of government, nor will specious, self-interested challenges normally carry the day. But in those close cases involving important competing values, the tenor of the time, the jurisprudential values of a particular judge or jurisdiction, and the judge-made weight of one issue upon the scales of justice as opposed to another will generally be the ultimate determining factor. This is indeed the true "balancing of the equities," the choice in a specific situation among legitimate competing values.

And so the police power will prevail in a period and in a judicial body realizing the need for public controls to balance private irresponsibility and to prevent public harm. The police power will also prevail in a situation illustrating demonstrable or reasonable public need for regulation even without the creation of problems by private activity. Private rights will prevail in situations in which public actions fail to consider the fact that in America the ownership of private property is a constitutional right which, though not absolute in nature, is demanding of the utmost recognition when it does not contravene the public interest. The healthy public desire to preserve and purify the environment must be balanced against the somewhat ignored public essential for sufficient energy to house a nation and to permit it to be productive.

The scales of justice do not usually weigh the sinner against the righteous or good against evil; they balance the accepted values of our civilization in a specific situation, at a particular time, in relation to a particular need, and with regard to the effects of a particular result.

It is so in this area of the law, and it is so in all areas of the law. Judges look to the problematic hills of a particular day, and if they are very good judges, to the hills beyond. This is what distinguishes poor judges from good ones and the good ones from the great ones. It is a matter of knowing the time and realizing the needs of this day and of the days to come.

*

INDEX

References are to pages.

INDEX
References are to Pages

[*353*]

†